King of The Castle

First published in Great Britain in 2002

1 3 5 7 9 10 8 6 4 2

First published by
Ebury Press, an imprint of Random House, 20 Vauxhall Bridge Road,
London SW1V 2SA

Random House Australia (Pty) Limited
20 Alfred Street, Milsons Point, Sydney, New South Wales 2061,
Australia

Random House New Zealand Limited
18 Poland Road, Glenfield, Auckland 10, New Zealand

Random House South Africa (Pty) Limited
Endulini, 5A Jubilee Road, Parktown 2193, South Africa

The Random House Group Limited Reg. No. 954009

www.randomhouse.co.uk

A CIP catalogue record for this book is available from the British Library

ISBN 0 09 188154 4

Cover Design by the Senate, London
Typeset by Lovelock & Co
Printed and bound in UK by Mackays of Chatham plc, Chatham, Kent

Jaques Prévert poem on page 5 © Jaques Prévert, trans. Laurence
Felinghetti, 1970 Penguin Books

Papers used by Ebury Press are natural, recyclable products made from
wood grown in sustainable forests

King of the Castle

martin plimmer

EBURY
PRESS

To Eve,

who put up with all this

Song

What day is it
It's everyday
My friend
It's all of life
My love
We love each other and we live
We live and love each other
And do not know what this life is
And do not know what this day is
And do not know what this love is.

Jacques Prévert

ACKNOWLEDGEMENTS

The action in this book takes place some time in the 1990s. This explains any references that may sound outdated. If anything should appear incongruously contemporary, then it is with hindsight, a prophetic insight. In some ways the world depicted has changed for the better; for example, Marks and Spencer now does sell size 12 shoes, though I don't see why it should be let off the hook just because it has belatedly reformed itself. This book is not a 100 per cent true account of my life but it is true to many things I have experienced in my life, and emotionally it's on the mark. Because I couldn't think of more apt ways of expressing certain passages, I have re-used certain bits and pieces that have appeared before in magazine and newspaper articles, so if you should come across a paragraph you've read before and think is the work of someone else, it's not. Thank you Reader's Digest for letting me use Umbrella and Snap, which first appeared in the UK edition of that magazine. Thank you my family, for supporting me with ideas, cups of tea and, yes, money.

Thank you Louise Greenberg, my agent, for having me. Thank you Hannah MacDonald, my editor, for sound judgement and patience, and the occasional kick in the pants. Thank you Amelia Thorpe, of Ebury Press, for playing such a pivotal role, both in the book and in life.

CONTENTS

PROLOGUE

This is the story of a year in the life of a man on the edge. I say 'edge', but the word already sounds out of place, because his condition is so amorphously middling as to make the idea of edges seem very remote. In almost every respect he is in the middle. He is middle-class, middle-aged, mid-career. His house, where he both lives and works, is situated in London's suburban midriff. He suffers middling complaints: fat ankles, thin hair, persistent children. Even his achievement is middling. Sometimes when he takes stock of his life, it seems to him that he is nowhere. The middle of nowhere. Handy, at least, for getting to other parts of nowhere.

In many ways he is unexceptional. There are many thousands like him, who sit at home all day, linked to the world outside only by their telephone lines and computer modems. He is a home-worker, a freelance; part of the greater contingency workforce; a mouse potato; homo-connectus. The lifestyle is unhealthy. It is at once all work and all home. He can work 24 hours on the trot and still be in his dressing gown. Conversely, he can *not* work for 24 hours on the trot and still be in his dressing gown. The unusual thing about him is the nature of the work he does at home. He writes funny articles for newspapers.

He sends these articles off by email. He gets paid by BACS. He rarely sees the people who commission him. They are voices on the other end of a telephone line. They ring at 11 a.m. and demand a thousand words on Chris Woodhead, or the clitoris, or sand gardens, by 3 p.m. If they like what he sends them he doesn't usually hear from them again until they ring to commission the next piece. It's like feeding a donkey strawberries.

If they don't ring again, ever, he knows that they hate him, or have forgotten about him altogether, or have begun commissioning the daughter of a minor celebrity instead, or else have made an editorial decision to drop funny pieces entirely in favour of first-hand accounts of exotic medical complaints.

Occasionally they will ring and say, 'Chris Woodhead: not funny.' And he'll say, 'Yes it is.' He used to say, 'Oh, isn't it?', but came to realise that it was easier to live with himself afterwards if he said, 'Yes it is', even though it means an intractable conversation of fat, tetchy pauses, which leads eventually to the editor saying, 'Frankly, no one in the office thought it was funny. Not even Brenda.'

'Well, everyone here thought it was funny,' he says, and he nods meaningfully at his cat, which is arrayed on the to-do pile on his desk like a three-tail pasha, peering back at him with the 'Who the fuck are you?' expression that is the result of thousands of years of evolution in conditions of exquisite idleness. '*Extremely* funny.'

There is a topic in Windows 98 Help, titled 'Deleting Remote Administrators'. He has forbidden himself to read it lest it should preclude the possibility that it is designed to deal with this very situation. He likes to think that somewhere in his computer there is a handy DRA routine waiting to be activated during just such a conversation. In a pull-down list of remote administrators all he has to do is select the name of the caller and click delete. 'Frankly, no one in the office thought ...,' they say, then disappear. Their coffee cup flops to the floor, their desk is vacant, people start searching the building with puzzled expressions.

Gratifying though this thought is, it's not compensation enough to stop him getting stroppy. Eventually he can't resist saying something like, 'Define "funny" then.' The editor tuts with exasperation and hangs up and he never hears from them again. No second thoughts, no recriminations, no goodbye; just silence.

I tell you this to demonstrate the nebulousness of the freelance writer's life. This man never meets his audience, if in fact he has one, which he sometimes doubts. The occasional letter percolates down to him, requesting the phone number of someone mentioned in passing in an article. He also gets the odd insult ('Are you a complete rhesus monkey?'), complaint ('I enjoyed reading your article "The Secret Life of a Penis" until I saw the word "Silesia" used in a bizarre context') and from time to time the incoherent ramblings of the mad ('My husband and I had not had any married life what so every but now we got a house after wait nearly over two year outside we got the worse mud area here but I am not complaint some of them want to walk three miles in to town where I used to live and back and I think that we sure have a phone on the estate because there are quite a few children and myself have got a bad heart ...').

This has made him wary of the public and unsure about how to talk to it. When people ask him what he does, he baulks at telling them he writes funny articles, because he knows they will think, 'I'll be the judge of that.' He can see them thinking it. This doesn't happen with other occupations. You don't think, 'I'll be the judge of that' when someone says they're a vet, or a bus driver (though it does apply to plumbers). Lately he's started telling people he writes *humorous* articles, in order to lower expectation, because humorous doesn't sound as funny as funny.

The best compliment that can happen is if a person says, 'I read your piece; *I laughed out loud*.' Imagine a stand-up comedian saying, 'I had a great show last night – someone laughed out loud!' People don't expect to laugh when they're reading, so in his job this is as good as it gets.

He has never seen anyone laugh out loud while reading one of his articles. He would love to see it; he longs for the sense of endorsement it would bring. He waits for the day when somebody on a bus, who, so far as anyone else can tell, is reading an article about the European Exchange Rate Mechanism, suddenly and helplessly erupts into laughter. Perhaps others might crane their necks across, trying to identify the piece lurking among the hospital waiting list stories like a joy bomb; perhaps the reader would tear out the article, put it in his pocket and pat it, still smiling to himself; perhaps he would stand up on the seat and read it aloud to the rest of the carriage. These would be great things to happen, though a single laugh would be enough to make him happy.

If (and this is rare) he spots a person on a bus or in a café reading a newspaper which contains a piece by him, he watches them like a

Newfoundland sheepdog observing a man eating a ham. I say Newfoundland sheepdog because he is that sort of size: he's six foot two inches tall. Dining chairs collapse when he sits on them; he can hold a baby on the palm of one hand. Physically then, he is not subtle, so anybody trying to read a newspaper in a confined space like a bus would be cognisant – even if it is only their sixth sense waving the distress flag – of this Newfoundland sheepdog-type presence gazing intently and with unrequited yearning through their newspaper and into their soul. It's quite hard to laugh under these circumstances, even mutely. Some people are inclined to emit a nervous gargle, but for him that doesn't really count.

Apart from the odd interview or press trip, he has very few contacts with people outside his immediate circle. This isolation may make his job seem as pathetic and lonely as that of an astronaut sent out of the ship with a cup to see if he can borrow some sugar. But in some ways it suits his temperament. He is after all, a man who can sit staring into space for an unbroken hour, no problem. He tinkers with small things for long periods of time, while the world storms hungrily past him. He can't see why watching paint dry has got such a bad press.

In fact nebulousness is integral to his personality. It's intrinsic to his philosophy, his working practice. Nebulousness is a vital element of his work – he's quite clear about that. Others disagree.

'Look,' he tells them, 'Clitoris today, Chris Woodhead tomorrow: not a lot of crossover there. You need to be versatile. Rigid mind-sets and dogmatic routines are not helpful. You need to be a butterfly.' He is a 17-stone butterfly.

The negative side to this gift is a certain vagueness. He is out of step with the nine to five world. He gave up wearing a watch years ago because it got on his nerves. It kept reminding him of the time. He is easily distracted from tedious chores. A cat can distract him just by waving at him. A pile of plates toppling over downstairs, a child crawling underneath his desk, a bumblebee needing to be put out of the window, a single idle thought flapping in his head – any small thing can divert him from a dull commission. And these are just the small things. Big things are even harder to resist: an unread newspaper, the arrival of post, a new stationery catalogue, the temptation to tea, the enticement of Marrakech Coffee House, the sound of au pairs gurgling in the bath, sex.

Sex is the distraction to end all distractions. It can arrive at any moment, even while otherwise interesting things are being considered. It hogs his brain, steams his glasses, floods his mind with big, libidinous flavours and forces him to forget he is working. An objective observer, watching him becalmed at the keyboard, might conclude that the writer's mind was in creative free-fall. The truth is: he's on a slow train with a fast woman.

It doesn't take much for his head to fill up with naked women. There is never a shortage of them and they are always extremely keen to please. They tumble about his imagination like Labrador puppies, knocking over all his carefully arranged good intentions. He sometimes wishes he had chosen the career of a figure artist, or underwear designer, or fundamentalist doctor, so that there would be a legitimate excuse for real naked women to be in his study.

This talent for wafting in the prevailing wind, which would be commendable in a butterfly or a dandelion seed, finds little favour among human beings. He is often accused of being gratuitously laid back. In the past some people (examination overseers, job interviewers, lovers) have mistaken him for someone asleep. When he has been called upon to read on the radio he has had to act manic in order to sound merely tired. Sometimes, when he has spent his day not talking at all, except to cats and children, he loses the power of normal speech altogether. In the middle of sentences he forgets what he set out to say; he introduces people to others as their sworn enemy; he says 'nightie-night' to nightclub bouncers.

If his cards had been dealt differently, he would have liked to have been an archaeologist, a warlord, a novelist, or appeared on *Top Of The Pops*, but the fact is – to the chagrin of those close to him – he has made only half-hearted attempts to carve his own path, create waves, forge success. Opportunities for self-betterment slip through his fingers like warm butterballs. He is not a shark. He is a grouper. He'll eat a little fish, but only if it swims into his mouth.

I hope I haven't painted too negative a picture. He is not entirely passive, nor entirely sad. He has his positive side. When happy he is invasively loud. He shouts, bangs lids and plays accordion music at plaster-cracking volume into the early hours. The unexpected flip-side to his insouciance is an obsessive streak. Occasionally, for no obvious reason, he will subject an insignificant writing project to such a relentless, unflagging concentration of intense energy (which nobody suspected him of having) that all meaning drains from it. Then he will take a month off.

I need to square the record here. This is a man who has never passed wind during a PTA meeting, never knowingly urinated in a yucca plant pot and, when called upon to do a party turn, never engaged in sexual intercourse with a water melon. When compared to war criminals and people who flick ear wax across crowded restaurants, he's got a lot going for him.

Let's give this man a name. We could call him Hermann Göring, John Prescott, the Aga Khan, Striker Maguire, Nimrod Ping, Bob Weatherwax ... any of these would do. But for the sake of simplicity let's call him me. He's not really me; I'm better looking, not so fat and better in bed; but for argument's sake, he's me.

Neither am I as lonely as he sounds. Not really. Or only in the sense that a man is lonely who is surrounded by people. For a start I have three and a half children in my life. I have a 17-year-old son Lowell from my first marriage, a 12-year-old girl Amelia and six-year-old boy Mungo from my current marriage, plus another child, Weeny, aged 5, who is not mine, but always seems to be here. These children come and go like express trains, sometimes not even stopping at the station, sometimes needing extensive refuelling, cleaning out and reconditioning, if not lifting bodily back on to the tracks, before they go screaming off again. They have lovers, friends, dirty washing, their own stereo systems, loud video games, a drum kit, a scree slope of teddy bears, and an alien monster which shouts out 'DIE HUMAN, DIE!!' in the voice of Professor Stephen Hawking every time you so much as nudge the toy pile.

As soon as children arrive in your life, your house and your eardrums are no longer your own. Your pain is distinctly and singularly yours, but everything else – time? privacy? biscuits? Kiss them goodbye.

Combinations of these children and their friends are required to be bundled into the car or on to the bus at various highly charged moments of the day and moved from one place to another place. They must be dropped off at school and brought home from school. They must have suppers made for them which fit their exacting dietary requirements. They must be delivered to and from each other's houses for nit-swapping sessions. They must be taken to extra-curricular piano lessons, extra maths classes, basketball, dance and dentistry sessions, hung around for and brought home again. I go for six eye-checks a year. I know the charts by heart.

The irony of being lazy is how incredibly busy it makes you. Here is the paradox of the indolent. Being lazy, I have to do all the things which other, more conscientiously hard-working people, haven't got time to do because they're working so hard. This sometimes gives me the disquieting sensation of virtue.

I have cats too. I have cats because I once didn't have children. A cat is what women get when they have no children. They lavish love on it. Then they get another cat. They lavish love on that too. Then they get a child, and from that point on they don't look at the cats. The cats turn to the man of the house. They know who they can walk over.

Because I have three and a half children and two cats, I have a cleaner and I have an au pair. I need their help. A cleaner is an old lady who comes in once a week and breaks things. An au pair is a big extra child who is supposed to help out around the house but can't cook, doesn't know how to clean and has never seen children before. She slops about in a turquoise shell suit and giant bunny slippers, crying with homesickness, sulking or entertaining murderous-looking men, eating everything in the fridge or not eating anything, staying out till dawn, having abortions and leaving oblations of toenails and hair balls on the side of the bath.

Because I have three and a half children, two cats, a cleaner and an au pair, I have a house. A big and trembling Victorian house, three stories, six bedrooms, cellar, loft: big enough, just, to cope with the human explosion that is my world.

Because I have a house I have workmen. There's always a workman hammering things about, cutting corners and demanding large sums of money.

Because I have workmen, I have the urge to Do It Myself.

Of course, I wouldn't have any of this – cats, children, cleaner, au pair, house, workmen, DIY mission – if I didn't have Martha. I have all this because I have a wife. It is the modern dowry, part and parcel of the gift of love.

A man without a wife enjoys an embarrassment of freedom. He is free to do as he will, or just to sit and wonder what to do. If the basin breaks, he uses the sink. Simple. He runs, he skips, he wears a crumpled shirt, he spends eleven hours straight playing Pop Music Hangman.

But he doesn't have Martha. And he doesn't have all this. If he once had Martha he wouldn't be able to do without her. I can't do without her and not only because I cannot imagine life without her. This termite mound of activity couldn't work if it wasn't for my wife's drive, vision and monthly salary cheque. She is a successful professional woman, but not a career woman. In fact she wants nothing more keenly than to be at home and devote her life to looking after her children. This is our special irony. It is clearly my fault. If I worked harder and earned more she could work less and be with the children. And we would all be happier.

Instead it's me who takes Amelia to the dental surgery to have two teeth removed and sits with her, hating it, when they inject her with anaesthetic. I watch horrified as, in a passing second, her will fades; her small conscious life dissolves. It is an unsolicited demonstration of how close is the divide between life and not life and it pulls me up short. One second I'm middle man, holding down an average day, the next I'm right out there at the edge. I'm shaking at the precipice. I can see over it into a world in which my daughter doesn't exist. I leave the room while they extract the teeth and when I return they've taken four. Had to go, they said. Four of my little girl's teeth have gone and for half an hour, so had she. Amelia is groggy, but she's OK about it. I'm traumatised.

Martha would love to be with Amelia at the dentist. Martha is good with teeth, interested in teeth, pragmatic. Instead I'm here and she's at work.

She was never professionally ambitious. She got where she is by being good; not by scheming or politicking or even by willpower, other than the determination to do her job properly. She rose through the ranks on the pure fuel of ability. She is reliable, she gets on with people, she is effective. And she is beautiful. I am a little in awe of her.

My dad always said, tapping his pipe out on the chimney breast, you should be on the mortgage ladder son and sure, I thought it was no mean idea myself. I knew people who lived contentedly in their own houses, with the smell of roast beef wafting along their battlements. They had stature, those people, a firm handshake, confident of their own permanence. They had their feet on the ground – no, they were rooted in the rock itself. They had a stake in the fundament.

Well, now I am one of those people. I can manage a convincing handshake but my gaze is all over the place, looking for cracks in the ceiling. I can't relax properly, not while I'm in the house, and if I had a pipe, I certainly wouldn't tap my chimney breast with it. I wouldn't tap anything. I know from bitter experience that if you tap something in a house it will likely crumble, or worse, be rent asunder.

The word 'rent' has an ironic chime to it here, a resonance of blithe and distant days when I did, in fact, pay rent and someone else did the worrying. Now that's all over. Now I own a house, though 'own', of course, is merely a form of words. I don't literally *own* the house, I don't have enough money to do that: I own a mortgage, which is a debt of lifetime proportions. I don't sit secure in a property, I teeter on a mortgage ladder. I can't look up because there's too far to climb and I can't look down because there's too far to fall.

I may not own the house, but I own its problems. I've lived here for five years and though I've done a lot, I have procrastinated too long on the major work that is needed. The outside urgently needs painting, pointing, gutter repair and some roof renovation. Inside, an upstairs room begs to be turned into a bathroom. The kitchen requires major work, including a loadbearing wall taken down to extend it to the back of the house, a French door to the garden put in, the kitchen range chimney breast dismantled and the floor levelled and made good. That's before we start talking about furnishings. Then there's decorating. We don't have knobs on the downstairs doors. We've grown used to the absence of carpets in the bedrooms. Every job needing doing is dauntingly expensive and we have no money. This makes me feel less secure than if I was out on the street.

When I go into town I am accosted by fit, youthful beggars sitting at the entrances to tube stations with signs saying 'ANY SPARE CHANGE?' in their laps. Of course I haven't got any spare change. If I had I'd be in a taxi. Adopting a shambling gait and wearing scruffy clothes doesn't fool them, though I have considered carrying a pre-emptive sign around my neck which says:

MORTGAGE OWNER, NEGATIVE EQUITY, THREE AND A HALF CHILDREN, TWO CATS, YOGHURT AND FRUIT EATING AU PAIR, LARGE INLAND REVENUE DEMAND PENDING, STRUCTURAL REPAIRS A NECESSITY, SECOND BATHROOM AN IMPOSSIBLE DREAM, CHANNEL TUNNEL ROUTE HEAVY RAIL FREIGHT PLAN CURRENTLY UNDER CONSIDERATION BY HM GOVERNMENT THREATENING LAST THIRD OF GARDEN, LAMBETH COUNCIL TAX. HAVE I GOT ANY SPARE CHANGE? – YOU TELL ME.

Not all these things have happened to me, but I think it's only fair that young people with absolutely no responsibilities have some sense of the paranoid fears home ownership confers.

As soon as I walked into my first mortgaged house I could see that it was less substantial in reality than it was in the imagination. As well as the soaring and steadfast bits, I also owned a fair measure of rot and fatigue. It dawned on me that this rock, to which I was to be financially tethered for the next 25 years, was crumbling, and that if I wanted it to remain strong and supporting, then it was I who had to be its strength and its support.

I have started to question that memory of my father tapping his pipe out on the chimney breast. I'm beginning to wonder if it happened at all. For one thing he never smoked a pipe. For another, it was his generation that wanted to knock all the chimney breasts out.

I too have sinned. I have removed one of the fireplaces from one of the bedrooms. This is an indictable offence in the Book of Yuppy, punishable by severe frowning. I don't care. I did it myself. It tore easily away from the wall with a dry wheeze. Bricks tumbled out and great dry gusts of dust: much more dust than I expected. Two mummified birds, stiff as Bombay duck, were lodged in the exposed chimney space, agonised and reeking, like props from a Hammer horror film, except they smelt authentically of death. I was startled, not so much by the corpses, but by the friability of the masonry.

The only wise but by no means only scary thing told to me by Bill, a shambling builder I hired last year to lay a damp course, was something he said the first day he came to my house. He took out his car key, which is no more than what all builders do, and stuck it between the bricks in the wall outside. Instead of mumbling about man-hours and VAT, as most builders do, Bill said clearly, chillingly: 'Dust.'

'Dust?'

What had seemed to be solid mortar was turning to powder. Holes were eagerly appearing under the twisting tip of Bill's car key.

'It's turned to dust, see. In houses over a hundred years old, see, the mortar turns to dust. It's no longer holding the bricks together, it's holding them apart.'

For a second he didn't look like Bill the semi-articulate so-called builder; he looked like King Lear.

This was news I didn't need. My house is held up by dust.

The whole truth is worse. Houses are against us. Those much-cherished symbols of domestic security don't actually like standing up. They don't *want* to be soaring and steadfast. They want to lie down. They're tired. They want to get back to the bedrock and they are alert to every opportunity that presents itself. They shimmy to the left, they shimmy to the right, they ease down, drop tiles, sag. They welcome hurricanes and bombing raids.

And railway lines. We have one at the bottom of the garden. We don't mind that every few minutes a train streaks by; we can make more noise than that. But twice in every 24 hours, at 3am and 11am approximately, a Grendel's mother of a freight train lumbers past, southbound from London, loaded down with stone aggregate. Where it comes from, nobody knows. Where it's going, nobody knows. All we know is, it's heavy as hell, and it makes the edifice shake. It makes Martha's scent bottles in the top bedroom chink against each other like the duty free on a cross channel ferry. Objects fall off tables, cats howl, au pairs shift in their slumber and dream uneasily of house fires in Budapest.

The other day on an otherwise still and uneventful evening, a pediment fell off the house next door and crashed on to the front garden path; 8.15 p.m.; just like that. After 110 years those bricks had had enough. They didn't care that they were supposed to be soaring and steadfast. They saw their chance and down they came. They didn't care how many snails were crossing the path at the time.

I may not own my house but I do own a lot of snails. I don't want them, but I like them. They are endearing little frigates, tacking with enormous endeavour across the path. Every evening armadas of them set off on inscrutable yet purposeful voyages, armoured yet defenceless, with as little apparent concern for falling masonry as if they were crossing an Emerson Lake & Palmer album sleeve.

I can't kill them. I collect them up by the bucketful and throw them over the bottom fence on to the railway embankment. I give them back to the aggregate. They live the rest of their lives sliding down the cutting in a vast snail scree, oozing and shifting, compacting slowly at the bottom of the pile. Eventually they will metamorphose into sedimentary rock from which, in times to come, aggregate will be hewn, cement powdered, houses built.

Part I

WINTER

Chapter 1 PIZZA

See Barnaby *run!* See Barnaby *crash!* See Barnaby *bash his sister!*

There is no person so liberal as the child of the liberal. He does what he wants, when he wants, if not before. He pesters his parents relentlessly, like an underage insurance salesman. He gets inexplicably angry about the garlic bread.

Everybody *scream!*

His behaviour might be tolerable in the setting of the Siberian steppe, but we are in the echo chamber of Clapham Pizza Express, whose shiny marble surfaces amplify every toll of the baby, every volley of the Megazord war sled. Normally I don't like to eat while fighting is going on, but I have no choice.

It's not just Barnaby. It's India-Jane (*'Eeeeeeeeee!'*), and Portia too (*'Aaaaaaaaaaaaaaaa!'*), and little Arkan (*Skruuunk!*). No problem: Pizza Express welcomes kids. All those wipeable acres of surface are just begging for it. Every Sunday, and particularly this Sunday, ten days before Christmas, the Pizza Expresses of London are magnets to the Espaces of Dulwich and Clapham and Putney, which arrive loaded with mobiles and bleepers and turbo buggies and fold-down cots – Whoops-ha-ha-sorry! – and Skogsblåbär baby bags and cussing plastic wrestlers and sound effects picture books and Power Ranger gloves that make a Taiwanese trumpet noise, and roller blades ...

Roller blades?

Yes, Pizza Express welcomes roller blades.

These people are not poor. The adults are mostly ten years younger than me, dressed in quality casuals. Their pullovers are tied by the arms around their shoulders. The men have proper hairdos.

Everything in their lives is under control, except their children. Welcome to the clattering classes.

What the children need, of course, is a good slap, but their super-dooper, all-smiling, super-absorbent liberal parents never slap their children. If you do hear a slap in Pizza Express, it's a Quattro Formaggi hitting the wall.

Here in liberal Clapham, the parental response is the forbearing smile, the whoops-ha-ha-sorry! mantra, and the dabbing ritual, with dabbing equipment retrieved from polka dot baby bags.

Curiously enough, these are exactly the sort of liberal middle-class people who came knocking on my door at 11.30 last night, complaining that my music was invading their right to silence (they're well up on their rights), and threatening to call the Lambeth Noisy Neighbour Police, who would come round and clamp me in muffs.

'But Ned Sublette is really rather good,' I told the man disingenuously, 'although at first it can seem an awkward coupling of Texan cowboy with Cuban percussion.'

'It's not the musical hybrid we object to,' he said, 'it's the fact we can hear it.'

'Oh really?' I said, pretending surprise. 'But it's Saturday night! Haven't you heard that Saturday night is for dancing?'

'Not when you have children trying to sleep.'

'Those are *your* children? I had Satan down as the father.'

The disappointing thing is, I didn't really say any of this. You see, I'm middle class too, and we middle class people are far too nice to talk to each other like that, whatever we might be thinking. We nod and smile, we even shake hands. If we were hippopotami, we would flick faeces into each other's faces with our tails as a mark of respect. We observe the niceties.

I've trained my children to expect a bit of ambient racket of a Saturday night. When the neighbour called last night, *my* children were fast asleep, apart from Lowell, my 17-year-old, who was at the top of the house playing ... oh, Prodigy, I think. It was probably his music that brought the neighbour round, but I like to think it was mine.

Martha was asleep too, but then she'd sleep through anything at the moment, rather than stay up and have fun with me. She's exasperated with me because my career has slewed to almost nothing and I'm doing nothing about it. I'm doing nothing about it because I don't know what to do about it. Martha's unhappy because I don't want to talk about it. I don't want to talk about it because I haven't got anything to say about it. That makes her even more exasperated.

That was my Saturday night. And this is my Sunday lunch. It's a family lunch, except that Martha isn't here either. She's the Marketing Manager of a retail clothes chain and she's working flat-out until the 24th. She's told me I am going to have to organise Christmas myself. 'It's about time you showed some Christmas spirit instead of sitting around being cynical.'

'Humbug.' I said.

We're a big table. My children are here of course. Mungo, aged six, is as here as he'll ever be. He lives in a dream, that boy, watching the world go past without seeming to be in it himself. Place him in front of a TV and he'll be there three hours later. More effective than manacles. He's still *my* boy though. Lowell I lost some time ago. He now has the self-absorbed indolence of the young and beautiful, which envious middle-aged people call arrogance. He only talks if he's in a good mood. We are on grunting terms.

And there's Amelia, once-darling daughter, former Daddy's girl, slipping, even now, through my fingers. Amelia's still 12, but she practises the affected can't-be-botheredness of the young teenager. In an instant when my guard was lowered, she slipped across the border into the teenage wasteland. I can no longer reach her there and she doesn't want me to. I can only watch her blundering about. She is prickly, awkward and distant, dressed in outlandish clothes. I have become embarrassing to her. I am proscriptive, interfering, antiquated and insufferably odd. A short while ago we laughed at everything together; now she blanks my jokes. She motions me to get lost when she is with her friends. If I persevere amiably she stares at me with *Please just go away* written on her face. When we greet, she launches an air kiss, each side of my head.

'You're allowed to kiss your dad, Amelia,' I say.

'I did kiss you,' she says.

Our friends Clive and Sam are here too, and their children, Tamara (12) and Rufus (4). Also here is Martha's father Hugh (80), who arrived by train this morning. He's here for the duration now, until Boxing Day. I'm lumbered. I had no idea he was coming so early. I've got nothing against Hugh personally, but it's going to be hard work shuttling him around with me as well as the children. He's six foot four, and now that he's getting frail, he's reverting to bone, which makes him seem longer than ever, with never-ending wrists and extended ankles sticking out of his suit when he sits down. It's like trying to get a deckchair in and out of the car. Hugh is an upright ex-RAF gentleman warrior with a white terrier moustache, and he smiles benignly through the chaos of Pizza Express. He probably thinks he's back at the Battle of Britain.

So the only person missing at this pre-Christmas family treat, is Martha. She'd love to be here, instead of working. I'm here, though God knows, I should be working. This is where equal opportunities has brought us.

Our children are reasonably well behaved, though the younger four have already made several visits to the toilet and I don't know how long their restraint can last, given the example all around us. Our table is an island of relative tranquillity in a sea of fighting bears.

What draws these families here every Sunday is the determination to live up to liberated European standards. They know that children are welcome in the restaurants of France; in Germany *gemutlichkeit* extends to the family dachshund (provided it is wearing lederhosen); in Greece even the waiters are children ... Why not here?

What they forget, of course, is that French children behave themselves. French children wait, quiet as honey, for the food to arrive, hands folded neatly under the table. They might have a secret sweet there, or a Gauloise – I don't know – but they wait like angels, for food is religion in France and throwing it is blasphemy.

English children don't understand waiting. The sight of tranquil cutlery disturbs them and makes them want to put salt in the sugar and sweep everything off the table with a satisfying kerralanga sort of sound. And they can't eat sitting down. Eating at Pizza Express involves a fair amount of running. If this level of mayhem were to occur in France, the Gendarmerie Alimentaire would come with pepper sprays.

All children love pizza. It's the meal that can be eaten in one hand, leaving the trigger hand free. And there's no cloggy potato-type food to muffle the shouting effect. Children can be themselves in Pizza Express. I can't. I'm not sure entirely *who* I am at the moment, though I feel like I'm turning into Adolf Eichmann.

Once, in a restaurant a long time ago, in a moment of infant fury, I lobbed a bread roll into my father's soup. There was a single exquisite, desperate moment of petrified satisfaction as my father's white shirt deliquesced to oxtail, then everything was fear and pain. My father yanked me by the collar from my chair, dragged me through the kitchen, past lines of chefs who raised their cleavers in adult solidarity, and out into the back yard among the chicken heads and cabbage ends, where he slapped my legs extremely hard. I won't ever do it again, tempted though I am to tip my house red over Barnaby's head.

Barnaby is invading my right to silence so much it hurts. Yet what recourse do I have? It would be pointless to ask the management to turn the children down, because clearly they don't know how to operate them. Who can I complain to? Who will hear me? I do not have a Taiwanese trumpet to command attention and I am no match for the vocal chords of Barnaby, who right at this moment is weaving through the tables, swiping at diners' legs with his pizza sword.

If it was just him and me now, out the back ... but sadly it's not. Barnaby has a team of endlessly patient back-up parents who are (not quite) keeping pace with him, following his trail with the Skogsblåbär, uttering the whoops-ha-ha-sorry! mantra, and dabbing at stained customers with dabbing equipment. These parents have more equipment than Xerxes. That's why they need those Espaces. What they really need, of course, is a good slap.

Fortunately for his nerves, my father-in-law Hugh has reached an age where he has forgotten so much of the past that everything is fresh and novel to him again. Even a clanging pizza house can inspire in him wide-eyed, childlike wonder. He points out a couple of families and remarks how marvellous it is, given the natural English reticence, how, because of children, strangers can be drawn together. That is true enough. They have to, for the table sets are fusing at the edges. Many Clapham friendships begin with the words, 'whoops-ha-ha-sorry!', and are cemented in the ritual exchange of tissues. And everybody mucks in when a waiter is injured.

For as long as I have known him, Hugh's conversation has consisted of reminiscence, but the present has caught up with him and enraptured him. Most of the time now he talks about Tesco. A new superstore has opened in his village and, stuck for something to do one day, he wandered in. Astounding. It was the first modern supermarket he had ever seen. He had been protected from that reality by his wife, who died last year. He never knew this stuff existed, and on such an enormous scale! He is a consumer innocent, whose shopping experience has been spiked with a powerful narcotic retail hallucinogen. Fresh fish from Alaska! Indian dinners all ready to eat!

Hugh pulls a scrap of paper out of his jacket pocket, upon which he has pencilled a list of items. 'Now what about these?' he announces. 'Who can tell me which four of these are chocolate bars and which four are household cleaning products: Oz, Logger, Omo, Kit-Kat, Bold, Boost, Stick-Up, Nova?' He chortles with satisfaction as we commit mistakes. He has a clear and beautiful smile on his face. 'By the way, what is a Lurpak?'

But it is getting increasingly difficult to talk, because a terrific baying has struck up. Some sort of extreme fight is taking place over a tricycle. A tricycle! Barnaby's face is beefeater red, his mouth the angriest O, his knuckles white. He is honking with unimaginable fury. So angry, so tense is his barking body, that the force of his rage flips him right over, and he continues shouting while lying on his back on the floor. I fear that soon I will have to shout as loudly as Barnaby in order for my kids to notice me at all. Given the freeform behaviour all around them, they can see no reason why they should be confined to the table talking to grown-ups about cleaning products, particularly as Clive and Sam have already given up on their two. Already Rufus is running up and down the aisle. I've told my two to sit down seven or eight times; soon, by the law of diminishing returns, repetition will render the words meaningless.

'Any ideas anyone ... ?' says Hugh 'Lurpak?'

A sudden remission of noise astounds the senses. At first I'm not sure what has caused it, but then I realise, Barnaby is no longer here. And not only is Barnaby not here, but over there, at the table by the window, is the father who isn't here either – a common sight at Pizza Express of a Sunday lunchtime. His wife is here, his Anoushka is here, his baby Theo is here, his glass of wine is here and his American Hot; but he is not. He is not here because he has been obliged to strap Barnaby down, wriggling, into the buggy and rush Barnaby out of the area when Barnaby went critical. And he will be halfway to Putney before there is any halfway decent chance at all of Barnaby cooling down, while here in the restaurant, his chair is being turned into a fort, his American Hot is cold and his doughballs are being kicked around by a surly mauve troll. Here too is the Skogsblåbär baby bag, containing Ruggy, without which Barnaby will never calm down, not in a million years.

'Come and see how the Internet works,' I say to Hugh later, after we've returned home. Mungo and I have something we want to look up. I've been going through Mungo's Romans book with him. I needed to sit down quietly with Mungo after the exhausting frenzy of the Pizza Express, for my own sake as much as his, as there are few things more relaxing than reading to children.

And now I feel guilty that I was less than patient with Hugh in my effort to hurry him out of the restaurant, which had so utterly beguiled him. I want to make it up to him. I'm assuming that the Internet will appeal to his newborn sense of novelty.

Mungo came across a picture in his Romans book that caught his interest, of a soldier holding a banner saying 'Veni Vidi Vici'. I told him it meant 'I came, I saw, I conquered' and that I thought Julius Caesar had said it. But that was all I knew, so I suggested we look it up on the Internet to see what else we could find out.

We go into the study and our new au pair, Europa, joins us. She has been with us a couple of weeks and seems like a good prospect. She's not as circumspect as the other au pairs were at the beginning; but then she's older. She's 26, and has already done a variety of jobs in her life. I'm not sure why she wants to be an au pair, as her English is already very good. She's a French woman who doesn't like France, and who can't cook either. But she's friendly. Friendly enough to pretend to want to see how the Internet works at any rate.

I type Veni Vidi Vici into the search engine, explaining to Hugh and Mungo how the system works. An impressive list of hits comes up.

'You see, somewhere here will be all the information we want.'

'Incredible,' says Hugh.

'Let's try this one.'

We are in a youth games site called The Alliance of Pain. The search term is contained in the motto of a member: 'Veni Vidi Vici Mutha Fucka, Eh?'

'You see, you never know what you might find.'

'Incredible.' says Hugh.

The second link takes us to a racehorse named Veni Vidi Vici, which ran in the Pinnacle Feeds Midsummer Classic at the Barbados Turf Club.

'Incredible,' says Hugh.

The next takes us to the Veni Vidi Vici restaurant in Atlanta, Georgia, and the link after that to the site of a metal band called Virgin Steele, whose repertoire includes the songs 'Voice is Weapon', 'Wine of Violence' and 'Veni Vidi Vici'.

My audience is looking nonplussed. Mungo yawns.

'Is that it?' says Hugh.

'No look – lots more to try.' I click on another link.

A picture loads of a smiling woman. Her face is covered with semen and she is holding an erect penis in her hand like a hot dog. The site is called Veni Vidi Veni.

'So you get the idea,' I say, shutting off the monitor.

Mungo and Hugh look puzzled. Europa is wearing a funny little half smile.

'What was that?' says Mungo.

'Incredible,' says Hugh.

Chapter 2 TNOHW

I have an article to write about sex in unusual places, but I've got a headache. Anyway, it's not as though I have nothing else to do. It's Wednesday, seven days before Christmas, and the first official event of the festive season has taken place: the cold water pipe on the bathroom basin has sprung a leak. You always need a plumber at Christmas.

I phone Pete, our regular plumber, on his mobile.

'Yeah I know,' says Pete, 'small basin under the window. Easy job, but, unfortunately mate, I can't help you out; I'm in Phuket, on the beach.'

I get another plumber – no job too small Paul – from our collection of cards that have been pushed through the door. Paul turns up flush with good intentions and disappears into the bathroom. He calls for a bucket, a cup of tea and, worryingly, a spanner. For a while at least, he clangs, and grunts and whistles in the approved manner of plumbers.

Then he shouts "Shit! Shit!" It resounds through the house, making the au pair dither. I become as tense as a bathing cat. This is what I would be doing if I'd tackled the job myself. I don't need to employ professionals to shout at my basin.

I pick Mungo up from school, dropping Europa off at the station on the way. She's off to France for her Christmas break so from now on all child and old-age pensioner care is down to me. Mungo has two of his friends with him, Toby and Sean.

Toby, a big stout boy with a sullen manner, has never been here before, but Sean has been back a couple of times. When it comes to cooking supper, Sean, a vegetarian, poses a special challenge. Meat is poison to Sean, but so too are tomatoes and cheese. And onions. He's also deeply suspicious of potatoes, and he believes that mushrooms are the vegetable manifestation of Satan. He won't go near mushrooms. He doesn't even like to be in the same room as them. When eating away from home he must be constantly on his guard, lest mushrooms smuggle themselves into his meal in disguise – in sauce or fleck form – to crouch behind other, more reasonable food, ready, the second his guard drops, to leap down his throat, killing him instantly.

I have been through the list of known foods with Sean and there is very little he will consider eating. He's even suspicious of sweets. He rejected the Twix bars I bought the boys to eat in the car. But pasta is OK by Sean, and Quorn. Sean actually *likes* Quorn. It's the one thing. He'll eat Quorn in any shape, size or colour: Quorn sausage, Quorn chicken, Quorn on the quob.

Unfortunately I have no Quorn. So I make cauliflower cheese. I make a very good cauliflower cheese, which everybody adores. I know Sean doesn't like cheese, so I put Edam in it – the cheese that doesn't taste of cheese – just enough to impart a savoury frisson. At my call, Sean comes into the kitchen with Mungo and Amelia, and sits down. Hugh follows, folding himself into a chair.

Sean approaches his plate cautiously, like a person at the lip of a deep and vertiginous pit. 'What's this?'

'Cauliflower er—'

'I don't like cauliflower.'

'I'm sure you would, if you tried it. Everybody likes cauliflower, don't they, Mungo?'

'What's this on it?'

'It's sauce. It's *lovely* sauce!'

He pokes it with a fork. 'Is that ... mushrooms?'

'No, that's cauliflower. Mushroom is normally darker, and mushroom-tasting. If you were to try a little, Sean, you might notice how very unlike mushroom this cauliflower is.'

Sean looks extremely unhappy, but fortunately at this point, Toby bursts in with the welcome swagger of a trencherman, and takes his place enthusiastically at the head of the table. Then he falters.

'What's this?' he says.

'Cauliflower.'

'Cauliflower? *Cauliflower*?' Toby looks around him with open-mouthed outrage and incredulity.

'Yes, cauliflower.'

'But I don't like cauliflower.'

'Are you sure? If you tried it, Toby, I think you'd find it was very, very nice.'

'I'm not a vegetarian.'

'You don't have to be a vegetarian to like cauliflower, Toby. Meat-eaters like vegetables too.'

'I don't.'

'Just try it, Toby. *Everybody* likes cauliflower cheese.'

'Cheese?' yelps Sean, pushing his plate from him with a reflex movement so violent it knocks Amelia's water into her meal.

'Now look what you've done!'

'I don't like cheese,' says Sean.

'It's not really cheese, if you want to know. It's Edam. All children like Edam.'

'I'm not a vegetarian,' says Toby. 'I'm not eating this.'

'Well, you should try it before you make your mind up.'

'My Mummy wouldn't make me eat this.'

'If you don't eat it up, Toby,' Mungo chips in piously, 'you won't grow big and strong.'

Ironically, Toby has big and strong sewn up already. I wouldn't pick a fight with Toby. I'd rather fight his father, who is slightly smaller.

'I'm *not* a vegetarian.' Toby is working himself into a fury. He has been insulted in the deepest and most offensive manner.

'Now look everyone. Don't you think you're all being a bit picky? You've had some nice cauliflower cheese made for you – thank you very much, Mr Plimmer – and your plates will be washed up for you afterwards. The very least you can do is eat it.'

'My Mummy wouldn't make me eat this.'

'Like it or lump it, that's all you're getting!'

'Tnohw!'

Tnohw is a child word, like brang and brung ('he brang', 'they brung'), part of children's own root language. It doesn't appear in any adult English dictionary, though it is composed of many English words and includes all their meanings. It is a reactive sound; a ricochet of disappointment, embodying dismay, chagrin and a tut of derision. In fact the pronunciation is so complex I have had trouble spelling it. I asked Mungo; he feels there should be an h in there; that's his only concern. I have no argument with that. We disagree on the t though (for *tut*: absolute contempt for all adult ways). He denies there's a t, though I can discern one 80 per cent of the time.

The fundamental part is similar to the American *aw* of disappointment, as in *aw shucks*, but is more of a squeezed, vexed *oh*. It could almost, under slightly different circumstances, be an *ow* of real emotional pain; it has that potential. There is also a *no*, of disbelief ('you don't say!') which is overlaid by a *w* (whine) of dismay. This can be extended and inflected, siren-like, upwards, to express severe psychological pain, and in one variation (the more extreme *Tnohw-wuh*), the word is finished off with a final *wuh* of sulky petulance, that can be made to sound almost aggressive. A child who has mastered this precisely nuanced expression can make an adult feel as though he has machine-gunned a family of rabbits.

'I'm not eating that.'

'Leave it then!'

'Tnohw-wuh.'

Hugh puts down his fork. 'I think I'm with the boys here. Have you got anything else?'

Amelia pushes back her chair and stands up. 'Can I go out now?'

'Out? Now? Where?'

I'm flustered. The stress of cauliflower cheese diplomacy has prevented me from noticing that Amelia is wearing a tiny midriff-revealing top. She has heavy black make-up round her eyes and blue eyelids. I tell myself it's only a phase, but it depresses me to see my fresh young girl, desperate to look older, aping the exaggerated make-up of older women who are desperate to look younger.

'Out with friends.'

'It's five o'clock. It's dark already. Where were you going exactly?'

'To the common.'

'The common! Like that?'

Tooting Bec Common, which starts at the end of our road, is worked on its eastern edge by rough-looking prostitutes with dirty knees, and expressions which seem to say, 'I've got my easy-to-get-your-finger-in knickers on.' The thought of Amelia standing there in her gaudy make-up sends a chill through me.

'Not our common.'

'What common then?'

'I don't know what it's called. It's near school. All the kids go there.'

'Why? What are you going to do?'

'Hang out. I dunno.'

'I don't think you should go.'

'Tnohw.'

'It's dark. And cold.'

'It's fun.'

To a child, fun is the ultimate justification; utterly persuasive, for its own sake. And Amelia is still a child. She's 12. She still says Tnohw. Fun is reason enough to put on your most vulnerable clothes, go to an unspecified open space and expose yourself to the dangers of the London night.

On the other hand, why shouldn't she go out? She's almost 13, it's only five o'clock, and isn't fun what commons are supposed to be for? When I was her age, I could go where I wanted in the evening, so long as I came back by a certain time. We live in a more dangerous time now, and in a more dangerous area, yet even so, should I not encourage her adventurousness, while advising compromises – for example, a thick jumper?

Of course I should, and I will, but there is another reason, apart from her safety, why I don't want Amelia to go out. I'm ambivalent about her growing up. I'm her father. I want her to join in the kiss chase, but I don't want her to get caught.

I am standing, watched resentfully by Sean, Toby and Amelia, frozen in indecision, staring deep into the bowl of cauliflower cheese on the table, as though it were the mirror of Galadriel, when suddenly an awful, rasping, choleric roar breaks out: "Fuck! Fuck! Fucking-fucking-fuck-fuck!"

The hair prickles on the back of my neck. I'd forgotten about Paul the plumber in the bathroom. The cry ends with a strangled groan that could be weeping. I can't ignore this one. I run upstairs to the bathroom. No job too small Paul is on his knees, wretched.

'Broke the basin,' he says.

It is clear to me that anyone can call himself a plumber. All he needs is to print out some cards and find someone gullible enough to suspend their disbelief. Paul is probably a writer of funny articles for newspapers, driven to masquerade as a plumber by a critical shortfall in competence and commissions, and possibly the motivating fantasy that one day he too might winter in Phuket.

Chapter 3 TURKEY

Jack presides over the desk like the satrap of a rich desktop province, perfectly at ease with himself in this position of exalted honour, on the throne of undealable-with-yet-unthrow-awayable papers, re-arranging them, at his leisure, in cat order, with annotations of fluff and cat dust and little black spots of cat grit. After thinking about it a while, he dabs idly at a paper clip. An hour after that exertion, he stretches on his side until his body is as stiff as a metal ladder, and a far leg pushes a jar of pencils off the edge of the table. Later, much later, he stands up and walks across the keyboard, writing an inscrutable cat remark, 'ksdhqw&$`3'#pnu – proi', on the screen.

Simpson sits on the window ledge, eyeing him balefully. She can't go on the desk because he doesn't allow it. When he goes in the garden for his lunchtime walk, and pats a bird to death, she watches him through the window, dribbling and sibilating, with her thumb down, like Mrs Caesar. This is his mother. She resents him and adores him equally. He does what he wants. A typical Friday, except that it's five days before Christmas.

Martha rings, shattering the calm. She wants to know how the Christmas preparations are progressing.

'I'm writing a novel,' I say.

I have done nothing towards organising Christmas at all, proving conclusively that Christmas hysteria was invented by women to make their traditional role seem more difficult and important than it is. I have worked instead on my novel:

'Codbucket!'

'*Codpot*, sir.'

'Oh, yes, Codpot – different kettle of fish altogether.'

That's it. So far. It raced along terrifically there for a while, but then I got blocked. I like this dialogue though. It has promise. It's pat. Well pat. I spent a long time fine-tuning the word order and punctuation to ensure my intended voice inflection.

The trouble is, I don't know what these two are talking about, and I don't know what they're going to do next. I don't know who they are either, except one of them seems to be called Codpot, though that could change, of course, as nothing is written in blood. It would be a shame if it did though, as the joke would go with it – the only joke so far in the book, which, on current evidence, seems to be shaping up as a comic novel, unless, of course, this is merely an episode of light relief. It would help to know what the book is about, but I don't. Yet. I know Codpot is subservient to the other person, whoever he may be, but for how long, and exactly why they came to be where they are, wherever that may be, is a blank sheet. If I knew anything about them at all, it would make my task a lot easier, though after two days kicking the thing around, I'm not certain now that I want to be stuck with these two for a whole book. In fact, I'm starting to hate them.

All this, depressingly, seems to prove that I have nothing to write about.

'Novel?' says Martha.

'Codpot.'

'Codpot?'

'Codpot – The Novel ...'

'Ridiculous!' Ridiculous is Martha's favourite word. The inflection can vary from a gentle glissando to an Uzi-like, staccato burst, as now, with particular scornful stabbing emphasis on the 'dic' syllable, signifying utter contempt. Martha is very agitated, but I see no reason to panic. 'You've got presents to buy, a tree to buy, a turkey to buy, decorations to organise, and a Christmas lunch for 15 people to plan, and you're sitting there fiddling about. Get it into your head: Christmas is coming!' She throws the phone down.

It rings immediately. 'And the goose is getting fat!' I shout.

'Mr Plimmer? Mungo's school here. I hate to disturb you, but as *always* on the last day of term, school closes an hour early. However, though most of the children have gone, Mungo is still here. It would be *so* nice to go home for Christmas this year.'

The sight of my six-year-old alone at school, with a term's worth of school work to show me and not a hint of reproach in his voice, would be chastisement enough for a Pinochet, let alone a petty misdemeanour like me. So I decide to get the Christmas ball rolling then and there. We make a festoon out of cornflake cartons and string – Mungo got the idea from a children's TV programme. It stretches across the room like a great string of rubbish, and detaches itself with a brontosaurian sigh the second Martha walks through the door, unpeeling a long strip of wallpaper.

Next morning, Hugh, Mungo and I watch a TV programme about the industrious and sensible beaver, an animal that, like us, builds an elaborate home, but unlike us, draws the line at putting up Christmas decorations. He does have a tree, however. I walk to Mitcham Lane, buy a tree and carry it home, children skipping and jibbering around my feet. We fix it up and get the lights going. I feel good: a man's job, well done.

'Not bad,' Martha says when she comes home. 'What about Christmas cards?'

'I thought we wouldn't send cards.'

'We have to send cards.'

'Not everybody does.'

'Who doesn't? Who doesn't send cards?'

'The sensible beaver ...'

Next day, on the computer, I draw up an alphabetical list of 239 potential Christmas card recipients. The projected cost is more than we have in the stamp tin. Also I've missed the second class post. So I trim the list to 50 and, instead of a card, I compose a round letter. It takes a while, what with the Poem Of Little Happinesses and all, but I'm pleased with the result. I read it to Martha over the phone.

'A turkey,' she says.

'What?'

'You *must* get a turkey. You're probably too late. They have to be ordered in advance.'

No they don't. There are hundreds of them at the supermarket. You just have to hoick one out of the freezer. I walk out exultant – children jibbering and skipping around my feet – turkey-wise. Also I've managed to purchase 40 silver metal pan scourers for us to unravel and make into Christmas decorations. I don't know where I picked up this trick, but I remember someone on television demonstrating how, with some scissors, string and just a little scourer lore, you can produce the elaborate shimmering garland they made earlier.

I sit the turkey in water in the sink to defrost. It's so big that not all of it fits in. The pan scourers refuse to be made into Christmas decorations, no matter how hard we try. Both Mungo and Amelia cut their fingers on kitchen implements in their efforts to unravel them. Still, we won't go short of pan scourers for a while.

The kids are bored. I promised them a treat today, and here they are, three days before Christmas, sitting bleeding from the hands with a pile of economy pan scourers and a frozen corpse. We make mince pies to cheer ourselves up, and then I take them all to the War Museum at Kennington. The War Museum is one of my favourite excursions, and it's great that Hugh is here to explain the aeroplanes to the children. I have to be careful, though, that Mungo doesn't see anything horrific, which might haunt his Christmas.

The visit's a success, but in the middle of the trench warfare simulation, I remember the mince pies, and we dash out along an unfamiliar passage leading through the concentration camp section. Turning a corner, we are faced with an intense, blown-up image of an emaciated Buchenwald survivor, staring bleakly, with cadaverous eyes, through a barbed wire fence. This is exactly what I didn't want to happen.

'Look,' says Mungo, 'it's Michael Jackson!'

The mince pies are acrid balls of grapeshot when we get home. Hugh is talking doggedly about the miracle of Marigold gloves, I don't know why, and the turkey is asserting an ominous presence. It too is giving off a smell – not a *bad* smell exactly, but an odour nonetheless, like that of a fat man after a shower. It makes me uneasy. You can't help but identify with something that big and that naked, which is bathing in your sink.

Martha is appalled when she sees it: it's too big to thaw in time, she says, and anyway frozen turkey is *not* what we give our Christmas lunch guests. Too late.

Martha cleans her teeth for five full minutes every night. No big deal, you may say. In fact Martha has said as much to me herself. Or rather she has said, 'Ho hiiih hiheaah', which is the language of people who are cleaning their teeth: a foamy form of Japanese. Their inscrutability, and the annoying way they count down seconds in their heads, so that they are unable to concentrate on the important things you have to say, makes their company trying.

Well, it may not sound like a big deal – five minutes a night – but when you've only got one bathroom, with one faulty basin, and you're weary and waiting in line, five minutes seems a lifetime. Five minutes a night adds up to 35 minutes a week. This may not sound much either, but think of it as 35 minutes standing waiting for someone to clean their teeth and the matter is thrown into a new light.

Consider too how little I see of Martha anyway. I'm not envious of her position. I'm not a competitive person. It thrills me when she comes home at night in her slick work outfit, parks her company car, phones Los Angeles. I follow her round the house. I want to know who she went to lunch with; what she ordered; what she said. She looks smart; she is smart. She deserves to be admired; I admire her. I love her even when she's prickly with me, like she is lately.

It's the teeth cleaning that drives me mad. It's squeezed into an already over-packed pre-bedtime activity slot, which starts at the point in the evening when we are too weary to stand up and ends the second we fall asleep. Into this matchbox of opportunity must be fitted many other rituals: house locking, cat organisation, child tucking-in, school bag packing, the making of beverages, attempting to read a page of something worthy, like James Mills' 1,165-page *The Underground Empire: Where Crime and Governments Embrace*, discussing an intractable problem, and having sex. More often than not, as it always seems to be the last item on the agenda, it is the sex which is carried over for consideration at a later date.

All I want to do, despite my tiredness, is pick her up and throw her on the bed, but that's hard enough to arrange even when she's not fed up with me. The fact that I have been busy all day catering to the needs of children and turkeys doesn't cut any ice with her either. Women may claim they want a man who takes out the kitchen rubbish every day without fail, but when it comes to the crunch, they don't want to make love to the sort of man who takes out the kitchen rubbish every day without fail. I want sex all the time, whether I'm happy or sad, alert or tired, stressed or unstressed; Martha wants sex only when all conditions are exactly right. Even then she cleans her teeth first.

Thirty-five minutes a week amounts to 30 hours 20 minutes a year. Now we're talking almost a complete working week. Add on the business with the disclosing tablets and the tiny SureSmile mint-flavoured cosmetic radiator brushes as well and you're running at well *over* a working week. I read today about a man who thinks it's healthy to drink his own urine every day. He must have to clean his teeth for 30 minutes so that he doesn't smile at people like a queer old Labrador. That's five working weeks a year and 10 gallons of Oral-B Extra-long Reach. You can bet he has to floss too – the worst dental habit of all – which involves putting one hand entirely inside the mouth. Habitual users floss in bed, making shuddery gasping and pluncking noises into the early hours. It's like lying next to a masturbating armadillo, which suffers from asthma. There's no time limit on this one.

'Thank God you don't drink your own urine.'

'Hiih?'

Sometimes, because I can't think of anything else to talk about while waiting there behind that self-absorbed dressing gown, I ask Martha why she spends a week of her life each year brushing her teeth. The answer is the dentist told her to do it. Actually the dentist told her to brush her teeth for five minutes every morning as well, but

Martha has defaulted on this part of the instruction. It's her way of rebelling.

I resent the hold the dentist has on my wife. And on me. Not content with nobbling my nightmares, he wants to fill up my sex allocation with teeth too.

We have many problems to discuss in bed tonight before we can go to sleep, and I am thankful for them, because they are a distraction from our main problem, which is the arid state of my career. We must discuss what presents I have to buy tomorrow when I go Christmas shopping, and the preparations I must make for our enormous Christmas lunch. As well as this family, we have invited our friends Clive and Sam, and Peter and Candice, who have two children each; also Sam's mother and father, who will be staying with them, and a woman named Margot, who is an old school friend of Sam's mother's, who lives in Hong Kong and is turning up in England for the first time in 30 years. She's been away so long nobody knows what she's like. I have to buy a present for her.

Another difficulty is Clive and Sam's boy Rufus, who is four, and has the looks and physique of a German U-boat commander. Despite this, his motivating passion is dressing up in girl's clothes. When he comes here he makes straight for Amelia's cupboard, emerging bejewelled, feathered and frocked. He thinks he's up on the catwalk with Naomi and Kate. Everyone claps and laughs, but this encourages him further. The trouble is: he's getting good at it.

Clive, who works in the macho culture of high finance, favours the sciences over the humanities and played rugby at school, has decided it's getting out of hand. He has asked us to help by buying Rufus masculine dressing-up clothes for Christmas.

Another problem: Lowell has gone to the country to spend Christmas with his mother, so I will have to take Mungo and Amelia and Hugh shopping with me tomorrow, as Hugh will never be able to cope alone in the house with the kids. Martha points out that if I'd done the shopping days ago when she suggested, I wouldn't have this problem. She looks at the present list we've made. 'God knows how we're going to pay for all this.'

'Credit cards again, I suppose.'

'Or you could get some work.'

I knew this was coming. 'You know my difficulties.'

She knows my difficulties. There's precious little work. I have only one commission pending: the piece about sex in unusual places, for the women's magazine *Perfecta*. Many of my regular outlets have dried up. Two magazines that used me regularly have closed down and my most supportive glossy magazine editor has gone freelance herself. Fees are being squeezed and on top of that, the climate isn't good for humour. Not that magazines have stopped asking for it; in fact it comes up at every editorial meeting where ideas are short on the ground: 'How about a funny?' someone says.

But they don't really want funny. The proof is in the brief. They ask for a *sideways*, or *lighthearted* look, at whatever it is. The subject is irrelevant to me, because any subject can be funny, but as soon as I hear words like *sideways*, I know I'm on dodgy ground: these are euphemism for funny. Humour is always unpredictable – that's the nature of the beast, and it flirts with doom. Most magazines don't like doom – it's too downbeat, and the unpredictable doesn't fit their rigid reader profiles. They'd rather settle for the predictable, which isn't funny.

I accept their assignments anyway of course, knowing that they will either ask me to rewrite the piece or will destroy it quietly or put it through a blender and *then* print it, with an important feed line removed, so the payoff doesn't make sense. 'Humour writing is like architecture,' I tell them. 'You can't just take out a joist.'

'Don't be pretentious,' they say.

Women's magazines are the worst, I don't know why. Sometimes they put exclamation marks (fittingly known in the trade as *screamer*s) at the end of every sentence in which they discern wit, which makes the writer come across like the Laughing Policeman. Worst of all is when an over-enthusiastic sub-editor tinkers with something and makes it funnier. That's unforgivable.

These, my gripes, I lay before Martha.

'I know all that,' says Martha, 'and I'm not saying it's not difficult. But it's beginning to sound like an excuse. It's as though you've given up, stopped caring. You used to be full of ideas for new projects. There was always the feeling that something good might develop ...'

'I still have ideas. I've got an idea for a magazine for househusbands, called *Coping Weekly*. And I want to do a book about hitch-hiking round Iraq with a fridge ...'

'You see, you're just facetious. We have to take this seriously. We already owe Barclaycard £6,000. We're in crisis here. You haven't done your tax return for two years and this house is a mess. How are we going to find the money to do it up? We've lived here five years and we still don't have a proper kitchen. There are no doorknobs on the downstairs doors; if you close them then you can't open them; if you open the oven door then you can't close it ...' She sighs. I hate it when Martha sighs.

Martha can go from prickly to despair in a second. It's the side of her I like least. She comes home a cool, glamorous, professional woman, and with just one wave of my magic wand she turns into a Kurdish war widow whose oven door won't close.

'So what if the oven door doesn't close?' I say. 'We've got a good house. We've got great children. We've got love ... Isn't that enough to be getting on with? In fact we should be making love now. It would be much more useful to me than itemising my shortcomings ...'

'How could we possibly make love now?'

'Yes, I'm naive. And you're always so serious, so doggedly ... sensible. Sometimes it would help if you just loosened up.'

'Believe me, I'd love not to be sensible, but someone's got to do it, and in this family it seems to be me who's drawn the short straw. You can sit around all day being as irresponsible as you like, but I'm the one with the sensible job and the sensible salary. You know, people at work think I must be reasonably well off, with my job. All my friends have carpets. They take them for granted. Even my secretary has carpets! I'm 46 and I still can't afford them. And you've decided to stop doing all the things which make money. Just like that. You've stopped doing celebrity interviews. A couple of those now would carpet the whole house.'

'They're boring. I'm trying to carve a niche for myself.'

'Sitting at home doodling with Cowpat?'

'Codpot. I'm trying to write a novel.'

'What's it about?'

'I don't know.'

She sighs. 'Look, does it really matter that celebrity interviews are boring – they'd earn us money and get you writing again.'

'I don't want to sit in a Park Lane hotel room for 20 minutes with a film star I'm not interested in, asking the same sordid questions about their private life that 15 other journalists have already tried on them that morning.'

'But you could do it, occasionally.'

'I can't do it occasionally – that's the point. You have to live it. I've been there and I don't want it.'

'It's all about what you want. What about me? What about the children? Why not do it for us?'

Martha has turned her back on me, curled up and gone to sleep in her purple pyjamas. She always sleeps curled in a ball, which is curious, because it was her sharp extremities I fell in love with first: the pointed toes, the elbows which stick in the air when she's on the phone, the sharp frizz of hair, the long, long, pointed nose. I love that nose, and the way she looks down it.

The least sensible thing Martha ever did was marry me. Winning her was a triumph in its way, but not a noble one: I lured her with false pretences. Technically, I was ditched. She'd already given me the big talk about being friends, not lovers; about her attachment to her independence; about, by the way, the other man who had turned her head with his sophisticated manner, not to mention fabulous salary and career prospects...

Through all the madness there was this uncharacteristic calculating, icy determination. Sure I was insanely obsessed, but I had nothing left to lose except my pride – and I didn't care a fig leaf for that – so I was going to give it my best shot.

I put all my money, and a lot I didn't have, on a Valentine's Day spectacular. I had inside information. Typically she dressed in black and white, but her pyjamas were purple. That seemed to be the key. I arranged a Purple Love Day. It would be both intimate and public. It would be do or die.

I made a card from a page of purple prose torn from a romantic novel. I signed it Mr Write. I had it delivered to her flat at daybreak with a great basket of purple and white flowers.

That was the easy bit. For a week I had been stockpiling presents: books of love poems and records with purple covers, things in purple boxes, a purple scarf, purple soaps and fragrances, a hideous purple liqueur called Parfait Amour and many little purple curiosities. I had spent a whole day individually wrapping them in yards of purple fabric, with elaborate bows, and handwritten notes.

One by one, on the hour, I had them delivered to her office. It was risky, because I had to assume she might be offended that I had gone public; might be seething in a sea of purple flotsam. Whatever, I had to see this through to the end, so to make sure she couldn't track me down and stop me, I kept changing my location and my courier.

The last purple persuader was a huge hand-blown glass bowl filled with chocolates, gold dragees, frosted violets and mini presents wrapped in purple and gold. When the taxi driver carried it in at 5 p.m. he blushed. The office clapped.

Later that evening she opened her flat door to my trembling knock and behind her, I could only see purple. Clearly now she was infected by the madness too, because she just shook her head and held out her arms. Six red roses – from the man with prospects – sat on a side table.

I felt almost guilty. I still do. The Purple Love Day broke her resistance, but also my worldly fortune. My credit cards were cancelled, my car repossessed.

That lovely girl married a pauper, and a problematic one at that. My present stumbling inactivity is making her unhappy and I'm not sure how much more patience she has.

Chapter 4 SEX

There's sex and there's sex. We've all had the first sort but it's the second sort we really crave.

The first sort would do right now though. Any sort really. I'm starving for it. I need it. I need to press its petals apart with my thumbs and gorge on it.

But my Martha is unintoxicated. She's immune to my madnesses.

I think these things while she sleeps. I'm too agitated by our conversation to sleep myself; too upset that I disappoint her.

It's not long, though, before my imagination reverts to desire. Is this avoidance, or normalisation? Does every man walk around with a headful of smiling vaginas?

If religious ascetics need to scourge the body to keep the mind on the subject in hand, why don't independent financial advisers have to do it?

The fact they don't makes me think it's just me; and that it might have something to do with the trains; the deep vibrations that fluster this dizzy house when the heavy goods goes by, whistling. I have read that in earthquake zones, tremors stir unquenchable passions in people; that children are conceived nine months after the earth moves. Well, the earth moves twice a day in this part of Streatham.

As a schoolboy, sex hijacked my every thought, yelled profanities at my finer impulses, tugged at my concentration like a young bitch on a short leash. Shocking, barbaric erections gatecrashed every school assembly, dissing the sermon, pointing rudely at matron. If every boy had been in the same state when we stood up to sing 'Onward Christian Soldiers', we would have rattled like a pike battalion.

In those days I used to think that by the time I was 45, the hunger would be waning. I saw that middle-aged men ran companies, governed countries, wrote books ... They couldn't do those things *and* think about sex all the time. How could anyone do brain surgery with a hard-on? Even harder – how could anyone study to be a brain surgeon with a hard-on?

Now that I'm 45 and still subject to the same urges I had at 16, I have to conclude that successful men don't think about sex at all. Those tirelessly wheeling-dealing Richard Bransons, those hyper-concerned Tony Blairs, those two-books-a-year Stephen Kings, are free to think of other things. This is – must be – the explanation for their relentless productivity. The fact is: successful men are undersexed. They can't get it up. They produce children, true, but don't they have aides for that sort of thing?

What a cruel waste it is, then, that so many women are so beholden to them. Perhaps now the truth is out, women will think again; lower their sights and their standards slightly, raise their satisfaction expectation, adjust their make-up and seek out the men who *really* appreciate them.

Because we do appreciate them, here in the pending and the out trays. We worship them; the curve of the bottom, the cool of the neck, the fabulous smile, the laughter. They are so fabulous we can't *not* look. They are salt on the tongue. They turn our legs to water, our feet to salmon. They are the reason we can't get on with our work.

Naturally, we fall in love with them at the drop of a hat. I fall in love, not exclusive, enduring-unto-eternity love of course, but idealised short-shift infatuation, easy-come devotion. I am romantically greedy. I fell for Helen Mirren by phone from Los Angeles, for Theresa Russell when she tucked her feet under her bottom on her sofa (perhaps celebrity interviews aren't so dull after all), for Fay Fife of the Rezillos when she balled out a member of her audience, for Jilly Goulden's nose via the telly, for a woman in the crowd at a circus whose face I had to stare at, but who didn't once, and never will, see me, for dark-legged waitresses who are damnably unbiased towards me, for a girl I didn't know who asked me to shield her as she peed by a motorway, for any woman who fixed my tie, for nurses, air hostesses – especially air hostesses – for glimpsed girls, pale girls, funny girls, for almost anyone called Lisa, for girls who were the best friends of girlfriends, for the sister, the mother, the maid, and the girl in the pub who put her hand on mine, wrapped her dark eyes around me and said: 'Do I disturb you as much as you disturb me?'

Did I really fall in love? I may have. I teetered sometimes, for sure. I looked over the edge into the abyss and savoured the exquisite moment of danger, knowing that if I were to jump (or even just to step), I would fall and fall and not be able to stop. And that would be it for a year ... or three ... or a lifetime. Does it make sense? Rarely. I was in love with Anne Frank when I was 13. I thought I could save her. I couldn't. She was dead. That's the problem with ideal love: reality gets in the way. Before long I was two-timing her with Tess of the D'Urbervilles. I wanted to save her as well. I wanted desperately to make her happy, to haul her out of the melancholic truss of fate and take her dancing to Den Angelo and the Midnight Set at Bracknell stadium. The trouble was, she'd been executed a hundred years before, and hadn't really existed even then. Lust and literature have led me down many a blind alley. Then I fell for a nymphomaniac. I thought I could save her as well, but she led me a merry dance to nowhere.

I discovered then that you can't change a woman to fit your ideal. You can only live with her. And if you live with her long enough, you are the one that changes. Gradually you give up everything to her. The woman you love most is the woman you end up with, not the woman who got away.

True love doesn't fear reality. It's the love that remains when the chips are down; when the telly doesn't work, when the gateau falls in the sink, when the sex has stopped, when her ugliest mood has crushed your day. You love the woman even when you don't like her. You do. You are *there* to prove it. True love is serious. It can end in death. It often does.

With luck it will be at the age of 90, wife in one hand and glass of Mortlach in the other. But it can get you before then. A woman I loved once attacked me with a knife, a bread knife fortunately. It was almost comical. If it had been the carving knife that had come to her hand in the drawer, I might not be remembering it at all. She hurt me more later. She betrayed me. I thought I would die then anyway. I behaved so recklessly I nearly did. I didn't know whether to murder her or, like in the folk song, weep a bowl of crystal tears to wash her deceitful face.

I don't really have time for Theresa Russell, Helen Mirren, all the Lisas, and Jilly Goolden, or even for that girl in the restaurant the other month, whose nipple winked at me under the edge of her blouse as she leant across the table to whisper a secret. I have too many women to love already. I have a wife and a daughter, and love is hard work. There are only so many people a man can give everything up for. Amelia gobbles up my patience, my energy, my time and my heart, but there is surely nothing I wouldn't give up for her (or that she wouldn't ask me for). One day I will have to make the ultimate sacrifice and give *her* up too, to allow some other sucker the chance to give her everything.

I've done it again: I start off talking about sex, and end up talking about love.

Chapter 5   STRESS

Years ago, before all this, before Martha and the kids, before this huge, ancient and trembling house, before plumbers, I lived by myself. I watched the time go by as it would, let things happen as they did, and abandoned myself to the gods of arbitrary and euphoric experience. It was a balmy, dreamy, four-year hiatus from the business of the real world; so balmy and dreamy that when I look back I can remember few concrete details. I seem to recollect clouds drifting slowly, gently amplified rock music playing in glades of thornless lote trees and almond-scented virgins bearing trays of sherbets.

I was jolted from this lovely lacuna by a traumatic revelation. It was my road to Damascus experience, except I wasn't on a road at all; I was lying on my back on a couch in a health clinic, having my nervous reactions measured as material for an article about stress. I had sensors on my head and hands and I was wired to a computer. A nurse told me to relax, but I was relaxed already. I was relaxed by nature. Some would say gratuitously laid back. I was expert at avoiding stress; too good for that machine anyway, which twitched, grew bored and fell asleep. The nurse scratched her head and said: 'You're either a Zen master, or dead.'

I was shocked; not that I might be dead – I had sometimes wondered about that – but that I might have achieved nirvana without even trying (which may just be the key, of course). I worried that it was affecting my sense of humour, making me boring. A cure wasn't going to be easy. I had to rid myself of everything that was safe. But discarding the comforts and cautions of a lifetime isn't easy. Then, out of the blue, I had a sort of epiphany. It came in the form of Hans Krebs, owner of the Grand Hotel Regina, Grindelwald, Switzerland.

I was on a skiing press trip, the only man in a party of six, and Hans Krebs was our guide. He was charming and convivial, but on the quiet a man of willpower, a wrestler of elements. He had successfully climbed that perpendicular rock triangle, the Eiger, from whose north face dead climbers, or what's left of them, hang from frayed ropes, and his eye contained, I realise now, a dangerous twinkle.

On the last morning, Herr Krebs announced a 'little surprise'. We were up a mountain at the time, looking across a deep valley towards the north face of the Eiger opposite. He had arranged a paragliding descent. My automatic response – 'I didn't get where I am in life by jumping off cliffs' – was drowned out by the spontaneous enthusiasm of my five female companions. They were delighted. One of them was 60. 'Ooh lovely!' she said.

And so it happened that, strapped to the harness of Joey – a paraglider operator who, I was distressed to note, was even taller and heavier than me – I leapt into the void. In an instant all the physical symptoms we now know as stress, which once enabled our caveman ancestors to fight and flee dangerous animals, took place in my body. Adrenalin surged, pupils dilated, pulse and blood pressure soared, oxygen rushed to muscles, testicles drew safely up towards the abdomen, bowels emptied.

Stress, and I can't stress this enough, is what makes us tick. Not just tick, but hum and whoop and yodel as well. I did that day.

Of course, there aren't that many mountain precipices in South London, which poses a problem for the man who has become addicted to stress. Besides which, there's stress and there's stress, and actually this sort of parachutey thing is child's play. Any man who reckons he can live a stressed-up life just by paragliding is, frankly, not really trying. He's kidding himself. He's in Stress Kindergarten. If he really wants stress, he'll get children.

Searching the cellar for the Christmas decorations, I come across Penelope Leach. She's lying under a bag of outdoor shoes; damp and skewed into the floor mulch like the preserved remains of an Iron Age bog person; a Tollund child-care expert, dented by the impression of thousands of years of wellington boots.

And that was how it went. The next week's session was much the same. And the next was the same as that. Nothing changed. Except me. I changed. I got sucked in. The weekly ritual started to woo me. As time went by and Martha grew bigger and more scarily imminent, the other students began to turn into almost reasonable people. The industrial relations expert gave us a lift home some nights; Mike the wine merchant took me to a Louis Jadot tasting. We still see Tony and Janet, the teachers (though our relationship is based almost entirely on a mutual need for DIY back-up), and Clive, the City economist, and his wife Sam, a photographer's stylist and costume designer, have became two of our best friends.

It wasn't friendship though, that reeled me in; it was the presence of the women. The magnetic women: so tranquil, yet so stimulating. The drama of their predicament, more intense every Thursday, electrified me. It was a buzz, frankly. That room was so full of feel-good pregnancy pheromones it was a drug trip. No wonder workers in prenatal clinics are always smiling like people who've been told they can eat as much ice cream as they want. It made the artificial stimulations I had enjoyed in my previous life seem tame. We left that house each week on a tide of euphoria and breastfeeding pamphlets. We were charmed. We were in this adventure together: the industrial relations expert, the wine merchant, the actor, the teacher, human genetic scientist, balloon women, Penelope Leach and me.

Then suddenly we weren't. One Thursday night a full fortnight before the proper end of the course, the wine retailer appeared in the doorway holding, stiffly, like a rare 1961 Chateau Lâtour, a baby. He had a baby! Jessica. We passed her round the room reverentially. She was the weight of a reasonable cauliflower.

The rest of us had to wait until the end of the NCT course, some longer. Clive and Sam had Tamara, Martha and I Amelia. At the point of birth our last shreds of independence vanished. Nothing would ever be the same again.

After that our NCT group met up occasionally at organised Sunday afternoon tea parties, to swap notes, while our new children hit each other over the heads with plastic buckets. Gradually, as we settled into our new families, the meetings grew less frequent. The last time we all met together was for the funeral of Thomas, the son of the actor and his wife, the only baby boy born to our group, who died suddenly of pneumonia. A single undertaker carried the white toy coffin through the church across his arms. There were no more teas after that.

Clive and Sam had a second child, Rufus, and we had Mungo.

Our children were not at all what we expected. Some children fight childhood, beat it back, hurtling ahead impatiently. Others indulge it. We had one of each. Amelia came out angry, roaring like a lion. Mungo arrived with a sigh, looking like Henry Kissinger, all wrapped up with knowledge. Amelia's an operator; she works the system. Mungo, slow, darling, sweet perpetual child, will suck his thumb for the rest of his life, metaphorically at least. They are chalk and cheese, and they hate each other. Amelia resents Mungo's arrival still, six years after the event, and after six years of being pinched secretly, he resents her too. It's like having a Palestinian and an Israeli in the same family.

Our children boomed; the mortgage burgeoned and at some point in the mêlée, Penelope Leach slipped unobserved into the cellar. Perhaps it all got too much for her, I don't know. Maybe we began to disregard her. Maybe we grew out of her, for there is a lot about babies, much of it unpalatable, which she omitted to reveal in her book. Perhaps she censored herself, so as not to put prospective parents off, though I think people who are typically at the time of life (misleadingly referred to as 'settling down') when loud noise is becoming less attractive to them, should be told (among other things) that what they are about to bring into the world is the loudest thing known to man.

Here are some of the other missing facts:

Babies may look small and helpless but one day they will take over the world. They've already won the propaganda war. They wrap adults round their little finger, and they have ten little fingers round which to wrap them. Even before they can speak, babies display natural leadership qualities. They communicate orders effectively with body language, fully expecting them to be carried out unquestioningly, any time of the day or night. These leadership qualities decrease with age: when adults give an order, nobody takes any notice.

Babies attract mothers-in-law to your house.

They monopolise your wife. Where once she was ready to roll across the bed at a moment's notice, squirming and giggling, now she is adrift in a sea of domesticity, children nudging against her like tugboats. At first you will resent this. Then you will decide they are worth any sacrifice. Then you are doomed.

The impression that babies are in control is not an impression. They *are* in control. Their whim is your command. If their whim isn't satisfied, they scream. Often they don't know what their whim is. It's your job to work out what it is. They make your life hell until you do.

Babies won't go to sleep just because they're tired. When they're tired, instead of going to sleep, they shout. It's your job as a parent to notice when they're tired and then make them go to sleep. They don't take being told to go to sleep lying down – especially when they're tired. At 4 a.m. when you want nothing more in the world than to be asleep, you have to stay awake trying to persuade someone who would rather be awake to go to sleep.

Babies don't care how incredibly important your incredibly important work is.

Babies are the opposite of burglar alarms: they're silent when you come into the bedroom, but go off when you try to creep out. You can cajole or shout, but the only language babies understand is the language of milk. When you do finally get them to sleep you can't go to sleep yourself for worrying about them. Sometimes they lie very still in their cots holding their breath, to see if they can give you a heart attack. Babies wake up randomly at any time of the night or day. They cry when they wake up as well, even though they didn't want to go to sleep in the first place. They are alarm clocks with no time control and no off button.

Babies grasp your lip with the grip of a circus strongman and twist it, making you look like a rainforest tribesman.

Order irks them. To babies a neat shelf of alphabetically filed CDs is intense provocation. They hide the car keys in a secret place and never ever tell you where it is. When you double up in pain from stubbing your toe on a chair leg, they laugh.

It's a parent's job to make babies wear their hat and their booties, but bear in mind the following: (1) they won't wear their hat; (2) they won't wear their booties. They would rather have frostbite than booties. You can't reason with them.

You think your baby is beautiful, but years later, while looking at snaps, you realise it looked like a potato. People who say 'What a beautiful baby!' are often thinking 'What a potato!' You can't believe the potatoes other parents get lumbered with.

That's not puppy fat in those cheeks, it's stockpiled dribble. To you dribble is a charming part of baby's expressive repertoire. To a stranger it's dribble. If Quentin Tarantino made a feature film about baby dribble it would be deemed too disturbing to be shown.

Without warning, babies smack you in the nose, making your eyes water.

Babies reject out of hand the carrot and chicken purée you have slaved over a hot stove to make them, but will happily eat earwigs from the garden. They also eat tulips. What they can't eat in one sitting they shred. They put everything in their mouth, except food, which they put everywhere else. At meal times they forget where their mouth is. They press food into their face in the hope some of it will go in. They eat the rest later when they find it under the fridge.

Don't be misled by the charming babycare book euphemism 'posset'. We're talking vomit here. Babies vomit a lot, and they never warn you when. That's because being sick comes so naturally to them, they don't know themselves when they're going to do it. Sometimes they don't know they have been sick. They can expectorate a gallon of warm milk into an open shirt front without being aware of it. Sometimes they are secretly sick down the back of your shoulder, making people think you own a parrot with gippy tummy.

They suddenly become so ill that you rush them to casualty. When you get there they get better. While sitting on Aunt Maud's lap at family dos, they stealthily undo her blouse buttons, revealing her giant brassière.

Anyone who says nappy changing is fun has no sense of smell. It's a fact that 99 per cent of adults are not interested in watching you change the baby's nappy and will resent being hauled upstairs to participate. The other 1 per cent are mad. Girl babies are preferable to boy babies because they don't wee in your eye. When you have an evil spready nappy to remove, babies go into a horizontal Riverdance routine.

They rip your spectacles off and fling them over your shoulder.

When carrying them in shops they lunge sideways without warning, making you knock over elderly customers. They start conversations with undesirables on buses. They arch their body like an iron bar when you're trying to secure their complicated car seat belt mechanism. At funeral services they hoot with joy.

A toddler is a baby with ten times the range and destructive power. Toddlers wake you at dawn by dropping a plastic wheelbarrow on your head. They take one bite out of an apple and leave the rest. Then they take one bite out of another apple.

Children take your youth, your wife, your sleep and your sex life. They drain your bank account, strain your marriage and stain your carpet. Ironically children wouldn't be here if it wasn't for sex, yet as soon as they are here, they do their best to make sure you never have it again. Lying between you in bed is one very effective deterrent. They know this instinctively, like they know of Elvis. Children don't have to learn Elvis. He has entered the hereditary blueprint, Lamarckian-style. Every child knows who Elvis is, what he looks like, and that he shakes his hips and goes A-wha A-whah, even though nobody has ever told them. If the accumulated knowledge of man were wiped out overnight, the survivors, 1,000 years from now, would draw pictures of Elvis and wonder what it was.

Children are supposed to inherit your characteristics, yet when they hammer round the house screaming, posting bananas into the video player, dribbling biscuit concrete on the carpet and scraping their feet down the walls, it's clear they've inherited the genes of Vikings. At bedtime however, when they bring out a checklist of exacting requirements – book, teddy bear of approved type, unique hard-to-find special blanket, pre-specified seating position, drink heated to regulation temperature, discreet lighting of pre-ordained wattage – they turn into tiny EU officials. Put a single foot wrong and back comes the Viking.

Children make you feel old. They show you how smooth your skin isn't, how cute your feet aren't. Birth 'experts' say you'll feel yourself again in six months, but it takes 16 years. Even then you don't feel yourself. You feel like an older person. Having someone depend on you 24 hours a day for food, shelter, moral guidance, and financial and emotional support is not the most rejuvenating experience. You feel even less young when your baby is not only taking the car keys, but generating parking tickets too. Once you have a child, the possibility of ever appearing on *Top Of The Pops* is diminished a hundred thousandfold.

When adults take children to the top of the house and say, 'One day all this will be yours!', they say 'Can I go back and watch *EastEnders*?' They already assume it's theirs. And so it is.

After you have children, the balance of your life changes. The deal is this: their needs, however banal, come first. You are no longer the most important person in the world; your needs are no longer (if they ever were), your wife's priority, they are not your priority, and depending how winning your child's smile is, they may not even be your mother's priority. Children teach you how it feels to come second.

All this though, is not enough, for children want something extra. Something huge. They *demand* it, and they'll grow up to be traffic wardens unless they get it. It's the biggest possible thing you have in you to give; the thing which, though bandied about often enough in promissory love songs, few are willing to give even to their romantic partner. It's Unconditional Love. The UL clause in the pact between parent and child would be thrown out of any legal contract. It's the no-limit, non-conditional, outsize-print insurance cover, the soft lining at the bottom of the cliff, the non-reciprocal ultimate gift. UL survives every kind of wear and tear. The IKEA chair back-testing machine cannot break it, nor can it be crushed by evil. It transcends murder and betrayal. It was there in the eyes of the Sierra Leone mothers whose execution by their brainwashed sons was the initiation ceremony to become a child soldier of the Revolutionary United Front. Preposterously, children demand UL, and get it.

There *are* returns for parents of course. Some are obvious, ga-ga in your face; others difficult to quantify. Like a certain madness that overcomes your formerly neat and predictable life. Is this good or bad? At first it's hard even to work out what's going on, let alone discern benefits, because children are hallucinogenic. If they came in pill form they'd be illegal.

A couple of months after Amelia arrived, a magazine sent me to Liverpool to interview some performers who were appearing in a TV rock concert, staged on a floating pontoon in the Albert Dock. An old sailing ship moored near the stage had been converted into a press reception venue for the evening. Given the amount of free drink available, I suppose it was inevitable that I would climb to the top of one of the ship's masts to get a better view of the final act, The Damned. The view was fantastic, but the last thing I saw, as the band came on stage, was my glasses disappearing into the Mersey. God knows how I got down. I interviewed Rat Scabies after the gig, staring fixedly at a blob I reckoned to be his head. The next day I felt my way out of Liverpool and scuttled home, eager to get back to familiar surroundings and shuck off the tramontane peculiarities of the outside world. I was anxious not only because I had suddenly been deprived of sight, but because I had to complete the Rat Scabies interview that day, and also another feature about potatoes. I led a glamorous life.

Turning my key in the door I became aware of a tremendous volume of noise and activity inside my house, of women hooting with laughter and babies belling. Some kind of nanny rave was going on. As I peered short-sightedly into the sitting room, silence descended. It was like the arrival of Lee Van Cleef in a Badlands bar. Nannies in tight pastel leggings looked up at me, their mouths open and full of Pringles. I could just about make out our new nanny there, in the middle, and Amelia on the floor. Children were everywhere.

After a moment, one of the senior boys (he was about three) strode towards me – a spokesman, obviously. He stopped, considered his words carefully, pointed to his feet and said: 'I've got my shoes on.'

I couldn't argue with that and there would have been little point trying, so I backed slowly – taking care not to step on anyone – into my study, shut the door and dithered. My house was crawling with homunculi. It had been taken over. I could hear them rattling around downstairs, upstairs; one of them, even now, in the toilet next door to my study, mouthing some nameless ululation. The noise abruptly stopped and after a bit of shuffling, my study door opened. A little girl appeared, about two years old. 'Ready,' she said. I'd never seen her before in my life.

'Ready?' I was irked by the intrusion, but I tried to affect a kindly tone, as I didn't want to frighten her. After all, I must have looked very important to her in my big grown-up study. 'Ready for what?'

'For you to wipe my bottom.'

Now here's a curious fact: though you will never again experience such hellish drudgery as that which children put you through, you will probably look back on this period as the most wonderful time of your life.

A few weeks ago Amelia came home after school with Jessica. Jessica the early bird, now a long, leggy 12-year-old with hairclips and opinions. By coincidence Jessica and Amelia are in the same class at secondary school. She's been back a few times since. I'm little more than a stranger to her, of course, but she's very special to me. I can't look at her without remembering the night 12 years ago – back when Penelope Leach ruled the world – when I held her in my hand and wanted her more than anything on earth.

Chapter 6 DOORS

I am woken every morning by a smirking cardboard Santa Claus lurching towards my bed, like a carnival float in a gratuitously cheerful nightmare.

It is an advent calendar, made in Germany. I know it was made in Germany because on the back is written a Teutonic enjoinment to dogmatic revelry: *Alle rechte vorbehalten* (all to the right forward-stopping). Noting Mungo's uncharacteristic punctuality as he crashes into my bedroom holding it aloft for the dawn door-opening ceremony, I know he has taken it to heart.

It gives me the creeps. For unknowable reasons the German artist has modelled this Santa, right down to its wire-rimmed glasses and malicious twinkle, on Benny Hill. Each dawn Benny challenges me to suspend my disbelief and blackmails me to suspend my cynicism. I loathe the thing, though I dare not say so, for Mungo adores it beyond reason. I know that with a single word of adult disdain, I could destroy everything.

Mungo's one criticism of the calendar is that the doors (incongruously located in Santa's stomach, beard, etc.) spring ajar before their appointed times. *Vorsprung durch technik* this calendar is not.

Squinting sideways, I could see, even before he opened them, that behind door 15 (in Santa's knee) there was an illustration of a maroon car. Behind door 18, there was a beige biscuit (or was it a roofing tile?). It was obvious that behind today's door, number 22, Mungo would find a pair of sad green socks with arthritic toes. These are the dullest of talismans. Nevertheless, a surprise is a surprise, or should be, for if it is not, it is not. In magic, mechanics are important. Even I know that.

I also know, from experience, that the magic of childhood is limited, and that eventually it runs out; faster if you peep behind doors before their due date. I warned Mungo about this in stern tones. 'Do not sneak a peek,' I said, 'or the incandescent wonder of Christmas (bound up, as is all magic, in ritual precepts) will not be vouchsafed unto you.' Or something like that.

He took it to heart, and now he is obliged to avert his eyes when looking at the calendar, as though it were a Gorgon's head he held in his lap and not a larger-than-life German Benny Hill bedecked with sad green socks.

Frankly, I didn't expect such self-control. We are talking here about a six year old who has not hitherto known how *not* to do anything. Every need in his life has had to be sorted instantly (the water's too hot, the jumper's too yellow, etc.). He can't bear to wait for anything.

He couldn't bear to wait to open today's door. His body trembled with tension. Yet he did wait. He forbade himself to look until the due time. Only the all-knowing, all-seeing adult beside him knew it was a pair of sad green socks which commanded his excruciating expectation.

'Oh! Funny little socks!' he chimed, entirely delighted. He didn't find them at all incongruous, like I did. Now one sock might suggest a Christmas stocking – at a stretch – but two? I can see no enchantment in socks.

Neither can Lowell, who is 17. He took one look and said: 'What's the point?' Yet even he is not entirely cynical – yet. He thinks that owning a car would give him the ecstatic liberty of a god, and he believes that incandescent and eternal joy would be vouchsafed to him by a single act of sexual intercourse with Kate Moss.

For me it's not so simple. I am too old to see anything approaching wonder in a cheap Santa calendar. But Mungo's eyes are wider than mine. He can see in this shoddy, mass-produced cardboard prop, all the numinous wonder of the season.

One day, I suppose, he will see a dull pair of socks for a dull pair of socks. He will see no transcendent joy in the almost surprise of a bad illustration of a biscuit. One day, I suppose, he will not run into my room in the morning.

Today the Benny Hill Santa advent calendar basks in the fickle spotlight of his approval. In this light I feel almost sorry for it. Its days are numbered.

I feel almost sorry for myself too, because when he says 'Oh! Funny little socks!' I get a sharp little pain inside me, and I know that the intoxicating, incandescent wonder of Christmas can reside in any object, but that I, the all-knowing, all-seeing adult, cannot touch it, except through him.

Already I know what lies behind door 23, and even door 24. I've seen it all. But I shall not tell my son. I have forbidden myself. The calendar has me in its sway. This Christmas, to Mungo at least, I am playing it strictly *alle rechte vorbehalten*.

To the old and cynical who don't believe in Santa Claus, the song 'I Saw Mummy Kissing Santa Claus' is at worst cute; to the young and innocent who do believe in Santa Claus it is about adultery. Either way you can't avoid it, for it returns each year like a cocky revenant.

You can't opt out, like the sensible beaver, who hides away in his humbug hole until the summer holiday brochures arrive. Your children wouldn't talk to you. Angel guano would drop on your head. Anyway Christmas is too big. It gets bigger every year. Preparation starts in January, when Chinese scribes set to work on the next batch of inscrutable cracker jokes, and new turkeys are born, full of hope. By August this year even I had been roped in, to write a sideways look for *YES!* Magazine about the tribulations of the festive season – the very pitch and yaw of which I am experiencing now.

I am in the middle of the Christmas mosh pit, at Oxford Circus, braced, at the epicentre of the Christmas commercial world, under the cheapjack product-sponsored lights, the pivot of the whole shuffling, grimly acquisitive multitude. I am the steel-hearted pin around which the Christmas carousel is doggedly gyrating, bashing me as it goes with packages of skateboards and eight-foot brass-look palm tree standard lamps, and robot dogs, and deadly holly bouquets, and grenadier guard tidy bins, and star mobiles, and unwearable saucy knickers (for Her), and unlikeable onyx desk tidies (for Him), and Bashin' Brawler wrestling dolls that scream 'Aaargh, you smashed my head!' (for Little One), while a scruffy Dickensian beggar, who probably takes more money in a day than I earn in a month, plays 'Stairway To Heaven' on an amplified accordion.

I have, on various fingers, seven carrier bags containing, among other things, long, bag-leaping rolls of wrapping paper, Go-Go Worms, a 10,000 piece jigsaw puzzle, some Mondo Water Wigglies, a pot plant, a Supersonic Ear, a big, expensive and almost empty box posing as a new board game, a heavy container of waxed play-sand, some Burples, some crackers, tangerines, chocolates and other seasonal necessities, and two dinner plates, glasses and sundry cutlery, purchased to extend the Christmas lunch capability. I am still looking for a present of some sort, a little knick-knack or furbelow (I can't decide which), for Margot, Sam's mother's colonial OAP ex-friend, who, nobody can remember ever seeing or knows anything about, yet who, nonetheless, will be coming to our house for Christmas lunch; something maybe not too modern-looking (for that may not suit her age), nor, yet again, too old-fashioned (for she may find that patronising), which could have, perhaps, some fancy decorative element (who knows?), of the sort that an old dear might find attractive, but which, on the other hand, is not over-fussy or unduly tasteless, and yet is relatively inexpensive, and also (this is important), can be carried on one finger.

I am clinging, with any fingers I can spare from the handles and holders, on to the fingers of Mungo and Amelia, and the raincoat sleeve of Hugh, cleaving them to me tightly, despite their protests, for fear they will spring from me like paper bags in the wind and be carried off down Regent Street by a contra-opposing human current, never to be seen again.

Martha was right: Oxford Circus is not the place to come with two children and a pensioner. She didn't remind me about Hamley's, the most crowded toyshop in the world, packed with irritable people shouting "No you can't!" to their children while being glad-eyed by Gummi Bears and hit on the head by boomerangs. Hugh is a lamb to the slaughter. Within seconds he is being chatted up by a talking fish.

Mungo and Amelia are stuck in an asking loop. 'Can I have a Noise Blaster?'

'No you can't.'

'Can I have a Squeezebag of eyeballs?'

'No you can't.'

'Look at this! Isn't it cute?'

'No it's not.'

'Can I have it?'

No you can't!

'Tnohw!'

They don't seem to realise that the spirit of Christmas is to give. Except when I'm giving. They are suckered by the 'squeeze me before I'm yours' come-on of every bug-eyed synthetic love-object going. Despite having the least money children are the world's best customers. Squirrels are more acquisitive, but they lack the logistical capability, and can't talk. Children can't compute the cost of an item, so expense does not mitigate their effort. Their purchasing power depends, not on income, but on emotion; on their ability to convince someone else that if they don't get whatever it is, they will wither.

'Can I have ...'

'*NO YOU CAN'T!*'

'*TNOHW!*'

What Mungo, and even Amelia, don't realise, is that some of the things they are asking me to buy for them I am buying secretly for them anyway, this being Christmas. Fortunately, children are easy to fool, because their natural assumption is that anything an adult is doing must by definition be boring, so they don't pay attention to me. Nevertheless it's hard work, because I'm dependent on Hugh to act as lookout. I stand him at a strategic point to warn me when the kids are approaching, but when I next look up he is in the thrall of a pink and yellow WuvLuv. The thing is toying with him. To his incredulous joy, it whelps a hideous mauve wuv-child into his hand, while singing 'I'm a Little Teapot'. This is where technology has brought us.

Next second he's beckoning me over to a cabinet of toys the same as the toys he himself played with as a boy. Here are lines of hand-painted Coldstream Guards in stiff cardboard packs, made by Charles Biggs Model Co., and carrying the quaint warning: 'Not suitable for children under 14 years of age'. Sadly there aren't many children over 14 any more, or even 13 or 12. Eminem comes in the night and takes their childhood away.

No wonder Christmas gets bigger every year. They never throw anything away. They just keep adding new stuff to the pile: more to see, more to sing, more to buy. As well as the fads of Christmas Present, all precociously articulate, luminous, banana smelling, stickable to walls, and made out of harmless polypropypinkyorangeygreenylene, there are the ghosts of Christmas Past: Thomas the Undead Tank Engine, Pinky and Perky, the Teletubbies with their genitals on top of their heads, and rows of Cabbage Patch Dolls, each with its unique personality, all looking like Mussolini. The sound track is Bing Crosby and Frostie the Snowman ... and here comes Mummy again, kissing Santa raw.

There are the sort of baby dolls Margaret Thatcher once played with, looking like Winston Churchill, some of them more lifelike than I feel, and next to them, busty disco chicks with impossibly thin ankles and transvestite eyelashes. Modern dolls pout and puke and pee profligately. They don't care who sees them. They show you their breasts on a first date. The genitalia-correct will go the full Monty. Disquietingly, on the packaging of one, it says 'I'M REAL'. I sip, I slurp, I wet: therefore I am.

Squeezing myself out of Hamley's mêlée on to the street, feeling momentarily as chilly and vulnerable as a lobster that has just shed its carapace, I seek out a newsagent and buy a copy of YES!, to see my Christmas feature. I flick through the pages at the bus stop, twice, but my piece isn't there. There is no sideways look; nothing. I phone the magazine immediately on my mobile. I try to stop my voice from sounding hurt.

'Let me try to remember – it's so long ago now, isn't it? Ah yes. No. We decided we were going to pass on that one.'

Pass. Of all euphemisms, this is the most hateful. 'Were you playing a board game of some sort?'

Her voice hardens. 'Look, if you want to know the truth, your piece just wasn't funny.'

'It was funny when I wrote it.'

'I'm sorry, but it wasn't.'

'It must have been the way you were reading it.' In this mood I am a volatile mix of arrogance and insecurity.

'Nobody in the office thought it was funny, not even Brenda.'

I've been here before.

'And my husband didn't like it either.'

I've never been here. 'Well, I say it *was* funny!'

I realise, as soon as I see Mungo, Amelia and Hugh's worried expressions, how pathetic I sound. I put down my bag of Go-Go Worms.

'Look,' she says. 'Let's agree that humour is subjective, and OK, perhaps we should have informed you earlier, but it really was unanimous. The tone was all wrong for us. We are a magazine that looks at life from a positive, *YES!* point of view. Your piece read as though you don't like Christmas.'

'I don't like Christmas. I wasn't meant to like Christmas; I was meant to glance sideways at it!'

'But there's sideways and sideways and yours came across as ... well ...'

'Sideways?'

'... bitter.'

It's a quiet bus ride home. I close my eyes. I let the children and the lights rattle and glitter in the background. It took the last of my energy to get Hugh up the stairs and into a seat while marshalling the children and the shopping. I'm exhausted.

I haven't bought a present for Martha either. I'd hoped to do that today, though I was being wildly over-ambitious. I've solved the problem of Clive and Sam's boy Rufus, at least. I've bought him a dressing-up kit comprising a Viking helmet, shield, breastplate and flaxen wig. Very macho.

But the magazine business drove the old lady, Margot, from my thoughts. I am just cursing myself when I remember that a similar aunt, or friend's mother, came to our house last year, and gave us a present of a tea cosy in the shape of a thatched cottage. It is the pointless product of a gormless rural craft worker's deviant mind. It will be perfect for Margot! What's more, I know exactly where it is. It's in bric-a-brac purgatory, the shelf of rejected objects at the dark end of my study.

I feel better by the time we get to Streatham High Road and, abandoning *YES!* Magazine on the seat to bring positive pleasure to someone else's life, I herd my charges to the top of the stairs. When the doors open, the sound of carol singers carries on to the bus. 'Little donkey, carry Mary safely on her way ...' The sweet melody and unaffected words, and the moving image of the donkey bearing the pregnant mother, catch me at a vulnerable moment. It's the second supercharged moment of spiritual euphoria this year. I get three each season. The green socks were the first and I know there will be another before the ball is over.

'Isn't it true,' says Mungo, 'that God is Jesus's Dad?'

I lean down to hug him, and from the top of the bag I am clutching to my chest, a stream of Brussels sprouts exits, and descends, like falling snow, on to the heads of the people below.

Chapter 7   **FUN**

Mark Borkowski is all bow-tie and bonhomie. His Christmas party this year is in an old slaughterhouse at Smithfield Market, now brightly chaotic and booming. There's the usual motley crew of show people, journalists, businesspeople and eccentrics. Guests are being encouraged to paint on large canvases. It's going to get messy. There's always an element of danger at Mark's events. Despite the fact that he's a publicist, Mark is one of the most genuine people in my professional orbit. We share a passionate appreciation of absurdity.

'Where have you been? I haven't seen you for ages.'

'I'm writing a book. I'm on my 11th word.'

Just a couple of hours ago I was weighed down with Go-Go Worms and woe, yet here I am, floating like a bubble through the party crowd, as empty-headed as a *Blind Date* contestant. Social functions are so few and far between nowadays that every one is like a dose of heroin. In fact this is the only work-related Christmas party I've been invited to this year. This is not just a measure of my growing isolation; it reflects the reluctance of publications to throw parties. Though increasingly committed to the pursuit of fashion, gossip and celebrity, journalism is fast losing its sense of fun.

'You know Gerry Cottle, don't you?'

Cottle, the circus owner, and a long-term client of Mark's, is complaining about a ban on performing animals by London councils. He's had to devise an animal-free show, which is particularly annoying to him, as he takes great care of his animals. Back home at Cottle Ranch, he maintains five-star luxury retirement pastures full of superannuated ponies, tigers and elephants. 'And now we've got a turkey too.'

'I've got a turkey.'

'I bet it's not as lively as mine.'

His turkey was acquired to make a point. When Cottle's Circus came to Battersea Park, he launched the season by reviving an old circus tradition – having a priest bless the Big Top. Of course his 'pet' turkey, called Lucky ('the luckiest turkey in London'), happened to be present too. This was a typical Mark Borkowski photo opportunity, designed to stir up controversy by pointing up the hypocrisy of politically correct animal welfare legislation, in the process getting maximum publicity for the circus.

After catching up with some old friends, I meet Lisa: dark-hair, bright-eyes, laughs a lot. Works in advertising. We seem to get on.

'Have you ever had sex in an unusual place?' I don't know why I think I can ask her this question.

'I made love once in the royal box at the Royal Festival Hall, during Mahler's Fifth Symphony.'

I've hit pay dirt, proving that procrastination is the garner of material. I make a mental note of the story for my article.

'We sneaked into the royal box during a performance. I had a summer job there at the time. It was always my ambition to orgasm during a live performance of Mahler's Fifth.'

'And you achieved it?'

'Yes.'

'There can't be many aspirations left for you.'

'There are a few.' She looks at me in a way that makes my gut shudder like a drawn cello.

'Wasn't it locked, the royal box?'

'It was easy enough to arrange if you worked there, and of course it was often empty, so you could sneak in and lie down under the balcony edge where nobody could overlook you.'

I like this Lisa. I like her a lot.

'The Queen had her own toilet too. That's where the gay men would go to screw. It was quite the done thing; something they all wanted on their résumé.'

'Did they have a red carpet in there?'

'I don't remember.'

'They probably have a special red carpet set aside in a nearby cupboard, in case the Queen gets caught short. Then they'd quickly clear out the gays and roll out the carpet. It would have to have a D shape cut out of one end of it, of course, so that it fitted round the bottom of the toilet pedestal.'

'How very practical you are!'

'I read in the paper this week that women are better at languages, but man have a superior spatial sense. D shapes are no problem at all for a man of my abilities.'

The party is swinging. Everything is bright and vital. Soon I'm telling her that I always fall for women called Lisa at parties. 'Lisas are always sexy,' I say.

'Are they?'

'You know you are.'

'Maybe that's what the Mona Lisa is smiling about – that knowledge.'

'No, she's smiling about something else.'

'How do you know?'

'I've seen that smile before – three times. She's pregnant.'

'What have pregnant women got to smile about?'

'Absurdity and wonder.'

'That sounds too romantic.'

'It's a romantic time. It's the *most* romantic time. And crazy. But that's not why she's smiling.'

'Why then?'

'She's doing her pelvic floor exercises.'

'Ah! – she's smiling because she's doing something intimate in public.'

'That's it! Pregnancy is intimate, and yet also so *public* somehow. Its a special combination. And she's tranquil too. That's crucial. She doesn't care. She's stopped being anxious about what she looks like. She's shed baggage. Her priorities have changed. She's funny. She's enchanted. She glides galleon-like through shopping centres, sending display stands toppling ... I'm sorry, I'm sounding obsessive now.'

'No I'm fascinated. Really. You're very fond of the pregnant woman?'

'Mm. I love her.'

'Even though you can't get your arm round her?'

'Even though she wears underwear designed for a horse.'

'Even though she throws up in the car?'

'Look, she's a star. She's luminous. And she knows it. She can do anything she likes. Nothing in the world is as important as what's happening inside her. Her body is the centre of the universe, and at the centre of her body is her baby, her new life. Nobody could give her a better gift. She's got it. She's got everything. She's the Queen Bee.'

'Would you make me pregnant?'

'I'd love to ... I can't.'

An illusionist who has been circulating the room performing tricks joins us: handsome, dinner suit, gift of gab, sleight of hand. He has been looking at Lisa for some time out of the corner of his eye and he's obviously keen to impress her. He puts a 50 pence piece in an ordinary wine bottle. I don't know how, but it's in there, rattling around. Then he gets it out again. Lisa loves it. Like a cat's, her eye alights on the trickery. She's snagged.

'Do another one,' she keeps saying. 'Do another one.' Eventually he says, 'Actually, I'd rather dance. Would you dance with me?'

'Yes I would,' she says, giving him the sweetest smile. She leans over and kisses me softly on the lips: 'See you later.'

I never do see her later, though I look for her. There is much that we haven't talked about. There's a whole lifetime of stuff. But I've lost her.

After many drinks and a whirl round the dance floor with an old friend who let me lodge in her house during a tight spot years ago, and now produces in-house magazines for the Ministry of Defence, I get a lift with a couple from Hortense, Missouri, as far as Kensington, where they are staying. I must be very entertaining because I'm laughing so much. I have laughed all the way from Smithfield, and the fug of conviviality inside the car makes me feel all the more abandoned when I step out of it. Kensington is quiet and cold.

But – it comes to me in a flash – there is a girl who lives here – Anna – a friend, a *particular* friend, with blue eyes, dark curls and a vinegar tongue. One summer, six years ago, when she was a sixth former, she did work experience with me – not that there was much to experience. She sat at the end of my desk for four weeks making sarcastic quips about me, and for four weeks I refrained from kissing her white neck. What serendipity! This is the perfect opportunity to call on her.

She's been through university since then, and now works as a freelance journalist herself. I know because we are in touch about once a year. Last time we spoke she told me she was living in London, at her parents' house. I know where her parents' house is too, because I gave her a lift home once, after working late. I met her father, a publisher, and we had a short, respectful drink together.

It's a big house, just behind the High Street. I don't remember the number, but it's a short road and I'm certain I'll recognise the house. Sure enough, here is a house which looks familiar. I climb the steps and ring the bell. I wait for what seems a long time. I am obliged to ring again. After a while there is a shuffling sound in the hallway inside. A face is dimly discernible through the glass.

'Go away, it's 3 a.m!'

This is very annoying. After going to all this trouble! I reason loudly through the letter box, but the person becomes more obdurate.

'Go away or I'll call the police!'

Tnohw-wuh! I knock hard on the door. My hand goes through the glass.

Chastened, I scuttle off to find the nearest cab company. I hear someone shouting after me. I am abruptly sober, appalled by what I've just done. All desire for conviviality has evaporated. I want only to lock the incident away in the black file of aberrations, which I keep in a dark cupboard in the box room of my mind.

At least they won't know it was me. They'll think it was some drunk.

I'm wrecked and I need to sleep, but I sense danger. I open my eyes to see Martha looking at me in a not very kindly way.

'What did you get up to last night?'

I am not immediately clear what I got up to last night, though I feel deep inside that I'm guilty of something. This doesn't necessarily mean I am guilty of something. It's my normal feeling.

'Nothing. Why?'

'You've got a black eye.'

'I have?' I have. A huge black eye.

I've come home with a huge black eye, and I haven't a clue how it got there. Martha is suspicious *because* it's a black eye. If I'd come home with a bleeding head wound, or even haemorrhoids, she'd be sympathetic. You can get a black eye by walking into a lamp-post, or most likely clocking a wayward piece of self-expression on a dance floor. But people with black eyes are culpable.

Even I'm slightly suspicious. I'm wondering if the bits I do remember about last night, which are bad enough, might only be part of the story. I certainly don't remember any fights. I remember a heated exchange about sherbet fountains at Mark Borkowski's, but surely blows weren't exchanged?

I ring Mark Borkowski's office, but nobody remembers the black eye. Nobody remembers a fight. Then I start to wonder if they are keeping something from me ... But this isn't healthy. This is paranoia, a common enough condition among freelancers as it is.

Around 10 o'clock the phone rings. 'Oh hello, it's Tom Kershka, Anna Kershka's father.'

What?

'Look I'm sorry to ring you out of the blue like this, but an extraordinary thing has happened. I might as well come straight out with it: the person who bought my former house in Kensington rang me this morning to say that – apparently – a man turned up on his doorstep at three a.m. last night, shouted wildly through the letterbox, and then smashed his front door down. And ... I have to put this to you ... the possibility has come up that you might have been involved ...' He tails off.

I pause. This pause is the only time I have to consider whether to come clean or deny everything; too long a pause, while scrolling through all the implications, would be tantamount to an admission.

To admit the truth now would make me look stupid, and I'd lose the respect of Anna and her father. This may be no less than I deserve, but on the other hand, maybe I can quash the whole thing here and now. I have a responsibility to myself to be cool-headed. I haven't time to compute the odds, but I put all my money on my innocence.

'How peculiar.' I pronounce the syllables slowly and vaguely, as though still trying to get to grips with the facts he's given me. I can't affect indignation – I'm not that convincing an actor – but I am aware that a true innocent would have a burning question to ask. 'Why on earth did you ring me?'

'Because the man at the door said he was Martin Plimmer.'

'That is ... peculiar.'

'Of course I knew it couldn't be you,' says Mr Kershka. 'Besides, the man had a black eye.'

'Ah.'

'I'm sorry if you think I've insulted you.'

'No, no. Not at all.'

And we say goodbye.

He believed me. I can't believe he believed me. Against all the logic of the evidence, Anna's father accepted my word. Why? The only possible explanation is that he trusts me. This doesn't bear thinking about.

'What was all that about?' says Martha.

'I have lied to a good man.'

'Is *that* why you've got a black eye?'

Chapter 8 ART

'Scotch eggs are finished,' says the Kennedy's sausage girl bluntly. She doesn't seem to be panicking.

'Finished!? For ever!?'

I live in fear that Kennedy's Sausages will close down, that this little half-size shop on Streatham High Road – this pork jewel – will start fatally shedding lines from its already tiny product range.

There are only seven Kennedy shops in South London, all as small and shy as this one, and they look vulnerable to me because they are idiosyncratic, old-fashioned, and serve the best pork sausages in London. They are not glossily packaged, not puffed in Sunday supplements, and not available in Hampstead High Street or Sainsbury's. There is a marked absence of the sort of moneyed foodies who might provide this little business with a lease on the future, in the queue of old people holding shopping bags (remember shopping bags?), and poking with a finger through their purses for a spare 10p: 'There – I knew I had one!' The plain scrubbed Kennedy shop, with its plain scrubbed Kennedy shop girls, has been run exactly like this for a thousand years, and its sausages taste the same as the sausages Martha's father ate 100 years ago, when he was a boy. No rocket and Sicilian caper crap here. Kennedy's sausage, like Kennedy's shop, is simple and unadorned and perfect. Life would be bleak without it.

'No, not for ever. The girl who normally makes the Scotch eggs is making Christmas puddings. She can't do both can she?'

'Ah! Christmas puddings!'

'Would you like one?'

'No thank you. So they'll be back – the Scotch eggs?'

'After Christmas.'

Problem resolved, I rush to Tesco's in Brixton. I'm on a last-minute Christmas Eve shopping run, garnering overlooked essentials, and I am fleet of foot, because for the first time in days I am alone in the daytime. Martha has at last stopped work and is at home looking after her father and the children.

What Martha doesn't know is that after scampering through Tesco I race up to the West End to find a present for her. From Brixton I am at Green Park in 20 minutes. I scoot up Bond Street to South Molton Street, looking in clothes shops. I am a streamlined shopping machine today. Pretty soon I am drawn to a glamorous hand-made, heavy-stitch jumper, of a sensationally elegant, daring and expensive design, which I am tempted to buy.

But caution stays my wallet hand. Martha is very clear about what she likes and dislikes. She has strict and particular standards and a strong sense of aesthetic dignity. You can't just buy her anything. A lot of things would look silly on her anyway, because of that refined and remote something about her, that sometimes comes out as arrogance, and sometimes is. I am carrying in my mind a picture of her two weeks ago when we were driving on a motorway. I thought she was asleep, but she said abruptly, scornfully: 'You've let yourself be overtaken by a *Twingo*!' I am trying to picture her saying that in the South Molton Street jumper. I'm not sure ...

Anyway, I have another gift possibility in mind. I have been considering buying her a piece of art; an impressive sculpture of some sort, or a painting. I race southwards. Very soon I am in the purring realm of Mayfair, among rarefied, priceless art galleries, all of them locked up tight, and indifferent to the casual browser (in Mayfair, even picture *frame* shops lock their doors).

I feel intimidated. I am remembering the one time I met Brian Sewell, the *Evening Standard*'s rarefied, priceless art critic. He said one thing only to me: 'You have large peasant's hands.' This is what you let yourself in for when you mix with art *cognoscenti*. They spot the visual flaw. I couldn't argue with him: this man had studied the hands of Dürer and Da Vinci. But I am reminded of what he said as I press my big potato fingers against the petite brass nipple of a gallery doorbell, and wait to be admitted by a discreetly groomed assistant with an 'Oh no, here's another one' expression.

It's like walking into somebody's private home. Inside, I become doubly self-conscious, for now I see I am the only visitor here, a lone trespasser. I am obliged to walk round by myself, trying not to drag my hands on the floor, acutely conscious of my Tesco carrier bag and the trail of wet footprints I am leaving on the dun carpet, while the gallery gauleiter stands at the centre of the room observing me, his own (refined) hands clasped in front of his chest in a gesture of aesthetic piety.

The first thing I realise, as the condensation clears inside my spectacles, is that the exhibition is ghastly. I would love to just walk out but I have to hang around for a decent interval (ten minutes is the polite minimum), wishing (as he does) that I was far away.

It's all down to attitude. What I should do is stride around pointing at things and making loud remarks. All you need is a bit of verve. But I left mine in Kensington last night. And I'm starting to sweat. I feel as self-concious – and yet somehow not quite all myself – as a Damien Hirst cow. And as tension builds I start to think that maybe I might break something. This is a ridiculous notion, but once admitted into my mind, it won't leave, and with appalling logic, starts to gain credence. I might for example, be the first person ever to slip over while standing stationary on a dun carpet, utterly crushing a delicate fourteenth-century cinnabar lacquered Chinese box.

At once the compulsion to do just that begins to grow. It's like the compulsion to step off tall buildings: to perform the one act which is certain to be disastrous. At any moment I might snap, go mad, uncharacteristically mistake myself for a helicopter, and whirl around this hallowed place, flapping paintings off walls and toppling the grim statues of marble babies with huge testicles. 'Wouldn't it be fun?' the peasant inside me asks, and the voice sounds reasonable enough.

Instead, I place my body in the grip of unprecedented will-power, point to a painting of a maroon smudge, and ask, 'How much is Denouement XIV?'

When he says '£8,950' I give a gay little laugh, and nervously remark, 'One can almost *smell* the denouement.' And as my words clatter about me like the chisellings of an epitaph, I summon up stupendous self-control and direct my body, like a man suddenly struck by severe constipation, towards the door.

I go back to South Molton Street and buy the jumper.

I am back home and writing up my article about sex in unusual places when Anna calls.

'Martin, I'm *so* sorry. My father's told me what happened and I don't know what to say. I am so sorry. I can't say *how* sorry. I'm shocked. I can't believe he rang you! *You* of all people! It's so insulting! How could he think you'd do something so idiotic. This has all the hallmarks of some sad, stupid, drunken escapade by one of my college friends. I'm so, *so* ...'

'No, please, no, please don't ... *please* don't apologise. There's no harm done and ... I'm really not at all insulted – believe me I'm not, and I'm sure I deserve to be insulted – for other things perhaps, so ... I'm just going to forget about the whole thing. That would be best ... Really. Let's just forget it, please ...'

Now I feel very strange.

Chapter 9 PETER

'Oh it's you,' says my friend Peter, picking up the phone at his end. 'What's the difference between a foundling and a dumpling?'

'A foundling has more gristle.'

Peter will be 50 this year, as he reminds anybody who cares to listen. Peter and I ring each other at least once a day. We never talk about anything serious, except by accident. We talk by the Men's Conversation Rule Book. We talk about trivia, or trade logical absurdities – the lingua franca of all my male friends. Women and children shake their heads, but this is therapy. It's man therapy.

Peter likes to read snippets to me from the newspaper.

'Have you read this? – "Mid-life crisis hits 20-somethings. Men as young as 25 are suffering over-the-hill depression normally identified with the mid-life crisis. Anxiety can be brought on by childhood pets dying of old age ..." Hah! "... or the strain of having children".'

Once we lived next door to each other in Brixton, and were in each other's houses all the time, until the trendy violence and window-rattling *I'm black and I'm loud* sound system cars got too much for Martha and me. Or maybe we got too old for them. Brixton is a young person's place. Apart from Peter, that is. We swapped it for the pale erotica of Streatham, up the road, home of famous Luncheon Voucher brothel queen Cynthia Payne, now a neighbour. Sold out, Peter says. Clive and Sam moved from Brixton too, to Dulwich. Definitely sold out.

'What crap!' says Peter. 'Wet behind the ears! Wait till they're 50 and they've presided over the death of a zoo ... And their children are old enough not to think they're gods. They wouldn't know over-the-hill if it came up and gummed them!'

My crutch, my sense of myself depends to a large extent on Peter. He's not overtly supportive, but in one sense at least, he makes me feel like a going concern. He has written no novel and not a single funny article, though he could certainly do either or both, if he were to put his mind to it. In fact he hasn't done anything. When I'm feeling denuded by overwhelming non-achievement, I look at him and think: I have done more than Peter. Also, he makes me feel young.

I'm still only 45, I don't say things like, 'Have I got my right glasses on?' and I am not yet a user of the Rejoice space-age incontinence treatment. I want sex all the time and I harbour a dim but lingering sense, a hope perhaps, that if I can shed past skins, the best, vocationally speaking, may be yet to come.

'I'm almost 50 and believe me, the world looks much bleaker from the grand circle.'

'If you can see anything at all.'

'Yes. It's no longer fashionable just to be short-sighted. You have to be long-sighted as well.'

'A technical impossibility.'

'Nevertheless made specially available to older people.'

Peter is half English and half Australian. His life is more complicated than mine and more desperate. He is as lazy as me, but he thinks he works hard. Though extremely clever, he knows himself not at all. He's in denial.

'They're still young enough to be able to read street maps after twilight. They don't wear bifocals! They can probably still see their feet!'

'They're frauds.'

'Malingerers. You know, I did a somersault playing with Cato the other day. I don't know what came into my head. It was like an articulated lorry rolling over. All the interior parts of my body slid from one side to the other. I was dizzy for an hour.'

Peter's always cynical. His memory is prodigious. He has a funny story to top every one of yours.

'Life would be more bearable if the desire to somersault left you as well. Then you could settle down and devote yourself to growing rhubarb.'

Peter is a kaleidoscope of intriguing flaws. One of them is material ungenerosity. This may be because he believes sincerely that he has nothing to give. All his generosity is cerebral. He is gloomy too. And though opinionated, in practice more indecisive than me. Another fault is a weakness for ruthless, manipulative women. There is always one in his life – over his life. At the moment it's Candice. Only once have I seen him with a sweet and sparkling girl, but he ditched her ruthlessly. He falls for the other sort with fanatical force. Rather than putting him off, their cruelty seems to feed his love. He merely falls deeper. This is pathetic, but he won't change. Part of the allure, I suspect, is that it lets him off the hook. It *allows* him to be pathetic. He can claim to be a victim of unjust circumstances. Being with Peter too long is always depressing.

'Wait till the dentist gives them the good news and the bad news: "Your teeth are still here, but your gums are going."'

Peter spent a large part of his youth trying to decide whether to live in Sydney or London. He hated London weather and Australian culture. Every so often during the British autumn, which is cold enough to bury him in depressive snowdrifts, he'd up sticks permanently for Australia. Then he'd return a few months later. I first met him during his second attempt to settle in London with his second wife and first baby. He stuck it two years, but when autumn came round again he took his family back to Australia, for good. I drove him to Heathrow and at the airport bar he bade tearful farewell to me and to British beer, which is the only thing warm in Britain in winter, and which he was loath to give up.

A month later the phone rang. It was him. 'What are you up to you bastard?' I said (that's how you talk to Australians). 'I bet you're lolling on some sun-fucked crazy paving drinking cold newt's piss and frying eggs on some blonde bird's bum!' Back came his reply, clear as a bell, as though he was just down the road. 'I'm at Heathrow. Put the kettle on ...'

'Well, you're keeping British Airways in business,' I told him when he arrived.

'Someone has to.'

I clinked his cup. 'Here's to the indecisive.'

'And the non-assertive.'

'And last but not least ...'

'The late.'

He'd come alone this time. His wife had given up on him and stayed in Sydney with the baby. For two days he sat in my house staring at the ivy plant with the eyes of Bela Lugosi, consuming nothing but nettle tea (he is an intermittent health faddist). Then he changed his mind again and went back to Australia for good. I drove him through the rain to the Heathrow bar, where I bade him a tearful farewell ...

'They aren't yet invisible to every girl under the age of 30 ...'

The ivy died. A year later Peter returned with a new wife and a new baby. She was Candice, 20 years younger than him, a receptionist; bottle blonde, vain and shallow. When Candice is not at the beautician she is indulging an unlikely fantasy to become a psychiatrist. We don't like Candice but we tolerate her. We never talk about this, though Peter sometimes alludes to it. He knows. He knows most things.

The first baby, Cato, was named, so Candice told us, after one of the big cats in a circus which used to come to Adelaide when she was a girl. Two years later they had a second son, Rocket.

'Why Rocket?' I asked Peter.

'Her favourite lettuce,' he said.

'Lettuce? But that's terrible!'

'She got it from the *Having a Baby Guide to Baby Names*. It could have been worse. It could have been Romaine, or Curly Endive.'

'It doesn't really go with Dawkins though – Rocket.'

'Bomber Harris, Blaster Bates, Rocket Dawkins – part of a long tradition.'

'At least Cato Dawkins sounds intentionally surreal. A challenge, a cultural contradiction. You'd have to watch your step with Cato Dawkins.'

'I used to know someone called Clint Eastbourne ...'

Peter may have settled at last on London, but he can't decide what his vocation is. He started off on a junior management scheme in a large corporation but quickly got the sack. Then he went to Nepal to start a restaurant, but decided to be a tourist instead, so he set off to climb a mountain, but changed his mind when he got near the top.

A few years ago he decided (rightly) that with his imagination he should be doing something more interesting and chose (wrongly) to go to drama school. Contrary to stereotype, not all successful actors are extrovert, but they are all good actors. Peter isn't extrovert, but I'm not sure he's a good actor either.

In fact Candice is a better actor than him. She has the Christopher Walken deadeye off pat. Candice can chill the blood. Peter can only do dejection. In fact you could say he's at dejection method school. So far, apart from college productions, Peter hasn't been in anything. For a time he attended a lot of auditions, though even these have fallen off now.

'These young people don't know they're born. And now they're trying to muscle in on our territory ...'

'Your territory.'

'It's all me, me, me with them. Well I'm telling you – if any of them try to give their seat up for me on the bus, I'll punch them in the stomach.'

'The best thing about being young is the luxury of blaming all your woes on the incompetent old people who are in control.'

'Ah, but when you get to our age ...'

'Your age.'

'All the incompetent old people disappear.'

'And the only one left in control is you.'

'And if it's not – you've missed the boat.'

Chapter 10 ALL YE

I've never dealt with any food this big before, or this human. I feel like an autopsy attendant at an amateur autopsy. My heart isn't in it. I know this turkey too well. We've bonded. At nine this morning – Christmas morning – I found his giblets wrapped up inside him in a shower cap. It was the final straw.

Martha has taken over. It's about time. Women are more attuned to such things. Rubbing melted butter on breasts comes naturally to them. And they can be much more cold-blooded than men. It's all very well for Nigella Lawson to tell me to test readiness by poking a skewer behind the knee joint of the thigh, but frankly, I can't.

We were up with the dawn today and we held back the tide till it was no longer resistible. We opened presents in our pyjamas in the sitting room. The children were delirious. Amelia undid her presents and stacked them all in a neat ziggurat in the corner. Mungo spread his throughout the house. Amelia's mini hi-fi was well received, and Mungo's Gameboy. I chose for him two beautiful Little Tikes cars; big easy rollers, made of heavy plastic, solid enough to sit on, and very difficult to sneak home from Hamley's. I'd coveted such cars throughout my childhood. They weren't cheap either. His Christmas smile faded as they came unwrapped. 'But they don't do anything!' Well ... not by themselves, no ...

He thinks any toy that doesn't speak, gyrate, twinkle, transform, reassemble itself after being smashed to a pulp, or have an 'attitude', is somehow shirking; not a toy at all really; an infiltrator from the dull real world of old people and inanimate objects.

But he was enraptured by his Supersonic Ear, with which he can overhear conversations from the other end of the house which he'd have heard anyway if he'd stayed in the living room. He hasn't read the User Guide – 'With good judgement and responsible play, you will enjoy many years of fun with your Supersonic Ear.' He intends to use it irresponsibly.

Amelia has a selection of multi-coloured make-up jars, which she will line up on her bedroom shelf and not use, and some chic perfume in a cool bottle that promises the moon and delivers a hint of jasmine, which she won't use either. Amelia likes *having* things.

The glamorous and elegant heavy-stitch jumper I bought yesterday makes Martha look short and dumpy. She gave me a beautiful marbled fountain pen that makes my hands black and my handwriting look like a five year old's.

At one o'clock Clive and Sam arrive, brimming with presents and children. Sam's mother and father, and Margot, her mother's prodigal friend, are with them.

'What have you been up to?' says Sam, instantly homing in on my black eye. She's mischievous. She can spot mischief a mile away.

'It's a long story.'

Margot is not as I imagined. She's a tall, elegant woman of around 70, with a severe haircut, a Chanel-type suit and the most lasciviously pointed shoes I've seen since the snakeskin cowboy boots of Texan singer Terry Allen at the Putney Half Moon in 1986. Margot is a published poet, it turns out, and also runs a magazine for ex-pats in Hong Kong in her spare time. She's cultured and well-spoken, and by the look of her, doesn't suffer fools. She shakes my hand firmly and looks at me straight: 'Oh the charms of those sprightly black eyes.'

If shoes can talk, Margot's shoes are telling me she won't be taking the tea cosy back to Hong Kong with her.

Peter and Candice and their two boys arrive, and everybody talks at once. I duck into the kitchen to pour champagne, followed by Peter. He has something urgent to get off his chest.

'Your Hoppa buses ...'

'My buses?'

'Yes, we have good, honest double-deckers in Brixton. Your Hoppas have dangerous hand rails. They're fluorescent lime and yellow. It's courting disaster ...'

Clive sashays in like Professor Higgins, full of brio, seizes my hand, 'Happy Christmas dear fellow,' he says. 'What a busy week!'

'Anyway, it makes them unsafe ...'

'I pulled off a deal this week you won't believe! I've got the whole of the Eastern Seaboard in my pocket.'

'It doesn't spoil the cut,' says Peter.

'You know there's not a consultant in the Square Mile comes close to me at the moment.' Clive is frighteningly clever, but his brilliance is dwarfed by his ego.

'Where's my champagne?' It's Sam, gliding in, looking for trouble. 'What *exactly* have you been up to?'

'Everybody out of the kitchen please!' This is Martha.

'It wasn't Martha who hit you was it?' This is Sam.

'Killed.' This is Peter.

'Who?'

'Who was killed?'

'Can we open our presents now?'

'If you all go out of the kitchen ...'

'The tropical naturalist. That's what I'm trying to tell you. He was killed.'

'Will we be eating first?'

'A dog ran into the road, the driver slammed on his brakes ...'

'By this time next year I wouldn't be surprised if I'm on seven figures ... Well, maybe half that.'

'Three and a half figures?'

'Can we open the presents?'

'But the hand rails are lime green and yellow, you see. In the Amazonian rain forest those are warning colours. On the tree frog they denote deadly poison.'

'Like Barclays Bank blue?'

'Worse even than that.'

'I think you've been kissing the wrong women ...'

'And when the naturalist reached his hand out to save himself, like anyone would, he saw only lime green and yellow, which after years of field work in the jungle, said only one thing to him: *Danger! ...*'

'A gin and tonic for Margot!'

'So he hesitated ...'

'You know, when the money does come in, the first thing I'm going to do is treat all my good friends to a holiday, you and Martha, Peter even ...'

'And shot head-first down the aisle and through the windscreen.'

'Who did?'

'Did he?'

'No.'

'Ah. Shall we open the presents? Children!'

'Hurry up in there!'

'Did he exist at all?'

'Who?'

'No. But if he had, interestingly, and all that had actually happened, he'd have been as much a victim of the Amazonian tree frog here in Streatham, as if he'd gone to South America and shaken one by the hand.'

'Don't do that, Mungo!'

Now the phone's ringing. It's Lowell from his mother's house in Somerset. He's so ecstatically happy he can barely talk.

'What's the best thing, Dad? What's the best thing that could happen in the world?'

'I find some shoes which fit me.'

'No, I've got a *car!* I've got a Mini! Mum's bought me a *Mini!* She bought it for £100 – and it *goes!* – You'll see it tomorrow! Happy Christmas!'

Since he passed his driving test earlier this year, Lowell has craved cars, dreamt of cars, talked only in car. Now he's got one. Thank God he's got one. I tell him to be careful driving home. Another sad fact about children: they turn you into dull policemen.

We drink our champagne and exchange presents. It's not clear whether Rufus likes the Viking outfit, but he hasn't overtly rejected it anyway. Margot gives me a bottle of pinot grigio and Martha a bottle of grappa (she's even bothered to find out Martha's favourite drink). I give her the tea cosy.

'Oh that's hideous,' she says. I know it will be behind the sofa when she leaves. I will put it back in bric-a-brac purgatory with all the other unwanted thoughts-that-count.

Lunch is a hit, though I can't bring myself to eat the turkey. Afterwards the children burn round the house in a froth of new toys, while we talk round the table. Howard and Beth, our hippy friends, who live in a flat a few doors along, walk round to share a drink with us. 'Been caught at it this time?' says Howard.

After fielding questions all day, I give in and tell them the story of the black eye, the door and the lie. They listen, and when they've digested this hors d'oeuvre they begin eagerly picking over the entrée of my career problem. I didn't intend this to happen but there you are, you don't choose your friends and you certainly can't control them.

'It sounds to me like you should be writing much more than you are,' says Margot.

'I could write for you, Margot.'

'You could write for me, but you should be writing for yourself.'

'He needs to write a book,' says Martha. 'His whole life is an act of avoiding writing a book. It's the one thing he really wants to do, and it's what he's most afraid of.'

'What's the point of writing a book,' I say, 'if it's merely rejected?' There is a lot of tutting at this, even from Peter.

'The trouble with Martin now,' says Martha, looking at me, 'and this is different from Martin in the past, is that he has lost the will or desire to do anything. He doesn't fight any more. He's cynical and distant, and grumpy.'

They all look at me. I don't know what to say. I can't deny it. The trouble is, I don't know myself what's going on. I know I'm rebelling against something, but I'm not entirely sure what that is. For the past few years I've been following the professional path of least resistance, and I don't want to do that any more. I'm even resisting Martha's contingency suggestions. I'm shucking off a skin, and it's painful. I know too that it hurts the people I love.

This is the positive interpretation of my behaviour. The negative one, which even I have considered, is that I'm succumbing to bone idleness. I can't tell them all this. The fact is, I'm confused. I can't tell them that either.

'I've had it with doing mediocre things, with mediocre results,' I tell them. 'I don't want *Quite Good* written on my gravestone.'

'I don't see the problem,' Clive says, pouring wine. 'Just sit down and write a bestseller. It can't be that hard. I'll help you.'

He means it too. Bless him. It's good, sitting here in this room, warmed by candles and endless wine and the company of friends. Rolling the warmth on the tongue, counting the drops.

They are fixated now on my epitaph. We've done this before. It's not really a game, but we do it at portentously drunken moments, inventing epitaphs that might be written on our gravestones were we to die that second. They can be funny, or perceptive, and as cruel as you like. For me, Candice says, '*Another Useless Bloke*', which is very Candice. Beth says, '*He Deserved A Break*', which again, says more about sweet Beth – undemonstrative, dreamy, full of good will, always assuming the best in people – than it does of me. Then Margot, who is new to us and therefore not expected to play, says, quietly, provocatively: '*He Just Couldn't Cut It*'. There are raised eyebrows, but I see the challenge in her eye and I like her for it. Clive says: '*This Stone's Too Good for Him*'.

It's Martha's turn. '*He Missed His Chance,*' she says. I look at her face and I see only worry and devotion, and for the third time, my heart turns to Christmas.

There is a sudden commotion in the hall. 'Tra-la!' pipes a little voice. We swivel round in our chairs. Rufus, rosy-cheeked and exultant, stands at the foot of the stairs, holding aloft the Viking sword, dressed in the horned Viking helmet, the flaxen plaited wig, the Viking breastplate, and a floor-length purple taffeta party dress. It's Brunhilde!

Chapter 11 PUZZLE

There is a fork in the Road of Life. One path is signposted, 'WRITE NOVEL, CONQUER WORLD', the other, 'DO CHRISTMAS JIGSAW PUZZLE'.

I choose the jigsaw puzzle route. It looks like it might take me as long. I'm at it most of Boxing Day, with only a short break to take Hugh to the station. I'm still doing it at 8 p.m. when the phone call comes. I will say in my defence, that I didn't want to start it. Martha started it, then dragged me in. She did it for 50 minutes, then stopped, saying she couldn't see any more. Mungo the Wise marked it down as a non-starter from the start. Amelia lasted until the straight bits had been accounted for. So it's just me, and the unending task.

Until the phone call. Someone is weeping grievously at the other end. It's Lowell.

'My car's on fire, Dad! My *car's* on fire!'

'Where are you?'

'I'm in Brixton. I drove back from Somerset and I went to Dexter's to show him the car. And I was just putting some speakers in he had, and now the stupid thing's on fire ...'

'Just stay there, I'm coming to get you.'

I get to Brixton within 15 minutes. The Mini is a drenched and reeking shell. The firemen have left already. I can't even see what colour it was.

I bring Lowell home and he mourns for half an hour. Then he perks up. It is as though he has been purged. His mail brightens him up more.

'Look at this, Dad!'

He passes me a jiffy bag. Inside are a pair of skimpy knickers.

'Who sent you these?'

'Look inside, Dad.'

There is an unambiguous message scrawled on the gusset, and the name of a girl at his college.

'Maybe I'll ask her out,' he says.

'Are you sure she likes you?'

I'm envious. I'm the sort of green you hope knickers won't be. I'd love to be sent a pair of knickers with a gusset message, or even just a pair of knickers – I could interpret them myself.

When I look at the modern world, I see many improvements, in particular the sexual mores of women, which are much more straightforward than when I was Lowell's age. This isn't the first letter he's had. One girl wrote to him suggesting sexual positions he might like to try. 'You are the criminal of my body,' she said.

If only it had been that easy when I was young. Girls were unattainable, or seemed to be. Girls had everything going for them: breasts, hair, legs – mystery. I didn't have those; certainly not the mystery, and I knew there would be no more significant hair. I was knobbly and white and unmanly. Girls were remote, beautiful, holier than I.

Young people know everything about sex now. Before their first kiss, they already know everything. Right now, Amelia is walking round the house revising sex for school: 'So: the penis goes into the vagina and ejaculates semen, containing sperm, which pass into the fallopian ... no the uterus, and then ...'

All I had was lust – wheelbarrows full of lust. I believed girls were above it, and I was somehow beneath it. Every woman I saw was grist to my lurid fantasy. I didn't think 'who?', I thought 'when?', or rather, 'please when?'

I passed my formative years in a testosterone fog, and if it hadn't been for a religious instruction teacher called Taffy Hughes, I'd still be rubbing against trees. He was a frightening man, a strict disciplinarian with the primeval skull profile of a goat. He liked to rip forth in fire and brimstone style about Yahweh and Pharisees, and in frivolous moments, Sodom and Gomorrah. Then one day, to our eternal surprise, he dropped the tedium of who begat who and moved on to how they'd gone about it. He'd realised that if he didn't tell us, nobody would.

There were one or two bits of information that Taffy Hughes wasn't privy to though, because he didn't warn us that girls had pubic hair. The line drawings of headless females he procured for us gave no hint of it. Neither did pictures in pornographic magazines, which in those days were censored by a little man in a hut somewhere with pebble glasses and a bottle of flesh-coloured ink. He had their nipples off too. Naked women looked like skateboard parks, with nary a snare to trip you.

Pubic hair was a hurdle I had to face alone, in the back row of the Regal cinema, Bracknell. I snatched my hand away with a shout of alarm, as though I had been bitten. It was difficult to explain at the time.

The first girl I nearly had sex with was a lovely redhead, who lay on her parents' couch invitingly. I decided to tell her jokes instead. That was my sex life. In my imagination I was a slavering creature, half man, half penis from Planet Lewd: in real life, a mumbling goon from Bracknell. My lovely redhead didn't pass me a message written on her knicker gusset, which is just as well, because I would have run from the room with my hair on fire.

It was a relief to learn that women are also interested in sex, and that sometimes they are slaves to it, though if I'm honest, disappointing as well. I am conditioned, you see. In my mind women swing from chandeliers, or disport themselves on cushions, akimbo and keen, but outside in the world, their sang-froid is an important part of my appreciation.

Lowell is relaxed about sex. It's not an issue. He's startlingly open about it, in a way I could never have been with my father. All through his life Lowell has come up to London every few weeks to stay with me, sometimes for a weekend, sometimes a week. Sometimes he'd bring a friend, Steve, or Sheldon, or Wedgie. I worried about Wedgie. Wedgie said he wanted to be a marine biologist when he grew up, or failing that, a master criminal. I wasn't sure he'd make that either, though he might have got as far as petty.

One week when he was 14, Lowell asked if he could bring Jack. Jack was just another boy until she stepped off the train at Paddington. I brought them home and they vanished. I went upstairs to find them and they were having sex in the bathroom. They hadn't even closed the door. There's relaxed and relaxed ...

By the time Lowell came to live with me two years ago, sex didn't seem to be on his mind at all. His priority was to establish a circle of male friends in the area. Girls haven't featured much.

He's certainly not interested in jigsaws. I'm on my own here.

My little boy was nine months old when I left him. And in the way men can, I shut myself off from him, pushing the problem he had become to a different part of my mind. The problem didn't disappear though; it became a guilty shadow on my life, which darkened ominously on the occasions he came down from the country to visit me. He brought to Brixton all the corrupting ways of the countryside. He read a magazine called *Oink!*, featuring a story about a decapitated head, he drank a chemical substance called Dr Pepper, and he told me casually that a man called Mohawk was living in a bender in his garden. There was nothing jarringly wrong about any of this, but all the same, I could see he was growing into something I might not want my child to be.

He was not unloved. It was just that his mother's expression of love was to let him run wild through the woods, in the free hippy way that prevails in parts of Somerset. This had seemed fine when he was small, romantic even, but in his teens his life became directionless. He kicked round the streets with a gang of boys and failed at school. He was wilfully uneducated. Once he told me how a friend and he stole a crate of lager from the backyard of an off licence. I told him that it was a stupid thing to do, and that now he'd done it once he need never do it again. He looked hurt. Then he said, 'I wish I hadn't told you now'.

My boy returned to my life a year and a half ago, when he came to live with me permanently. The idea was that he would attend a vocational course at a London college. It was an opportunity to be a proper father to him at last.

But I was appalled by what he had become. Perhaps all he had become was a teenager, but at the time it seemed appalling. And it seemed to me it was all my fault. He slept in much of the day, and once asleep it was impossible to wake him. When he wasn't asleep he watched television horizontally from the sofa, scattering crisp packets, dirty cups and shoes across the carpet. Standing up didn't feature much in his life. His room smelt like he'd got a dead bear in there.

He ate white sliced bread and peanut butter. And ice cream, which he flicked from the freezer with a wooden spoon because he didn't like the feel of ice on his other-worldly hands. He had no interest at all in the everyday conventions. One day he left a letter to his mother on the hall table with a nine pence stamp on it. I told him it wasn't enough. 'No,' he said, 'but I don't mind how long it takes to get there.'

He could see nothing of interest in my world of writing. He had never read a newspaper. He thought the IRA was an American TV network. He told me he didn't read books because his friends might spot him doing it and think he was the sort of person who read books. He communicated in broad Somerset, which he quickly converted to all-right-then-mate South London. We seemed to have little in common.

He had thought that London would be an easy option. Whenever he had come up to see me we had done fun things. He thought it would be fun all the time. At the end of the college interview, the tutor asked him if he had any questions. 'How much time off will I have in the week?' he asked. The answer was none. This was a surprise to him.

Of course he failed his first year. Looking back, I realise how tough it was on him. He had no friends here. The college was in Ilford, an hour and a half travelling time each way. He was the youngest student on his course. He was only 16. Worse, he had no discipline. He'd never worked in his life. He didn't know how to wash up, let alone write an essay.

I was in despair. I'd been lenient with him because I was terrified he'd just walk out. Now I shouted at him. I ranted. I accused him of not facing up to his responsibilities. I chastised him for not knowing what I had neglected to teach him. He stood in my study in tears and then he apologised for letting me down. I couldn't tell him it was my fault.

He didn't walk out and they let him do the year again. Gradually, very gradually, he began to change. He added tomatoes to his diet: 'By the way, I like tomatoes now.' I resisted the urge to cheer. He started to see the point of his college course. 'This IRA business has gone beyond a joke,' he suddenly declared from behind a newspaper. One afternoon I found him up to his elbows in ice, throwing away food we'd put in the freezer, because it was past its sell-by date. He said he wanted to help. He converses. He's got a part-time job. My little boy is growing all the time, in every way. He knows now which direction his life is headed, which is more than I can say for me at the moment. When he finishes his course this year, he'll be going to university. That's when it will get hard.

I'm still working on the jigsaw when Wendy, who lives in the upstairs flat next door, bangs our door to tell us, wide-eyed with new vistas, unfurling brochures, that she has won a dream kitchen in a competition. Her plain face, which is a child's drawing yet to be coloured in, almost glows. Martha is vicariously ecstatic.

'My dream come true!' says Wendy.

I have never dreamt of kitchens. Never run, like Wendy, across the Corian plains. In my dreams I'm chased by killers through knee-deep quick-hardening cement in busy burger bars, naked. But Wendy is an innocent, a pale spirit protected from life's too crude realities by a spick and span lifestyle agenda. If I *were* to dream of kitchens then Isabel Adjani would be in them, arrayed on a white platter, her body adorned with pale slivered cucumber slices, through which her flesh would gleam like salmon terrine. And Helen Mirren (to hell with the consequences) would be there too, leaning on the fridge, fixing me with that look that says: 'I'm here, leaning on your fridge.' My dreams tend to be organic.

Wendy's aren't. In every brochure she shows us there is not a human in sight. Not a trace of food. Not a cookie. Just a stainless, scratchless landscape from wall to shining wall. My kitchen, if I were to dream it, would *explode* with food. And vile-smelling cheeses. And sweating skivvies. And a commis chef employed exclusively to slice cucumbers to the point of transparency.

We've been to dinner in Wendy's house so I know she has no love for food. She has come to an accommodation with it, for the sake of survival, just as I suspect she's come to an accommodation with sex. She tolerates it so long as it's neat.

It's the equipment Wendy loves. She has never, like me, looked into a blender and seen only menace. In Wendy's dreams she dances ergonomic golden working triangles twixt hob, fridge and work surface. Stainless is her vision (and you know she's cleaned behind the vision too), peopled by machines; knobless.

'You don't pull these cupboard doors to open them,' she says. 'You *push!*'

'We have knobless doors too,' says Martha. 'And they rip your fingernails off.'

'Look at that oven!' says Wendy. 'Now is that or is that not impressive?'

It's impressive. It has the sleek gravitas of a stealth bomber. Martha gasps at it, then looks at our sad oven and laughs. We have never owned an oven which doesn't require a heavy stool to be propped against the door in order for it to work. Oddly enough, all our friends are the same. Even Clive and Sam's new oven has a faulty door. The oven door stool seems to be something which, like herpes, friends catch off each other.

I point out that we are on an improving curve. The oven in our house in Brixton wouldn't work, even with a stool leaning against it. We got so used to making hob-cooked food that we forgot it was broken. The first Saturday night after we moved to Streatham, the new owners at Brixton rang us at 9 p.m. They were having their first proper dinner, they said, their guests had enjoyed the starter, and they had opened the oven to serve the roast pork loin, only to find it was raw. Was there a switch they'd overlooked?

Martha is starting to dream now. She has that visionary look about her. I'd like to discuss whether a new kitchen can make that much difference to anybody's life. I don't believe dreams become real, even one as concrete as a cupboard door which you push. I believe dreams slip under the door of your consciousness at night, kick you round the room a bit, then get bored and abandon you.

I think Wendy really does believe that her dreams will be made real in her house, by men with special spanners. I fear that the reality will be less than the dream, so I tell her a cautionary tale about a man who fell asleep on a beach in Morocco, and dreamt he was performing cunnilingus on a beautiful woman, but woke to find he was being kissed by a bearded man.

'Good gracious!' says Wendy. 'Is that the time?'

Now Martha wants me to discuss my plans. I don't have any plans.

'Why does it have to be now?'

'Because you're not doing anything. You're doing that stupid puzzle.'

'So I am doing something. It's 11.30 at night and I'm trying to relax.'

'I'd like to relax too. I'd like to go to bed knowing that we are taking some positive steps to get us out of this mess, but I won't be able to sleep because I'm so worried, and because I know you're going to stay up all night doing this stupid puzzle, which really is the last thing you should be doing right now.'

'It won't be all night. Anyway, I'm not doing it for myself. I'm doing it for the sake of the family, so we can put it behind us before the summer arrives.'

She walks away in disgust.

Martha is desperate to plan. She wants us to decide what our aims and objectives are before the new year cranks up. I've never been big on planning. I've been for taking risks or doing nothing. Those are the attractive alternatives. Planning is hard. I'm in favour of letting it ride a little: see what comes up. We're in a bad patch: they happen. That's my manifesto.

But I know she's right. Our life has got to change. *I've* got to change. I've got a lot to face up to, difficult decisions to make. It has to be a brave new year, if only because it was such a cowardly old year. And because I'm 45.

We can't go on living like this. It's not hand-to-mouth exactly – we don't deny ourselves a social life or go without piano lessons – it's just that we have no surplus. We can afford the mortgage but we can't afford to paint the house. We scrabble around and every major expense, like the summer holiday Martha is worrying about, leaves us gasping.

I'm in no mood for facing up to things. It *is* all night.

'Life is like a bowl of All Bran,' sang the Small Faces. 'You wake up every morning and it's there.' I think life is more like a jigsaw puzzle. You wake up one morning and it's finished. And then there is only emptiness and desolation.

And a picture of a cow in a farmyard. And you think: 'Is *this* all there is?'

And you cry out to the unhearing dining room chairs: 'IS *THIS* ALL THERE IS? – a picture of a cow in a farmyard? Is *this* why I've laboured so long. Stayed up all night?

Here is the Zen of the jigsaw puzzle: when the puzzle is completed *it is a bigger puzzle than when it began.*

It's not proper a picture anyway: you can't pick it up.

They say it's not the destination that counts, it's the journey; it's the drive to create order from the arbitrary. I kidded myself it was an achievement of sorts. I was creating the picture, I was rendering it *bitless*, I was returning it from chaos. I was obsessed.

But actually the journey wasn't much to shout about either. And now I don't know what to do ... Well, deep down I know what to do. I must smash the thing which beguiled me with its promise of Oneness. I must kill the Sacred Cow. One day we may want to eat off the kitchen table again.

Yet what a terrible sacrilege it seems. A single stroke will render my recent past pointless. I see now why people who run bed and breakfast establishments in Ilkley cannot bring themselves to face the horror of Jigsaw Breakyupyday, and in their confusion and desperation, resolve to preserve the cow for ever, a mummified relic, cunningly glued in a special frame – a laborious process that involves doing the entire puzzle again with Pritt Stick – neither picture really, nor any more puzzle; worshipped daily ('Oh felicity! Oh great interconnecting scheme of Oneness!'), varnished. And thereafter everyone who enters the room – Mrs Brackish from next door, all the guests, those dreadful people the Smithsons – see it and say: 'Why didn't you just buy a picture of a cow if that's what you wanted?'

'You miss the point,' they answer bitterly.

But you know, the Smithsons know, and the cow knows: they are lost, hopeless. They are but randomly scattered matter, arbitrarily spinning in the void of space.

Did I dream the Smithsons? I don't know. All I know is that I have been asleep slumped over the jigsaw puzzle and someone is knocking at the door. I'm disgusted with myself. I didn't think I could sink this low.

It's 9 a.m. by the oven clock. Everyone must be still asleep except, by the sound of it, Mungo, watching the *Big Breakfast* in the other room. During holiday periods, only people who never work come knocking on your door at 9 a.m., so I know it must be Howard at the door. I can tell by his silhouette – skinny, trim – that it is. You'd never know him for a hippy, except perhaps for the little woven thong around his wrist. He is always impeccably dressed, in his way, in his blouson and scarf, soft shoes and immaculately clean cords. Howard was never your scruffy hippy. In fact there is something about his management of himself – all-of-a-piece and curiously upright – that brings to mind a military officer on his day off.

In comparison, I am a hairy monster.

'Nice puzzle,' says Howard, one eyebrow raised.

'It's the children ... they love it.'

'It's a mindfuck,' he says.

'You're telling me.' I start pulling the puzzle apart.

'Don't do that ...' he says.

'Why not?'

'It seems a sacrilege.' He looks hard at me. 'Particularly when you've been working so hard on it all night.'

'What makes you say that?'

'Your eyes betray you – they're all ... jigoid.'

'You've been smoking too much dope.'

'You haven't smoked enough.'

Howard comes to see me once a week. It's part of a royal promenade that may take in the library, the social security office, the Oxfam shop, and a friend in Shrubbery Road who owns a novel hubble-bubble pipe designed in San Francisco, and makes definitive houmous. A ritual tour. Howard is a man of routine.

'Congratulate me,' he says.

'Congratulations. Your birthday?'

'No, not that, though I was 45 yesterday.'

'What then?'

'On my retirement.'

'Retirement?'

'I'm now officially retired.'

'But Howard, you haven't done a stroke of work in your life.'

'That's a very unkind thing to say.' I pour tea. Green tea: acrid and euphoric.

'But it's true. You've been a hippy all your life.'

'That's just it. I'm retiring from being a hippy.'

'How can a hippy retire? Hippies don't do anything.'

'We do a lot, which is why we retire young. Hippies retire at 45. It's in the contract.'

'But how can you retire? I'm 45 too, and retirement has never crossed my mind.'

'Ah, you're still a student.'

'A student of what?'

'A student of life.'

I snort. We drink tea. A squirrel runs along the fence holding a whole apple in its mouth. 'What are you going to do?' I say.

'Grow some weed, relax, practise guitar, re-read *Illuminatus* maybe ...'

'No change then?'

If I am slow, Howard is static. If I have no sense of urgency, then Howard has no sense that he has no sense of urgency. He has never suffered from ambition. He is blissfully uncompetitive. He is untouched by the nine to five world because, having never been a part of it, he has only a dim conception of its privations. He doesn't bother it and, by mutual arrangement, it doesn't bother him. He is a man of boundless inertia.

He lives in the top floor of a house down the road. He rents the attic too – his pride and joy, for it is here, under artificial lighting, that he harvests his marijuana crop. Here too that he spends most of his life, among the drapes he has hung there, his bed, his superb hi-fi, his TV and his collection of remote controls. It is a den of cushions and books and candles and bundles of marijuana leaves: a Turkish-style fire risk. If it went up, the whole of the road would giggle as he burned to death.

Howard lives with lovely, sweet-natured, long-skirted Beth. She is an elf. She has a quick yet tranquil smile and a pale, limpid complexion. You can almost see through her ears. Beth is forever quietly busy about something or other in a corner. Unlike Howard, who never moves unless he has to.

The last thing Howard did requiring physical effort was when he built the last shelf. 'The Last Shelf,' he said portentously. It was for his bananas. In the corner where his bed is, he has a shelf space for everything he needs in order to avoid getting out of bed. Every item required for the reclining lifestyle was within reach of the reclinee, except bananas. Because of some oversight in the planning stage, there was no shelf allocation for his favourite fruit. He tolerated the omission for years, being obliged, when he felt the call of the banana, to get out of bed and walk over to the fruit bowl, or else get Beth to fetch one for him, which she was always willing to do (though he tried not to take advantage of her good nature; he is essentially a kind man). Finally, after considered design and careful construction, a dedicated banana shelf was fitted. The Last Shelf. Now Howard's lifestyle is replete.

Howard is a hippy from the Class of 70, a vintage year. In his youth he blew his mind, dropped acid, read a magazine called *Strange Faeces*, tried to grow a third eye, copulated promiscuously while reading aloud from the *Druid Book of Words*. He hung out in a Chelsea commune with a hedgehog, some geese, a seven foot hand and a machine that blew bubbles into the road. He grew runner beans up his street sign. At one point he built himself a Reichian box for hiding away in, lined with foam. Spiritually he graduated from the Paramahansa Yogi, who advocated sitting with all the body openings closed up, listening to the inner sound, to Guru Krishnamurti, who taught his followers not to follow gurus.

Of all the people I know, Howard is the most organised. Though Clive makes a lot of money and is a veritable success, it's hard to know exactly what he's doing most of the time. I'm not sure he fully understands himself. Clive works in a chaotic whirlwind, so he is always stressed, and most of the time he also seems to teeter on the brink of catastrophe.

Howard has never worked and sees no reason to do so. 'Somebody's got to be unemployed,' he says. 'It might as well be me. Give those gizzajob people my job and leave me in peace.'

If he'd wanted a career, Howard could have picked his profession. He's clever enough. But he turned his mind instead to exploiting the benefits system, brilliantly. He analysed it with academic rigour. He's an authority on claims forms and the nuances of claimants' rights, and he carries the detail of all the appropriate legislation in his head. Though hounded often, he is a step ahead of social security officials.

There are no rules in his life, except those he has imposed himself, and he's allowed to break them if he feels like it. In theory he is a vegetarian, though I've noticed, when he comes to my house and rummages through the kids' lunch box supplies in the fridge, that he makes an exception in the case of the cocktail sausage. He is not at all embarrassed about this. 'It seduced me,' he says.

And though, if you ask him, he will say he believes in total equality – men, women and squirrels – he is more chauvinist than anyone I know. Beth does everything: pops down the shops, runs the washing machine, cooks. In conversation she espouses the fashionable liberal causes, but she does exactly as he bids her. They have no children and appear to have no need for that complication.

'This is a *big* change in my life,' says Howard. 'Before I retired, that was duty. Now it's pleasure.'

'Ah.'

'You say "Ah", but I worked hard at being a hippy. It was a revolution, remember. I've made my mark. I've blazed my trail.'

'You've sat smoking dope in the attic.'

He looks at me sternly. 'I've blazed my trail.'

Clive is forever hankering after things: recognition, riches, respect. Peter wants the impossible – to be loved by Candice – and therefore has suspended his claim on happiness indefinitely. I'm still trying to find out what it is I want to do.

Howard knows precisely what he wants, and he's got it. In his quiet way he is more resolute than any of us. All his powers are geared to achieving the results he has defined, and Beth concurs. They look at the chaos and contention of this household with astonishment. Their lives run like clockwork.

We rib Howard, we laugh at his innately absurd lifestyle, but sometimes it's hard not to envy him.

Chapter 12 INNER

Howard is the exception among my male friends, but if you were to take Clive, Peter and me to represent the male sex, then you would conclude that men are either surging through life moving and shaking, laughing and hooting, getting filthy rich and rolling with dogs on lawns, or else sitting at home with sad jigsaw puzzles, bemoaning their tough luck, eating peanut butter from a jar with a dessert spoon, and watching late-night TV programmes they don't even like. It's a success/failure see-saw, with no reliable middle state.

Martha's ambitions for the year about to start are to knock the kitchen through to the back of the house, fit an upstairs bathroom, buy carpets, exercise more, and maybe, if she can remember, plan the summer holiday in advance for a change, so we don't end up in Brittany again. She'd also like doorknobs on the downstairs doors, in fact she *craves* doorknobs – but that is more problematic than it sounds, because the second-hand doorknobs we bought for them are lacking the tiny screw bolts which lock them to the spindles. Also the door wood round the handle needs filling ... Put it this way: it's fiddly and it involves me.

'And now,' says Martha, 'what do you want?'

What do I want? I don't know.

Men don't know what they want. Well, we know what we *want*, but we don't know what we can feasibly get. We want the moon, but we can't have it. We get disillusioned when we don't get it. Men are romantics. I don't mean in the remembering anniversaries sense, I mean in the deluded dreamer sense. My instinct tells me that life is a Great Adventure, and Great Adventures do not compromise: you are either on one or you are not. If you are, then yippee; if you're not then you might as well watch *The Jerry Springer Show* eating peanut butter with a spoon.

Most of my boyhood options are now ruled out: impossible with current wife, children and abilities. I'm too old to train for archaeology and I don't have Schliemann's fortune. And I never got the breaks to be a warlord. That leaves the novel I've always wanted to write. I want to write it still, passionately, but what would it be about, and even if I did spend a year writing it, would anyone want to read it? Would Martha be happier?

At the moment she's happy just to be talking about it. I don't know why I ever tried to deny her this. She's in her element, laying plans, analysing practicalities, suggesting possibilities. She's in her sharpest mood – all elbows. I can only admire her.

Martha's ambitions are more realisable than mine. This time next year she's likely to have fulfilled more of them than me. Like most women, Martha has a tight grip on reality. Sometimes, like when I want to stay up all night chasing a conversation, or dancing on the lawn with a friend's wife, this can be a drag, but more often than not it's a quality which pays dividends.

Martha knows that the best way to reinvent your life is not to stay up all night drinking, but to worry away at the dull grey stuff that is everyday reality, tweaking timetables, bending budgets, organising child help, memorising birthdays, preparing picnics ... Men don't see these things as priorities because they don't believe they have the power to change lives. They do.

When life slaps Martha in the face she takes the blows on the chin, collapses, reassembles herself and carries on. Me, I need intensive care and lengthy convalescence. I know why men who get the sack after 30 years come home and roll into a tight ball, some of them never to emerge. Men can harbour pain for years and then suddenly, at an unforeseeable moment, they cry. They cry the way bears cry; great barn-shaking sobs in the crook of the arm at dead of night. Often they don't have a very clear idea what they're crying about; all they know is that the world is ending.

Women have a fundamental belief in rebirth; in everyday transformation. They see themselves as ongoing projects. They are packages of qualities, some good, some bad, but all open to the possibility of improvement through work and application. Men's magazines concentrate on entertainment; women's are full of things to do; not necessarily easy things: LOSE 40 LBS! BAKE A CAKE! LOOK LIKE A SUPERMODEL! GET IN TOUCH WITH THE INNER WOMAN! They go to evening classes, yoga, do aerobics, aromatherapy, massage, bossa nova, consult horoscopes, consult counsellors, rearrange furniture according to deviant oriental practices ...

Men might say, derisorily, that they are forever fiddling about, but women's goal is a noble one. Women have faith in the Inner Woman, the illusive panacean person waiting patiently beneath the surface of the outer self, eager to be released from the bonds of everyday limitation. Women poke around in their hearts and minds to find her, fully expecting that with the appropriate technique, a calmer, happier version of themselves will emerge, unfearful of getting trapped in lifts, never saying *'Because I said so!'* to children, able to cook exquisite bouillabaisse and resist the come-ons of debonair chocolates. They know she's there. Sometimes they find her.

Are men ready for the Inner Man? Some of us can't even control the Outer Man, the one who drinks too much wine at dinner and breaks chairs just by sitting on them. What kind of monster might this Inner Man be? Will he approach us in dayglo popsocks? Will he insist on a bout of bare knuckle fighting? Or force us to sing 'On the Good Ship Lollipop'? Or will he make us cry like a bear? As the great (male) guru said, 'In life's adventure a man meets many strangers and the strangest of all is himself'.

We spend New Year's Eve with the usual array of friends at Clive and Sam's house. Afterwards, Martha and I bundle our sleeping kids in the car and drive home, wake Amelia and prod her up the stairs. I carry Mungo to his bed, remove his outer clothes and tuck him in without him knowing anything about it. He could be in Athens or Teotihuácan for all he knows, in the year 400 BC or AD 400 for all he cares. I lean down and kiss him. *'Die human, die!'* shouts Professor Hawking from the toy pile.

I put Leonard Cohen's piano instrumental, 'Tacoma Trailer', on the study hi-fi. I play it in enchanted late night lacunas like this. I like the way it fills the house with lugubrious portentousness. The children have only heard it during their sleep. It is ingrained in their souls.

And now everybody is asleep. I'm just soaking up the sound. I'm rich with piano wealth. This is my house. It needs a lot of work. We can't afford a builder. So what! My professional life is moribund. I will work full time on house improvements! I've been doing some DIY at weekends, so I know I like it. It's easier than writing and involves less decisions. Martha will be pleased. I'll earn my keep by building the house. It will be a holiday from writing! It is a noble task. I'll buy myself an electric screwdriver to celebrate this decision, and with it I shall make cupboards and convert bathrooms. I shall fix things to walls! I shall build a New World for us to live in.

Chapter 13 WEE

The New Year celebrations are over and the world has gone back to work – well, most of the world apart from me. *Perfecta* Magazine rang this morning to say they didn't think my piece about sex in unusual places worked.

'Oh, what didn't work for you?'

'It's not that we didn't like it, but when we said "unusual places", we weren't really thinking about the royal box at the Festival Hall.'

'That's unusual, isn't it?'

'No, it *is* unusual. But our readers wouldn't think it was very nice.'

One of these. *Perfecta*, the magazine for the faint-hearted. I *know* it was nice. Very nice. 'Where were you thinking exactly?'

'We were thinking, the kitchen, maybe.'

'Did Brenda like it?'

'Who's Brenda?'

'Did you think it was funny?'

'Oh yes, it was funny.'

'Well then run it, and fuck the kitchen.'

'No, I'm sorry, it really was too *outré* for us. But we're prepared to pay you a kill fee of 50 per cent.'

'That's very nice of you, but I'd rather have the amount you agreed to pay me.'

'But this is the normal arrangement if something doesn't fit the brief.'

'It's not my arrangement. And it fitted the brief exactly. If you didn't want unusual places in your article about sex in unusual places, then you should have told me.'

'We do have the right to kill the piece.'

'You do. Pay me the money you agreed to pay me and you can kill it as dead as you like. You can torture it with pinking sheers if that's your fancy, in whatever unusual place you choose, the kitchen, the ironing room ... I couldn't care less.'

'There's no need to be like that – you really were very near the knuckle.'

'I don't think that was near the knuckle. I could have suggested Canterbury Cathedral, or Ann Widdecombe's vagina ...'

'That's not very nice.'

'Your assessment, not mine.'

'I don't think there's much point continuing this conversation.'

'Agreed. And I expect a cheque for the full amount as per our verbal contract.' Strange how anger can turn you into a bureaucrat. Well, that's another magazine I'll never work for again. Do I care? No. Yes.

'During the war the Chislehurst cave system was Britain's largest bomb shelter. Only one child was born there, christened Caveina, though she later changed her name. History doesn't record why.'

It's the day after the *Perfecta* debacle and I have actually started panelling the bathroom. But I am interrupted by Peter, who has cycled over on his bike, complaining about having to come this far south. He has brought the newspaper along to read to me. This is fairly normal behaviour for a Thursday morning.

'Tea?'

'I went for an audition yesterday.'

'Milk?'

'It was for a Winalot dog food advert. The voice of the dog.'

'How'd it go?'

'I was the 59th dog.'

'They got a whole pack in then?'

'Rocket was sick in our bed.'

'Poor Rocket.'

'I had to change the sheets at 4 a.m. Candice said it was my fault.'

'You made him sick?'

'She said I fed him bananas.'

'Did you?'

'Yes.'

'What's wrong with bananas?'

'Don't know. Piss weak tea.'

'Earl Grey.'

'Look at this: "Scientists have discovered women's brains are richer in grey matter than the brains of men, whose brains are more densely packed with less efficient white matter."'

'That's depressing. We are better than women at some things though, aren't we?'

'Oh yes.'

'What?'

'Strength.'

'Strength.'

'Putting bumblebees out of the window.'

'Yes.'

'And of course, that all important *spatial ability*; vital for, um ...'

'Darts?'

'Yes.'

'The darts champion is truly a role model to be proud of. Anything else?'

'Well women can do everything else. Being prime minister, driving, making decisions, showing emotions of course ...'

'Identifying little things about the house which are wrong ...'

'There must be some things they're hopeless at, apart from football.'

'Urinating.'

'How can you say that? That's shocking. But you know, you're right! That's the white matter talking now.'

'Hopeless at it. Urinating is where men come into their own. It's one of the intrinsic male talents – along with all the others.'

'It should be on the CV: "Good urinator".'

'A wee superiority.'

'But an important one.'

'The equipment's better for a start ...'

'Aim is no problem.'

'The ergonomic "hose" type arrangement gives better directional control.'

'Longer range.'

'Yes, and faster in-out operation ...'

'Finger-tip control of, oh, a variety of effects ... Jet ...'

'Mist ...'

'Though there is no swivel head attachment.'

'No, but the female urinary department on the other hand...'

'Is very ...'

'Very ...'

'Unsatisfactory.'

'Yes. It's as though God lost interest in women at this point and concentrated all his attention on men instead.'

'Personally supervising trials.'

'At the test wall.'

'Sending volunteers to the wind tunnel.'

'It's a triumph.'

'Women will never catch up.'

'Envy us though they will.'

'However hard they practise.'

'How hard do they practise?'

'Good point. Not enough!'

'When was the last time you saw a woman peeing in a wind tunnel?'

'Exactly!'

'With women, it's hard to see what's going on at all.'

'It's all confusion and fog.'

'And when you look close up, as most of us have at some time or other ...'

'Have you?'

'Haven't you? ... More tea?'

'No thanks ... The slogan was Livalot, Wagalot, Winalot.'

'Catchy ... It's a most unsatisfactory affair, more like watching a lemon being squeezed.'

'No range.'

'If you had a tap that did that, you'd sack the plumber.'

'When caught short outdoors, women are obliged to adopt that undignified squat position ...'

'With the feet splayed at obtuse angles.'

'Like an elephant trying to sit on a very small invisible chair ...'

'The vexed question of tights doesn't bear thinking about.'

'On a windy motorway verge it is a maladroit and forlorn spectacle.'

'I've seen the moment of truth, you know.'

'Truth?'

'When a girl becomes aware that she's inherited a raw deal. It was heartbreaking really. We were at a picnic. Amelia was three. Three little boys walked to a hedge and she followed. She positioned herself at the end of the line and copied everything they did: faced the fence, legs apart, eyes straight ahead; then she gripped an air willy just below her belly, and weed down the side of her leg into her shoe.'

'A hard lesson.'

'I had to explain to her that life had a different role for her – a sort of squatting one. And that one day she would receive breasts as compensation. Don't they contain ethylene gas – bananas? Would that make you sick if you ate a lot of it?'

'I don't know.'

'It speeds the ripening of other fruit. It rots them. They say you should keep bananas separate.'

'Really? In the naughty fruit room. They'd be lethal in the hands of terrorists, wouldn't they?'

'Yes. They could just send a bunch of bananas to the Oval Office in an innocent-looking parcel.'

'And all the presidential advisers would ripen.'

'Howard's built a special shelf for bananas by his bed.'

'So they don't curdle his sensimilia.'

'Men don't beat about the bush, do we?'

'Thirty seconds and we're back in the car.'

'A woman takes 21 minutes, or more.'

'And sometimes she decides to give it a miss altogether.'

'But we get no credit.'

'Just the opposite. We have to wait outside the ladies' lavatories in the rain with the shopping.'

'And never a word of thanks.'

'While we have the efficient urinal!'

'The Concorde of sanitary ware.'

'The perfect architectural corollary to the male point-and-go system.'

'Way outside women's experience.'

'They can't comprehend them. They say: "How can you do it standing next to someone?" "Do you look at each other?" "What do you say to each other?"'

'What do we say?'

'It's a problem to know sometimes.'

'Especially when you're standing next to your boss.'

'Or a chief constable.'

'Or a violent crack dealer.'

'Do you look at his penis?'

'Not likely! You don't even look at his face.'

'That's the cardinal rule – *no staring*.'

'You look straight ahead only.'

'And up.'

'That is the origin of military bearing. If it's an important principle not to look at your neighbour's penis in a civilian toilet, then in a military one it's number one principle.'

'With a bullet!'

'Foolish is the soldier who tries to take a peep at his sergeant-major's little man ...'

'And blurts out: "That's a tiny penis you've got there Sergeant-Major!"'

'He'd forfeit his own.'

'Any sergeant-major worth his salt will be carrying a larger weapon somewhere about his person.'

'It's a great leveller, the urinal. Men of every race, creed, and station in life, standing shoulder to shoulder at the porcelain face.'

'You might be next to Colonel Gadaffi ...'

'Or Woody Allen.'

'But never, note, Madeleine Allbright ...'

'Or Oprah Winfrey.'

'In other circumstances these men might not even deign to talk to each other.'

'But in here they are simply men ...'

'Equal in the sight of God ...'

'Despite huge differences in wealth, privilege...'

'Penis size...'

'Thirty seconds!'

'It's about time we were recognised for it.'

'Ask not why we never put the seat down!'

'Ask rather why they never put the seat up!'

'Men are from Mars, women are from Venus.'

'They tinkle ...'

'We hose.'

'Respect!'

'Any luck with Winalot?'

'You're joking. I was the 59th dog.'

Chapter 14   ISAMBARD

It's true of course. Men are from Mars and women are from Venus. I've always known men are from Mars – that's why we hate dusting. And there is credible evidence to suggest that women are from Venus. My mother used to say: 'I've only got two pairs of hands you know!' I never worked out if it was a slip of the tongue or a statement of fact. If a slip of the tongue, what caused her to make it? Was it some vestigial memory of her distant origin on a planet of four-armed women? It's undeniable that women can do two things at once.

They can fill out a tax return while watching *EastEnders*, phone a friend while making a cake, talk while cleaning their teeth... They can do that up and down and round and round on the head and tummy thing with two hands. Or is it three? Some can sing 'I Will Survive' at the same time. Women can fillet a fish while talking down hostage holders, or whatever it is they do for a living, while part of their mind which is reserved entirely for private tasks is simultaneously planning a child's birthday party and considering Heavenly Mango for the back dining room wall. When I say 'women' here I'm generalising of course. I just mean all the women I know.

Men can't do that. Men can't do *those*. We can't even do the up and down and round and round head and tummy thing. Not properly anyway. That's why women are always criticising us. We can't do it because we can only do one thing at a time – and *that's* because we can only think about one thing at a time. It's not necessarily sex we think of, though that does, of course, creep in from time to time. Often it's something quite innocent, like how many Polo mints can be fitted in a 30 gallon tank, or how they make Scotch eggs, or what it would be like to be Asterix, or have Helena Christensen walk across the conservatory roof with no underwear ...

But one thing at a time – that's the point – we're single-minded. We may not be capable of watching TV at the same time as cooking a meal, but we could manage either reasonably well. We have tunnel vision, like Isambard Kingdom Brunel, the patron saint of tunnel vision.

All men have some Isambard in them. At B&Q every Sunday morning you can spot men wandering the aisles, lost in 'project trance', eyes glazed, scratching their chins, pondering the awesome possibilities of MDF, while at home their lunches go cold on the table.

Every single thing we do is done intensely. It may take us an hour to thread a needle, but we'll get it done even though the room's on fire. Bring a man a cup of tea and he will either ignore it altogether, or else drop everything and devote his whole attention to it. A woman on the other hand, can drink tea while operating a church organ, at the same time composing a letter to a nephew in Trondheim in her head.

Isambard Kingdom Brunel had the benefit of the domestic division of labour. There just isn't time in the modern household to devote the male intensity of attention to all the jobs the modern man has to do, so inevitably he gets distracted. When that happens the job he was doing goes back to the bottom of the attention list. That's the reason there are no doorknobs. Or else he gets preoccupied with method.

Women are more interested in getting things done than exactly *how* they will be achieved. That's why they don't read product manuals. They just want to know where the on button is.

Some mornings Amelia wakes herself up at six to bake a cake before school. She prepares her sandwiches and finishes her homework at the same time. She practises her dance steps while waiting for the kettle to boil.

Mungo never wakes up early and when he does he hunkers in front of the TV with his thumb in his mouth. To get him out of the sofa you need a big sofa lever. You can't get him to put his clothes on at the same time as he is watching TV. His hands don't work. They're like Pooh bear's hands. You have to point at them to make him realise they work. Even then they don't do much. He can sit for half an hour holding his trousers on his knees in front of him in the putting-on position.

I despair, but he's not so different from me. I do have my trousers on now, but then I'm much older than him. And it's gone 10.30.

It's fair to say the female body has many more functions, and what I can only describe as *places*, than ours. Unlike us, women can carry objects in the armpit, the crook of an elbow, in that small area just behind the ear or balanced on the hip. They can operate machinery with the knees, mouth, feet or nose. No wonder children are drawn to them: they know a proper lap when they see one, especially one with built-in throw cushions.

Sometimes, when Sam phones me to while away a slack moment during her working day, much of which is spent in her car, I am aware of many things going on at the same time: an assistant asking questions from the back seat, a Greek salad being consumed, an A to Z studied, adjacent van drivers bellowing at her to get off the road... Occasionally when she's hard-pressed – let's say she's doing her nails as well, and there's a tricky junction coming up – she says, 'Hold on!' and everything goes muffled. I know exactly what she's done because I've sat next to her in the car when she's done it. She's tucked the phone between her legs. I'm between her legs! I can't tell you what this knowledge does to the concentration of a man who is supposed to be fixing doorknobs.

Women's multitasking facility gives them such a devastating competitive advantage that for centuries far-sighted men of all nations, races, classes and income groups organised a universal embargo to keep them out of the workplace, afraid that if the truth got out, men would be forced out of the market, and left to get by as best they can writing funny articles on the fringes of society. The male accord has all but collapsed, though a brave rearguard struggle is being waged by Islamic fundamentalists.

The best thing about male single-mindedness is that when it's time to relax, we relax single-mindedly. Given the right kind of settee cushions, alcohol supply and television programming, men have been known to relax so superlatively that the last rights have been initiated.

It's even harder to rouse a man in this state than when he is digging a tunnel, though there is a method involving a pointed stick and children with trumpets.

I sometimes wonder if women ever relax in quite the same way. Even when they say they're relaxing, they're making tablemats for school fêtes, organising a share portfolio on their laptop, or wondering what to get someone for their birthday. Maybe, because they are also psychologically ambidextrous, they are incapable of doing one thing at a time.

Then again, maybe they don't want to. Maybe life with two pairs of hands is richer than lying slumped on a sofa like a dead Zen master.

Not too long ago women had a thing called 'women's intuition', an indefinable psychic power that enabled them to say 'I knew that was going to happen!' Now that women have started becoming prime ministers and going on space walks, I've noticed that they don't talk about women's intuition any more, probably so as not to make men more alarmed than they already are about women's powers.

Women do have powers don't they? They suddenly go clear-eyed and other-worldy and the next thing you know they're having a baby. Over the years the male medical institution has been at pains to promulgate a role for men in this process, devising clever cutaway drawings of our various parts to postulate possible correlations, and shaky theories about something significant the man may have done one night nine months before, after that Giant Sand concert. Frankly it's all a bit far-fetched. The inescapable fact remains that women spend nine months quietly metamorphosing without any help at all from men (though they try to make them feel better by pretending to need it). Anyone who has been at a birth knows that it's more fantastic and spooky than anything in ET (though certain scenes from Alien come to mind).

Also, women can smell things no one else can smell. Funny things. 'What's that funny smell?' they say in the middle of ER, and the men spend ten minutes searching for something that might be defined as a funny smell, fearful of finding Mr Bean chewing raw onions behind the sofa. We never do find it. Neither do we find out what happened to the woman with the back-to-front stomach, or whether Jerry ate Dr Green's pizza.

And there is the fact that women are not the slightest bit self-conscious about making themselves look beautiful – something men do shamefully and in secret. Women answer doors with white stuff all over their face, as though it were the most normal thing in the world. Well, perhaps it's normal on Venus, but in Streatham it just looks scary.

It is a universal truth that everyone – both male and female – wakes up in the morning with a face like a Rolf Harris painting. What happens next demonstrates a fundamental difference between the sexes.

A man looks in the mirror and thinks, 'So that's you. Hard luck. Eat some peanut butter.' A Woman looks in the mirror and then, with willpower and the application of coloured paints, miniature chimney sweep brushes, pheromone-heavy scents in talismanic bottles, creams and semi-precious transparent unguents in tiny rubber pods, endeavours to transform the Rolf Harris to a Rembrandt (or Picasso, depending on her mood).

If all that fails to make her look effortlessly beautiful she has foundation – a substance predicated on the notion that if beauty is only skin deep, then here's something thicker.

And if *that* fails, then she has the diet, the dental make-over and the depilation programme to fall back on.

If *they* fail, then there are many creepily discreet cosmetic surgery clinics waiting their opportunity in the Yellow Pages, next to Corsetry, Corrugated Cases and Corrosion Prevention and Control. Roll up for liposuction, enlargement, implantation, augmentation and … (this is creepy) eyelid surgery. Suck out fat: squeeze in collagen. It's an ugly business.

But we're talking extremes now. At least we hope they're extremes. Most men like to think that beauty is a natural magic. We are horrified to see that so much engineering is involved. The litter of beauty in the bedroom is disquieting enough: the grubby brushes, ravished tissues, pots of human-coloured cream, exhausted dabbing pads, dead razors, nail ends, sloughed skin, rejected hair. There is a claustrophobic smell in there, which reminds men of their mothers wiping their faces with something from a handbag, licked. And there are things which are downright sinister: lewd lipsticks with perversely sculpted ends, like little alien penises, and puddles of concertinaed tights-and-knickers sets that men come across unexpectedly on the carpet, still warm, as though the wearer had suddenly been catapulted naked into space by their own underwear – back to Venus, probably.

Men are wont to dismiss the beauty machine as empty-headed and superficial, but on the night, when the women walk out, we are not so glib. It works you see. On the whole it works. From our perspective women are alarmingly good at changing the way they look. So good that we sometimes don't recognise them. We are bewildered by their ability to metamorphose from power woman to vamp to hug bunny at the flick of a new wardrobe (or a night of tears over a bucket of boiling henna wearing a New Guinea bongo man clay mask). It plays hell with our emotional responses. Shocked and bedazzled, we are drawn moth-like into their light.

Without appearing to do much to achieve it, Sam, Martha, and Beth are all handsome women who manage their appearance well in individual ways. They have an assurance which is attractive in itself; a sense of dignity that is aesthetically pleasing. They are coolly edited versions of themselves.

They each have their interesting idiosyncrasies. Martha's is her shoes. Unlike her attitude to life, her shoes are utterly impractical; delicate and fine. Martha eschews sensible shoes. Though I salute them, I worry about the price she must pay to wear them; the discomfort, the inconvenience. These are shoes to wear in high class salons. I worry about her going off for a whole day on such tiny shoes, as she ventures on them into the maw of Brixton tube.

Candice is not so successful, though, unlike the others, she spends a lot of money at beauticians' shops. She is a poor judge of style and everything she does to herself is marred by a sense of underlying desperation. She's obsessed with her looks. She fears wrinkles more than illness. Fundamentally she's pretty, but she craves to be spectacular. At best she looks wrong, at worst atrocious. Always she looks vain. I would pity her if she wasn't so cruel to Peter, who wants more than anything, for her to be simply *her*. He loves the *her* who wakes up next to him in the morning with tousled hair and milky breath: the real *her*. He wants only to be her privileged post-cleansing cream companion, jealous of her secrets, bonded by a love so profound that appearance is irrelevant.

He's sincere. Like most men he's happy so long as his wife has a vagina and a personality (not necessarily in that order). The rest is negotiable. He doesn't want a glossy seductress squeezed from a tube. And when she looks in the mirror and says, 'I look *gross!*' he tells her, 'You're perfect the way you are.'

'There you go again,' she says, 'putting me on a pedestal!'

This is unfair, for though Peter *would* put Candice on a pedestal if he could, his criteria of pedestal-worthiness count for nothing in her eyes. Meanwhile she labours night and day to get up there on her own terms: the wake-up routine, the bedtime routine, the 20-minute touch-ups in motorway toilets, the pre-breakfast aerobic flap …

Not long ago, Candice arrived home with collagen bloated lips that she claimed made her look like Julia Roberts. Peter was appalled. It was an act of sacrilege. He was close to tears. I think he actually shouted at her.

'You should have told me first!' he said.

'It's my body.'

'You're not the one who looks at it.'

That's not true actually, Candice looks at it more than anybody else.

'If I'd wanted Julia Roberts, I'd have married Julia Roberts and not you.'

What can he do? He can only hang around the periphery of the boudoir with cups of tea, trying to find a place for himself in all of this, idly twiddling lipsticks. 'What is E'Spa Pink Hair Mud exactly?'

He might as well give up. He can't compete with the entire glamour industry. The only way he could get her attention would be to bring out a stylish yet reasonably priced summer collection of his own, or develop his own-label skin hydration improving moisturising ceramide. His looks, his personality, his lover technique are not enough any more, for she is driven by an imperative more pressing than the sex urge. She's obsessed. She's gone. She says she does it for him, yet *he* can't stop her. She has her face pack on, not talking to him, her fingernails are viscid, not touching him, her body carries the haunting aroma of hair-eating chemicals, not turning him on.

'She won't give it up just because it's tearing our relationship apart,' he says.

There's something else about women. Call me naive, but I didn't know this. I always love talking to women, you see; especially *these* women. But I had no idea that when they were alone they talked a different language. Well, they weren't exactly alone – I was there – but for most of a week of evenings, when Sam stayed here while Clive was in Canada on business, she and Martha talked about bras and celebrities. It was all right at first: we talked about many things round the table, and laughed, all three of us; but after a couple of evenings I realised I was being increasingly overruled, and that the scope of subjects had narrowed. One evening they did bras, another, celebrities, with a long coda on wrinkle cream. I tried to bring the conversation round to Great Pyramid theories, but was firmly repressed. It was as though I wasn't there. I wondered if all these years I had been merely boring Martha with my Great Pyramid theories.

A few weeks later Martha and I were at Peter's house when Candice was away somewhere. For some reason Peter had invited two single men and another man whose wife couldn't come. So there were five men, and Martha. The conversation crackled back and forth like gunfire, but at 2 a.m. I noticed Martha asleep on her hand. I realised then that we'd talked for five hours about musical trivia, with half an hour of light relief on the pyramids. When I told this story to Eloise, a woman friend, she curled her lip and said: 'anoraks'. Sadly there is no equivalent derogatory term for women with fixated interests.

Despite all this I don't want to believe Martha is from Venus. I'd hate to think there's such a gulf between us. I've counted her hands carefully and found only two so far, and I would surely know if she was emitting signals in her sleep. She could be from Tonga though:

somewhere hot enough anyway to explain why she watches telly wrapped in a blanket when the central heating is on.

I've come to the conclusion that men and women need each other to prevent the other sex from being boring. Those are dull old places, Venus and Mars, and it's not surprising nobody lives there any more. Segregate the sexes and you get Freddie and the Dreamers hit-lists or Raquel Welch's wedding anecdotes. Mix them up and you have life.

It's 1 am. I've been waiting for Martha to go to sleep. I have to fix my hair. I noticed scurf in it yesterday and I went into the Body Shop and bought a preparation of scalp oil. Martha is asleep now, so I won't have to stoop to this activity in front of her. I baste my head in the pungent and viscous oil and then sneak into bed beside her.

I am just dropping to sleep when Martha sits bolt upright. 'I can smell burning fruit!' she declares, then sinks back down to her lovely dreams of Tonga, where the sun is hot, and rock star wives gambol in their bras, and the fruit smoulders in the trees.

Chapter 15 CHAR

When people die the most difficult thing is to remove them from your address book. I can't cross Mrs Gems out yet. I should have crossed her out a long time before this anyway. We didn't need her because we had an au pair. For years the only reason we had a char at all was because we had Mrs Gems.

You're not supposed to get close to your cleaner. She's supposed to be untouchable. She's supposed to be peripheral to your life. Oh, she may tut at it occasionally and tell it to lift its feet, but she is meant to be as ignorable as the rag under the sink.

Yet she shares your world in the most intimate way. She knows what's in your cupboards and under your bed, she dusts your secrets down; she sets the room right after every sort of domestic disharmony. And she has in her handbag the keys to your door. You are vulnerable before her in so many ways. Yet you pay her a pittance.

In fact she is so poorly paid she is just like one of the family. That's why it is so difficult to get rid of her. We got rid of a couple before Mrs Gems.

There was Ella an extrovert West Indian cleaning woman with a happiness condition. Ella was 50, with three grown-up children, but she glowed with the gung-ho euphoria of one who has just discovered sex for the first time. This was because of a new boyfriend, Michael, a British Rail engineer, who could reach the parts other men can't.

Ella shared her bounty of pleasure with everyone. Every day she rhapsodised to me about the previous night's erotic adventure, while teasing the mantle with a duster.

'What that man do for me, Mr Plimmer!' she shrieked. "I'm 16 again!' Oh, the things Michael did. What's more, he paid for her tummy tuck.

One morning, caressing the doorpost of my study, Ella described how Michael had pleasured her on the kitchen floor. This sort of information can be distracting on a Monday, and made me envious. Ella never got down on the kitchen floor for me. Or for Martha. In fact the closest she got to the kitchen floor was the end of a long and languorously waved mop, which sketched clean doodles on our dirty tiles.

Ella had an over-developed respect for objects, which she treated as a cyclist treats bollards, skirting them with as wide a berth as possible. If we didn't keep moving things around, they accumulated verges. Ella didn't really clean at all; she was too full of passion. She merely excited the dust. The trouble was: we liked her. That's why it took six months to fire her.

In the end I had to lie to her. One day when she arrived, Martha was curled up on the floor, trying to ease labour pains. While Ella vacuumed the profile of a pregnant woman into the dust, I told her that, as my wife would be at home after the birth, we no longer needed a cleaner. I felt like someone tricking his grandmother into an old people's hostel.

Blind Betty, who followed, was much worse. Betty was so blind that she would let the vacuum cleaner lead her across the room until it hit something, then turn round. One day it crashed into a cabinet and a wedding present decanter fell on her head. In a previous incarnation, in the Sixties, Betty stood next to Mick Jagger at a peace demonstration. How the paths of those two have yawed since!

Blind Betty was a vegetarian hypochondriac, and wore an anti-dust mask over her mouth. She would only use expensive 'green' products. She used to cover the wet kitchen floor with sheets of the day's newspaper, then go home. This was specially annoying because it made the paper hard to read.

That was Betty's trademark. All cleaners have one. Mrs Gems, who followed Betty like a dose of salts after the gripe, always left a single flaw – a duster on a table, or bucket in a corner – which, like a potter's thumb-print on a vase, we took to be the signature of a master craftsman.

Mrs Gems was a different kettle of scourers altogether. She didn't waste time with talk. Mrs Gems had signed the pledge against dirt and pursued the stuff relentlessly, like a crusader, grim determination etched on her face. She was in her sixties and thin as a Hoover pipe. The only thing that ever stalled her was a chest cough that made her clutch the banister. At half-time she sat in the kitchen in a fug of cigarette smoke, with a mug of tea, frowning at the children.

Mrs Gems broke something each week methodically, as though it were part of her contract to do so, with never an apology or explanation. She arranged the shards on the kitchen side like battlefield dead, so we could inspect our losses when she had gone. One week we found there the remains of an Aalto vase. This wasn't wanton destruction: it was gourmet destruction.

One day Mrs Gems turned up with a heavy blanket of patchwork squares that she had knitted out of scraps, to wrap Amelia in. That was a long time ago. She has deigned to smile once or twice since then. She has been gone three months. She phoned once, explaining that she had to go to hospital for tests. I bought her a get well card which I never got round to sending.

I had a phone call this morning from a man who said he was Mrs Gems's son. He had in his possession some keys which he believed to be ours, he said, and he would deliver them. Mrs Gems died of cancer yesterday. I have the get well card in my drawer here. I can't bear it being there. I take it outside and put it in the dustbin.

Europa is not meticulous. She'll be back from holiday tomorrow, not that it will make much difference. She hates cleaning. And she is idiosyncratic. Nothing on earth will persuade her to put the carpet attachment on the vacuum. The carpet attachment is anathema to her. Instead she scrapes at the pile with the end of the tube. She leaves trademark striations on the carpet, as though a glacier has passed over it.

She throws things away too: magazines, socks; two days ago, a big pile of papers, which constituted my collected research for a possible project, disappeared. I can get over that; I can get over the Aalto vase. Most of the paraphernalia in a household is dispensable when it comes to the crunch. But Mrs Gems's blanket is part of the family.

Part II

SPRING

Chapter 16 GHOSTS

This house is visited by gorgeous ghosts. They are not ghosts in any morbid sense. These are very much alive. They are professional women in their forties. They are all single.

They are ghosts in the sense that they are unresolved souls. They are limbo women, detached from the *Sturm und dräng* of partner relationships: mysterious, other-worldly and utterly fascinating; desirable, yes, but untouchable (though they admit to a longing to be touched). Sometimes, when they look at me from some distracted inner part of themselves, they send a shiver down my spine. Spooky. If I were a dog I'd bark at them.

Single 40-plus women are a growing phenomenon. We used to count just one of them among our friends. Now we have seven: Eloise, Mo, Wendy from next door, Nadia, Laura, Katherine, Eithne. Some have children; some are childless. Either way, they seem to like coming here. They relax in the informal atmosphere of our chaotic conjugality. They turn up with bottles of wine, they eat, gossip, chew over problems, then fall asleep. That's the pattern. It's Friday evening and Eloise, who is the deputy editor of a glossy women's magazine, and Laura, a TV producer, whose nine-year-old daughter is upstairs with Amelia, are here now, sipping wine.

On high days and birthdays, when they overdo the wine and I crank up the stereo, I get to dance with one, or even two of them, but that's as far as my specifically male contribution to their lives goes, apart from maybe carrying their sleeping children to their cars at 2 am.

They are clever and funny and they're all attractive. They may have lost the bloom of youth, but they are at an age of easy elegance.

They no longer strive to impress. They know what suits them. Looking good is simply a reflex. To me they seem a delicious mix of experience and potential. Yet though they may be more desirable than they have ever been before, they are far less approachable. Single men are frightened of them.

Every now and then we tell them to go out and grab a man: get a life. This is hardly provocative; they tell themselves to do the same thing. They resolve to do it. They don't.

They already have a life actually. A very nice life. That's part of the problem. In all seven cases, and in widely differing ways, they are women of substantial achievement. They hire and fire, travel the world ...

Their professionalism extends into their lifestyle choices, which are ruthlessly discriminating. They have the right mobile phone, the right car, the right house and the right furnishings, each item laboriously selected out of thousands of possibilities. In restaurants, if their meal does not delight them, they send it back. One of the seven once left her cinema seat to demand that the projectionist turn the sound down. They are not pushovers.

They are so used to having exactly what they want, in the size, shape, colour and vintage they want, that they have become very fussy about men. Gone is the impetuous passion of their youth.

Yet they know in their hearts that marriages are not made in the satisfactory fulfilment of some detailed checklist. They are made in reckless, spur-of-the-moment decisions, followed by years of trying to match unsympathetic elements, until some magical symbiosis is achieved. Or not.

In any case, single men of their age are hard to find. This is odd considering they are supposed to be in surplus. They are certainly keeping a low profile. Occasionally one of my women will ask me to track one down for her. I'll follow a single man's footsteps to a lonely pub, corner him at the bar and weave dreamy images of my seven gorgeous spirits. It makes the men depressed. 'What a cruel waste of vaginas,' one of them said, mournfully.

Once I invited a single man to dinner and I sat him next to one of the seven. They got on like a house on fire; shared a passion for

Truffaut and wines of the Alsace. But did he fling back the rug and call for hot Latin music? No he didn't. Did he insist she leave her Audi at my house and drive her home in his Ka? No he didn't. He slunk home early with a sudden headache, claiming a heavy day ahead. I was disgusted.

Sadly, men don't see these women's elegant autonomy as a come-on. They see it as a problem. They run away. Yet if men don't do the chasing, nobody will, because though my women have overturned every other traditional role pattern, they still expect to be pursued. They see it as their birthright. They are baffled that they are not, but they carry on looking lovely anyway, being fantastic, being there. To no avail.

A man in their position, with their power, might go for a docile partner, someone he doesn't have to compete with. But they aren't interested in docile men. Women haven't changed that much. They still fantasise about a man who will sweep them off their feet. They fancy something hard between the sheets.

Neither do men know the subtle skills of insinuating themselves into a powerful person's life. They take one look at my seven women, with their magazine-perfect homes, and they think: 'Where would I put my racing bicycle? My electric guitar that I play only when I'm drunk?'

Getting her into bed might be the easy bit. The hard bit would be telling a woman who has ordered a cinema projectionist to turn the sound down, that you think your Captain Beefheart album collection would look fine on her minimalist zinc shelf.

One of these seven women has a house rule forbidding anyone to enter her sitting room with shoes on. And she's got two children! How those kids are going to turn out without the sensible influence of a man, God only knows.

The one thing the years have managed to take from these women is their spontaneity. They no longer lift up their skirts and fly, as they were urged to do in the Sixties – not without knowing the destination first anyway. They're old enough to have been messed around before and they don't intend to be messed around again. So they rewrite the partner job description, inserting tougher clauses; and in the meantime, sink their passions into redesigning their bathrooms. There isn't a man alive who wouldn't compromise their lifestyles.

In our house though, they can relax their standards. They don't have to be on their mettle here. We've compromised already, so they can keep their shoes on, or kick them off, as the whim takes them. There's nothing they like better than coming round to watch a video they've been dying to see. Within ten minutes, they're asleep. Ghosts.

Tonight I stop the film, make coffee and wake them – very gently, or they might tell me off. Laura demands that I précis the part (an hour) that she's missed. Eloise denies she's been asleep at all.

'I can't understand what the critics saw in this film,' Eloise says.

'They saw it,' I tell her. 'That's the difference. In their waking hours.'

'I was awake!'

'Film critics watch the film with their eyes open – trick of the trade.'

Martha doesn't share this need to sleep in the company of others (we do it every night) but sometimes she becomes infected and drops off too. Like tonight, during the second half of the screening. I am alone in the room with three sleeping women, arrayed across sofas like lions of the Serengeti that have eaten too much wildebeest.

This makes me feel lonely. At such times I might just as well be a sad single man; the only difference being that his wish might be that he had three women in the room with him, whereas I have, all making gentle prrpwah noises with their lovely lips.

Chapter 17 AU PAIR

'There it is!' says Mungo. 'It's small!'

'It's very far away.'

But the closer you get to Stonehenge, the smaller it becomes.

It's the last Sunday before school term begins, and we have spent two days with Martha's father Hugh, at Salisbury. We are visiting Stonehenge on the way back. Mungo is keen to see it and so am I. I've never made the pilgrimage, though all my life it has loomed large in the imagination, up there with the Great Pyramid, throwing its monumental profile across the English psyche, embodying and obscuring everything we may not know about ourselves.

Stonehenge is our great-great-grandfather clock, our sun temple, our primal cathedral; erected in the murky pagan forest and surviving 3,000 years to dominate the tractable Christian plain. This is Thomas Hardy's Temple of the Winds, whose sombre hum, 'like some gigantic one-stringed harp', lulled Tess of the d'Urbervilles to sleep on her last night of freedom.

It was with a sense of numinous expectation that we approached across the windy plain, scouring the horizon for our first glimpse of the stones. We find them on a traffic island in the fork of the A303 and the A344, so subsumed by the everyday might of modern road vehicles that they bring immediately to mind the 18" Stonehenge prop in Spinal Tap. It doesn't do much for the gravitas of a 40 ton sarsen when every minute a lorry carrying that weight in MDF kitchen doors breezes past at 60 mph.

And then there's the underpass. Built for the best of reasons – to hide the access route from the car park – it is the most unenigmatic of things, which doesn't inspire you to ponder what you may not know about yourself, but rather awakens the sensation that you might be in Milton Keynes.

Still, Stonehenge is puzzle enough to draw 750,000 ponderers every year. So many that they threaten to obliterate it. British Heritage has been obliged to protect the stones from their fans, who at one extreme, would take bits of it back home to rockeries in Godalming, and at the other, would indulge in sex rituals with underage goats, making the place stink of charred virgins. Which of these two groups most resemble Stonehenge's original devotees even the most sage of academics cannot tell us.

We have to view the stones, which are as mournfully isolated as elephants in a zoo, from an orbital gravel path. This is the closest to a trilithon as we can get, and we stand there for fully five minutes in the freezing wind. Stonehenge may be perfectly aligned for viewing the Midsummer sunrise, but (speaking as a DIY expert here), the draughtproofing is way out.

Mungo holds his arm out and squints between his thumb and forefinger. 'I can squash it between my fingers,' he says.

Quarantine may save Stonehenge from 7,500,000 fingerprints a year, but it's a disaster for people. The temple isn't an intellectual experience. You can sense that, even from a distance. It is the most tactile of artifacts, like Plasticene, utterly, irresistibly hands-on. You want to connect with it; paint the children and wife blue and run through the stones naked. You want to be part of the history, not someone standing on a gravel path in a raincoat.

But it's not allowed. If you were to perform a sacrifice here (and by some accounts the site has an honourable tradition in this respect) you would have to do it on the gravel path, and even then I think it would be frowned upon.

I can't blame English Heritage for our disappointment. Anything they did here would be a compromise. No, to hell with it: I can blame English Heritage. I can blame it for the visitor centre, where Stonehenge enters a new concept of smallness, passing through the border control of Spinal Tap absurdity and straight out the other side. Here are Stonehenge tea spoons and Stonehenge fridge magnets and tiny Stonehenge models 5 centimetres wide. Give me sex with a goat any day.

We arrive home tired and disillusioned. Lowell makes us a cup of tea. Europa serves biscuits. It's nice to see everybody being so considerate for a change.

They have something to tell us. They seem bashful.

'We've become friends,' says Lowell. '... Well, more than that really.'

Amelia's eyes grow huge.

'Yes,' says Europa. 'It's been going on for three days now, but after this weekend we are sure. It's a big thing for Lowell and me.'

It's a *fait accompli*.

We never thought this would happen. We never thought a blonde French girl of 26 would look at a spotty English boy of 17. How wrong we were to stereotype them.

She has been through three boyfriends already. She brought home two smart black men who worked for the drugs squad a couple of times, making Howard nervous. Then there was a one-nighter with a juggler called Ramon, who took her with him to Covent Garden the next day and chucked her. Lately it's been a pale man who works in the health food shop. I never dreamt she'd even look at Lowell.

Without Edam the whole au pair system would break down. It would be too expensive. Doubt it though you may, it has always been the case that au pairs don't like good cheese, which is expensive, but they eat a lot of Edam, which is cheap. This seems to me to be an important part of the trade-off between au pairs and their employers. If they don't eat Edam you can point out to them that it is the law.

No one can quite know what it's like to have an au pair living in their house until they've done it. We all have preconceptions and mine were quite the rosiest, encouraged by au pair agencies with names like Bees Knees Problems Unlimited, and receptionists called

Sandrine, and the poignant applications of the au pairs themselves: 'Dear Family, Hallo my name is Kathrin. I'd like to see you and your children and I wish we were friends ...', 'I love to read children a fairy or a poetry, to teach them to love the nature, the trees, the flowers, the meadows ...'

I had a quasi-paternal fantasy. I expected au pairs, unlike Stonehenge, to be small. I pictured an idealised little girl, neat, with plaits probably, nibbling a diet bar, baking strudels, and when she wasn't reading the children a fairy, filling the house with laughter and flute music. What I got was a big person in a turquoise shell suit and giant bunny slippers. They all wear giant bunny slippers, even the ones who intend to join the police force. Au pairs are not neat little plaited flute girls. They are always much bigger than you think, with their own complicated special needs and orange towels and body bags containing abused teddy bears, and talcum habits and depressions. And you have to accommodate them into your family.

We've been through seven au pairs in three years. We've had two abortions, a bail visit to a police station at dawn, rejected boyfriends prowling the garden at night, and now to cap it all – a baby-snatched son. Even so, no experience has been as stressful as the first two au pairs, who lasted, between them, four weeks. We weren't very good judges of character then, but we learnt fast.

It was clear the moment we set eyes on Alzbeta, that she was going to miss the merriment she had so emphatically left behind in Slovakia. We fussed around her, showing her the newly painted bedroom with its nice new lamp, but she curled herself up on the sofa in as close to a foetal position as adult conventions would allow. She was allergic to cats and ate much fruit.

If you've ever had a large, depressed, fruit-eating au pair in the corner of your living room, you'll know how disquieting it can be. What she probably needed was a hug, but it's hard to hug someone in a turquoise shell suit and giant pink bunny slippers. Besides, I got the feeling that bodily contact might be dangerous.

Teenagers, as we know, are alien creatures anyway. To have a teenager in the house who doesn't speak English and has a happiness problem is to be thrust into the forefront of interplanetary relations.

Alzbeta was sad for three weeks and then suddenly, mercifully for us, her sister rang from Slovakia to say she'd had a still birth. Alzbeta left the next day. Two days later a family rang from the next borough to say she had applied to them for a job and could they have a reference. This was odd. This meant that Alzbeta had been depressed about something specifically to do with us; something that she thought she saw, or misheard, or misunderstood – or worse, something she actually did see, hear or understand. We will never know what it was.

Miserable au pairs are bad enough. Happy au pairs are worse. Piroska, whose letter of introduction said, promisingly, 'I love the famous English sense of humour', filled us with fresh hope. A bonus: she could drive. What she didn't mention in her letter was that she came from a region of Hungary where people drive screaming through the night with their eyes shut.

She was so keen to get into the car that on the second night I suggested that Lowell, who had just passed his test, take her for a spin. They arrived back at 6am the next day. Both wing mirrors were smashed and there was no petrol in the tank. It was as though all her life she'd been locked up in a cellar and this was her first taste of freedom. Lowell was pale. He couldn't remember where they'd been; all he knew was, it had been at high speed. I told her this sort of thing did not accord with the famous English sense of humour.

Piroska had lots of washing. When one cycle finished she loaded another. After six days her agency rang us to say they felt duty bound to tell us that they thought she was planning to leave. It was true. She was planning to leave the next day. She'd found a new job with a family who had a swimming pool. She hadn't warned us, she said, because she hadn't wanted to annoy us. Martha took all her bags of wet washing and put them in the street. I was proud of her. The car breathed a sigh of relief.

It settled down after that. For one thing we dispensed with the regular agencies and their tiresome fees. We found a little second-hand au pair agency in Thornton Heath, which fixed us up for a fraction of the cost. It specialised in au pair, whose placements had not worked out. This was sometimes the au pair's fault, but more often than not it was because they'd been abused in some way. Some of their stories were heartbreaking. I would sit in the waiting room with the other customers, who always seemed to be men, and who looked as shifty as I unaccountably felt, waiting for girls to be brought in. We could at least assess them face to face. It was a strange affair, like getting a dog from Battersea Dogs' Home, though with less checks on our suitability.

The first one was Hungarian and most of those who followed were too. Each one tended to recommend someone to take their place. Sam and Clive also had Hungarian au pairs via the same connection, so they all saw each other socially. Sometimes they had their friends and relatives over to stay, bearing gifts of Tokaji. One summer seven Hungarians, one called Attila, turned up at Clive and Sam's in a battered Mercedes and pitched a tent in their garden. Once I came home to find a sultry girl, Zigana, who was working for Clive and Sam, standing in the middle of my kitchen lazily consuming an enormous sandwich.

'Ah Martin,' she said languidly. 'I am *so* glad you are here.'

'Why?' I said.

'Because *that* is on fire.' Sure enough, the toaster was in flames.

And now there's Europa, who breaks the mould. Europa is sloppy, dreamy, *petite*, rather sexy, a bit sullen sometimes, but I like her, which is just as well, because now, for better or worse, she seems to be part of the family. I am beginning to realise that her life is on hold, she can't decide what to do with it. That's why she's a perpetual au pair. I have to say in her favour that already, after just a couple of days after she moved in, Lowell seems to have smartened up his act considerably. Is it just my imagination, or does his room smell better? He looks jauntier too – probably the prospect of taking his 26-year-old, blonde, French girlfriend to meet his friends at the pub after college. Stereotypes still matter sometimes.

But the gap in Europa's life isn't large enough to accommodate hard work. She hates cleaning particularly. She is resourceful though and I like that in her. Already she has sub-contracted out the cleaning part of her job to a fat French boy called Bernard, who au pairs for the widow who owns the house one down.

Bernard is a character. He stands at the front gate with his feet apart, smoking cigarettes, looking up and down the pavement and nodding at passers-by in a way only French men do. I am told he has not been out of Streatham.

Bernard sits in our kitchen gesturing expansively. He's a convivial character. It appears he wants to be a film director. I ask him what sort of films interest him.

'V.O. Lance,' he says.

'V.O. Lance?' I am baffled by this. An obscure French film director perhaps? I shake my head.

Bernard raises a finger, then gets up and goes out, returning minutes later with two copies of a glossy Japanese film magazine called *Aghast!*, which specialises in pictures of sawn-off limbs.

'Ah! Violence! You like violence! We have a lot of that in London.'

He smiles. 'I do not like London,' he says.

Chapter 18 SHOP

'Katie here at *Weekend*. Martin you don't know me but we've *really* been enjoying your pieces in *The Times* and I wondered if you'd like to do a piece for us here at *Weekend*?'

I've never written for *The Times* in my life, but I'm not one to scupper a compliment, and even though I am currently Mr House Fixit, repairing my way back to Martha's heart (though she remains suspicious of the whole plan), I would be foolish to look a gift horse in the mouth.

The commission is to write about a reward holiday for ten members of a retail company's management staff, who have consistently bettered their personal objectives. It will be four wild days of high living at a schloss hotel in Austria. 'You know what it'll be like,' says Katie the gift horse, 'lots of indiscretions, practical jokes, bed-hopping, soul-searching ... We want to know exactly what those paragons of business really get up to on these reward junkets. The company will be sending a PR to look after you – Zoe at Peter Crawford Associates.'

Zoe at Peter Crawford is posh and rough at the same time; breezy with a dirty laugh. She confirms the dates and tells me she'll meet me with the tickets at the Heathrow check-in. 'You won't miss me, I'll be the one with the big hair and the clipboard!'

'I'm tall and I've got no shoes.'

'Oh!' said Zoe. 'This is going to be *whacky*!'

I fly on Monday. It's short notice but never mind. It's not as though I'm snowed under. The only problem is that I really haven't got any shoes. So I've come up to the West End this Saturday morning with

Martha, Amelia, and Mungo, to find some. It's not as easy as it sounds.

I'm big you see. I'm the one who passes down the serving dish from the top shelf, the one who pins up the streamers. At the Lord Mayor's Show I wear a small child on my head. I'm up here among the clouds and cobwebs, and the low beams, built by small-minded carpenters for short people. All I did was eat up my carrots as a boy, and now that I'm grown up, I find the world is biased towards people who didn't eat up their carrots. Everybody's looking out for the little man. Well what about the big man?

I have heard a rumour, or was it a dream? or was it a malicious trick by small people? that Marks & Spencer is now stocking size 12 shoes, and so I am here, in the Temple of The Great Provider, St Michael, with an eager wad of money.

I am in the store which caters to every conceivable demographic. Here are loud dressing gowns for retired criminals, and brown wool ties suitable only for Dundee librarians. Here women of substance buy insubstantial lingerie. Here, for small businessmen, are racks of small suits, for drunken wives, satin slips in dark wine. Here are gay socks for rent boys and muffin and beige single check shirts in easy-iron cotton twill, for people who sit at plastic garden furniture writing why-oh-why letters to newspapers. Here too are soft-soled leather moccasins for men whose calling it is to pad soundlessly through forests at night. Wait long enough and you will spot Margaret Thatcher, who famously buys her knickers here, on her way to the Political Underwear Department.

But, call me blasphemer – and may St Michael drown me in a rain of speciality coleslaw if I lie – I am beginning to get strong intimations that the store which is all things to all men is ostracising me. There are no size 12 shoes. At the end of the shopping day at M&S, unsold walnut salads are rounded up and distributed to the walnutless. So much for the little man. What about the big man? What about Terry Waite and Arnold Schwarzennegger? What about me?

Big men are not a small minority, yet can we buy size 12 shoes? No we can't. We have to buy a pair of size elevens and limp. My main concern is simply to get something which goes all the way round my foot. For this rarity I am grateful, even if it is maroon.

The shoes I have worn for five years, my lovely Grenson's that I cherish, have had it. They happen to be size 12 and stylish, and not maroon – a priceless rarity. But they are dead. I have to face this. They have started to smell of wet pony. People look at me on the bus, as though expecting to see a wet pony sitting there, and I have to resist an urge to wink at them. My shoes are dead. The welts are grinning, the heels hanging. Yet I'm still wearing them. That's because they fit.

M&S has 20,000 men's shoes, laid out in the order of maximum difficulty. The small sizes are on the top shelf, where the small men can't see them, and the large sizes are on the bottom, so the big people have to crawl like men who have come to fix the carpet. The shoe sizes are displayed secretively inside the heel of each shoe, where they are hidden by the shelf above. You must serve yourself.

After a fruitless half-hour on our knees pulling shoes in and out, Martha and I are hot and exhausted. Amelia has sloped off somewhere and Mungo has reached that point children get to, where he is so bored it's starting to hurt him. He's lying on his back on the floor, in the middle of the aisle, moaning. It seems churlish to tell him off, seeing as Martha and I are also lying on the floor in the aisle (though sensibly, on our fronts).

I corner a member of staff. 'The 12s,' I say, 'I can't find them.'

She must have heard the rumour too, because she says: 'Have you looked under?'

I say I have. 'No, *under*,' she says emphatically.

Either I am delirious or there is a logic to this: if the biggest shoes are on the lowest rack, then even *bigger* shoes might somehow be *more* under. Sure enough, I have only to lay on my stomach on the floor and stretch my arm out underneath the display stand to feel the tantalising toes of other, distant shoes, in a kind of inner sanctum, a shoe ur-space whose existence is only rumoured, even among sales assistants. Here, surely, are the size 12 shoes of myth and legend. Sweating and struggling, I manage to hook several out. They are all size 11.

Now the assistant is standing over me. 'I'm afraid we don't do size 12 after all,' she says, crushing my hopes with a smile. I roll over on the carpet and stare up at her. From here I can see exactly why small people feel an exaggerated need to assert themselves.

'And why not!' I shout. 'What has Margaret Thatcher's bottom got that my feet haven't?'

She can't answer that.

So I buy a pair of size 11 Oxfords for Austria. And as I squeeze my feet into their mean confines, I become aware that someone has left an ancient pair of battered brogues on the bottom rack of the stand. Even from my great height I can tell they are a good size 12, and that they smell of wet pony. The tongues have fallen out, yet they speak volumes to me. A casual observer might think they have been dumped, or are evidence of a shoplifting switch, but I can see that they are the final expression of a desperate act. I can picture the man who once wore them. He has been through this same charade, before me, but in his case, disappointment has driven him over the edge.

And here is his shoe suicide note. He has left it here on the rack for others to interpret as they will, and he has run barefoot out of the store, screaming silently. He has run to the river and thrown himself off the bridge, where even now he is standing with his feet on the river bottom and his head sticking foolishly out of the water.

I take what must pass for comfort in my new size 11s. There but for the grace of the god of pain go I.

'Get up quick! It's *Yesterday in Parliament* already!'

Martha, a Radio 4 morning person, wakes me with a riddle.

It takes me a full ten seconds to work out what this might mean; then I bound from the bed. I make it to the airport forty minutes before take-off, anxious.

There is no one recognisably big-haired, or holding a clipboard, to be seen. I scan the concourse for five full minutes, checking other airline counters, checking the time, checking the check-ins. Nothing.

They must have given up and gone air-side. I am about to ring Peter Crawford Associates, but I check my ticket first. The time is bang on. The date is a week out. Today is the 16th: the flight is scheduled for the 23rd. I'm a week and 35 minutes early.

Being early is a new experience for me. What's more I'm *really* early. I'm *so* early it's no longer creditable. I'm earlier than the early bird. I'm earlier than the worm. I'm here with the amoebas! Already, one week and 35 minutes before I've even left, my Austria shoes are killing me.

Being early is worse than being late. There's a huge hole in your life, a sense of having vaulted into limbo. I have to go home and face all the people who've only just given me a special send-off. What's more, because I haven't been anywhere, I've got no presents. For a week I tread water. I can't concentrate on anything. I'm obliged to slide through the house like a shade. I have nothing planned to do and the things I do occupy myself with don't seem real. Time passes infuriatingly slowly.

'You'd be early for your own funeral,' Peter tells me, trying the idea out. He drops it immediately. It's too horrible. You'd be there, but there'd be no mourners. Just a mounting sense of horror.

Martha normally likes to take Mungo in to school on her way to work, but she has to be in early all this week. Europa was going to do it, but as I've got nothing to do now, I go instead. I don't like the playground ambience in the morning. Mungo's school is in the heart of Brixton, but it's a good school, so inevitably, it's turning middle class. I'm uneasy about being surrounded by so many middle-class people. Individually they may be OK, but when they herd ... All that self-satisfaction, that embarrassment, their cynicism, false modesty, ubiquitous manners, their declared concern, their 'inverted commas', their habit of taking over the world, their camouflaged egos, their alternating designer and liberal labels, their declarations of poverty, their wealth. They remind me of all the most tedious aspects of myself. I don't want to talk to them, particularly in the morning. I like good, honest, working people: craftsmen and stevedores, firemen and fisher-folk. We could do with more fisher-folk in this school.

I particularly don't like their eco-friendly bikes with shopping panniers and strapped-on lights, their elbow protectors and plastic helmets, which make them look like rock climbers in the playground. I'm not ungreen – I've taken a box instead of a carrier bag at Tesco's – but some of these cyclists bring their children to school on little seats fitted on crossbars, with pull-along matchwood trailers at the back for baby siblings, fitted with a wee flag to tempt the traffic. They cycle through the buses and lorries on one of London's busiest feeder roads, by the side of which, several times a year, you can see flower shrines to people who have been knocked down. These children are at the cutting edge of the Green Revolution.

Also I'm wary of teachers. Ms Carroughough teaches Mungo; she used to teach Amelia. I've grown up a bit since Amelia's days there, but still, when I bump into her in the school corridor, I start to mumble.

When I was a boy I assumed one of the compensations for growing old, looking horrible and becoming boring would be that teachers would no longer be around. I was wrong. They're around whenever I take the children to and from school. I still have to deal with them. Outside the school gate I can kid myself I'm an important citizen, but in *there*, assailed by that peculiarly evocative aroma of pencil shavings and damp trousers, I am as a child. I am rendered small again. I am always late of course, and I have always forgotten something important, but I am *desperate* to please, to be liked, to be correctly turned out with the correct gym kit/picture of Henry VIII/homework/book bag/child. I want to be teacher's pet parent.

I suppose what makes me regard teachers with exaggerated respect is the influence they once had on my life, for good and bad. They opened doors, but they closed doors too. They illuminated and they blinkered. They were saint and bogeyman, judge, jury and jailer. And now they have my children.

No matter that Ms Carroughough, in the convivial mêlée at the Summer Jumble coffee counter, tells me to call her Jane, the word sticks in my throat. Somehow Carroughough is easier to say. Her invitation to informality may just be another formality. Why else, when I go to see her on parents' evenings, does she make me sit on a very small chair with my knees around my ears?

I nurse a secret fear that I will be caught out with the wrong book bag in the school corridor one morning, and Ms Carroughough will rise on her heels to ceiling height, and focus her attention on my feeble pretence at adult status. 'Mr Plimmer ...' she will say in a clear and strident voice, and the corridor, which a second before had been booming with activity, will fall silent. 'What are seven nines?'

'58' I will say and all the children will laugh derisorily, guessing that I am wrong, and I will stand there with my pitiful grown-up person's burden of gym bags and lunch boxes and pictures of Henry VIII, feeling bleakly foolish.

'And another thing. Tell the school what you are trying to hide in your head.'

If exaggerated respect for teachers is one extreme of my mental condition, exaggerated resentment of them is the other. I have a smouldering sense of grievance that needs little prodding to jump into the ring and seek active revenge. Given the right circumstances, any teacher may become representative, spokesman and spirit incarnate of every teacher who has wronged me in the past.

During her first week at secondary school, a teacher issued Amelia with a detention. The class had been noisy and he made an example of her. It doesn't sound much, but it crushed her. This was a little girl who had never been punished before, who had never knowingly done anything wrong, and who wanted *painfully* to do everything right at her new school.

The teacher acted heavy-handedly, but the hatred it stirred in me was out of all proportion to the slip of judgement it was. He was a monster. I wanted to barge in there and strangle him.

We did meet three weeks later, at the first parents' evening. He didn't have two heads, or that habit of putting his tongue round your neck and popping your head off. He was a young man trying to do a difficult job as best he could. Suddenly I could see that clearly. He wasn't a bad teacher either. He had worked out a cunning study plan for Amelia, which showed a considered understanding of her weaknesses and abilities. I didn't mention the detention.

Chapter 19 FLY

'Hello old Fruitus!'

Zoe from Peter Crawford Associates is incontrovertibly, unmissably here this time round: hair, clipboard – the works. Larger than life. Waxy lips. Hard to imagine the airport without her now. The management high-fliers are here too, a grey bunch, still in their work clothes, by the look of them, huddling with each other like sheep, as Zoe jollies them through Departures, to be furthest away from her hyperbolic fabulousness.

'You're late!'

If she only knew.

Deep down everybody is afraid of flying, though each to a different degree. The hardened test pilot only gets scared when *both* engines are on fire. I get scared when the wings wobble. Or when cabin staff make engine malfunction noises with catering equipment. Ever since that paragliding experience in Grindelwald, flying has made me nervous.

The fact that I am heading back to the Alps doesn't help somehow, plus there have been bad omens: getting the date wrong was one, having a graphic premonition of my own imminent death another. Does this mean I'm psychic? Or does it mean I am over-imaginative? If psychic: is it too late for me to alter anything, now that we're taxiing down the runway? If over-imaginative: can I stop myself screaming?

Logically, we *know* humans are not meant to fly. Apart from the buffalo or the slug, humans are the least aerodynamic of all the animals. The finest human athlete can manage only six metres, and that with the help of a stick.

We *know* that sitting on air is supernatural. Air is not the most reliably supportive of stuff. If you leave a book on some air and go for a cup of tea, it won't be there when you get back. We all *know* this, yet we kid ourselves we can 'fly' (to Vienna, for instance!), just like that.

Perhaps the 'miracle' of flight (as even rational scientists, in sloppy, yet revealing, moments, sometimes refer to it) requires an act of faith – a suspension of disbelief. What would happen if we, the passengers on this flight to Vienna, collectively stopped believing? Would the plane slide into the sea, unable to remain aloft on the crew's faith alone?

What if everybody on the plane ate a heavy sort of porridge for breakfast. What if they're all concrete salesmen, heading for a Concrete Convention in Konstanz, trying to outdo each other in the range of samples they've brought along.

There's only one thing to do at times like this, and that's to distract the mind by concentrating on the air hostess. Unlike au pairs, air hostesses have instant access to my deeper feelings. It's something to do with the uniform, but more to do with the way they hover over me. This partiality is another consequence of my size. I'm so used to being the tallest person in the room, that when the tables are turned it can be disorientating, though pleasantly so. Nurses are mother figures, air hostesses angels.

There are other reasons to watch the air hostess. She is an icon of airworthiness provided by the airline to instil confidence. She is living proof that flying is possible. We scan her face, as though checking a barometer, for signs of concern, and are comforted by her equanimity, even though we suspect that she is so well trained (she has poured coffee standing upside-down in a flight simulator for God's sake!) that she would still be smiling in a tail spin. On the other hand, she has flown many times before and she is (still here!) a model of tranquillity, without earthly care, all the while balancing a little origami hat, specially designed to increase the impression of weightlessness.

She is beautiful. This one is beautiful. She is dressed to kill, in a uniform of figure-correcting navy blue polyester that declares simultaneously: 'Something softly desirable inside' and 'Don't try it!'

She is a star. However sparkling the passengers in Clipper Class, she is the only one allowed to stand. She has a captive (if not strapped in) audience, and barring the retch of an engine, or the halloo of a rogue sidewinder, absolutely nothing to upstage her. She is enviably remote from our humdrum earthbound existence. She is a loner, restless and rootless, as romantic in her own way as a cowboy of the Western frontier.

To us she is a sexy fantasy, tangible as a whiff of duty-free Gigi on the slipstream of an aft-bound croissant truck, or the briefest glimpse of an airline livery bra elastic, as she leans over to oblige a window sitter with a perfect arc of tepid coffee, or rarely (very rarely) perhaps, the sharp delirium of two blouse buttons pressing against the ear as she leans close to allow a fat man with a felt donkey pass down the aisle behind her. It is an ephemeral thrill, for next second she is gone again; to restrain a Euro MP or chastise an unbelted bishop. Power is the perk of her job, and I'm not just talking here about withholding salted cashews from a naughty tycoon ...

The plane lurches. I became aware that my feet are incredibly painful in my new shoes, and all thoughts of angels leave my mind. The pilot announces a patch of bad air turbulence, but the air hostess carries on smiling. Is she really bending to check a seat belt ... or count the wings?

I daren't look out. I must be seen to have faith. I daren't risk offending the *miracle*. The plane continues to bump along, as though airlanes are strewn with sleeping policemen. Reading is good. What can I read? I have my ticket to hand. 'WARNING, DANGEROUS GOODS' it says. 'Do not pack containers of compressed gasses (flammable, non flammable or poisonous), corrosive materials, including wet batteries, oxidising substances, magnetised materials or OTHER DANGEROUS GOODS, such as offensive or noxious materials and items in IATA Dangerous Goods Regulations.'

Too late: in my suitcase I know that my shampoo has leaked over my razor, causing corrosive salts from the batteries to seep into my notepad, igniting it and burning freely, making revolutionary concrete treatment chemicals in the suitcase next to it to become unstable, and release a flow of oxidising substances and flammable (not to mention non-flammable) liquid gasses, that even now are burning their way out of the case and magnetising the undercarriage causing, in the process, untold additional unspecified noxious mayhem, as listed in IATA Dangerous Goods Regulations.

Even crew members, come to think of it, harbour secret doubts. You don't hear them cracking gravity jokes. Why else do pilots wear wings on their uniforms? The design isn't chosen at random: otherwise it would be a slug, or an anvil. No, the wings are *lucky* symbols. *They* know, and *I* know: we will only get to Vienna if we believe we can fly. We must believe that we are as light as feathers, and we must blindly trust that the 200 porridge-stuffed passengers, the 61,000 litres of highly volatile aviation fuel, the two garage-sized engines, the lead undercarriage, the 150 cast-iron catering clang-pans, the 500 items of exploding, seeping, corrosive IATA Dangerous Goods Regulations-busting baggage, concrete samples, kitchen sink and all, will all quietly follow suit.

I can't just sit here with all this going on. I stand up. My feet are numb. I take three paces down the corridor, and faint.

I see a strip of carpet stretching off like a highway, and close by a giant cloppy shoe. There is a woman 40 feet tall, rising from it, a polyester vision with black tights and slim legs. An air hostess. A nut goddess. The Goddess Nut. This is how I meet Ursula.

'He's coming to,' she says, and bends over me, pressing something against my forehead. 'Are you all right?'

How could anyone in this position not be all right! I have been snatched from the jaws of death, and I am lying in the arms of a beautiful air hostess. Apart from the pain in my feet, I am blissfully happy. What's more, I know that for precious minutes, all her normal duties will be on hold, while she ascertains that I have come to no harm. I have her undivided attention.

There are many questions I want to ask her. Do air hostesses have their periods in the same time zone? Was she once Miss Guildford? Has she got 23 varieties of hotel soap in her handbag for distribution to Third World Children? Does she nurse a secret desire to be talked down at the controls of a Concorde, running on one engine in a thunderstorm, while the pilot lies unconscious in the galley? Has she ever made love to a pilot standing up in the first-class toilet during the screening of *Home Alone XIV*? Can she say 'Put the cup on the tray' in Japanese? Do her sanitary towels have wings? Does she wake up in Cheam at 4 a.m. on her day off, full of life with nothing to do? Would she like to own a little dog?

But we don't discuss these things. Instead we talk about children. First I tell her not to worry about my fainting – I have a history of it; it's something else I used to do in assembly. I'll be fine in a minute, if she could just tell Zoe from Peter Crawford Associates to go back to her seat.

Ursula has a little girl of five, Natasha. She's looking for a new childminder right now, she says. It's a headache, especially in her job, with such irregular hours. Her husband's in the airline business too – they rarely see each other! I tell her about Europa, and that the au pair system works fine if you can find a good one, though Natasha probably needs extra attention at her age. I'm at home most of the time, I tell her, and some days I pick Mungo up from his school in Brixton.

'Well that's a coincidence,' she says. 'Natasha goes to school in Brixton!'

And that's it, more or less. Ursula sees me back to my seat and I give her my best smile. She's fabulous. I think we've bonded, but I see that her lovely smile, when she smiles back, is not real.

After that, the Austria job is an anti-climax. Schloss Fuschl is a magnificent castle hotel, spectacularly arrayed on the shore of a mountain lake, but my ten middle-managers are immune to its enchantments. They do not let their hair down, or romp about. They never take their jackets off. They can't giggle. Despite Zoe's vigorous efforts to whip it into a froth, their conversation is polite, guarded, and so full of business jargon I haven't a clue what they're talking about.

'They've become so process driven, they've taken their eye off the customer ball,' one says.

'Absolutely,' says another. 'Though if they don't buy into this then they're not really at the races.'

I almost prefer Zoe's gabble. She is relying so heavily on me to keep the whacky conversation quota up that it's making me depressed.

The days go by with outings to Salzburg, and into the mountains, which are at least diverting, but the evenings, sitting formally at dinner, are deadly. If anybody does venture an anecdote or joke, the whole group listens at once, dutifully, and without enthusiasm, putting a terrible onus on the speaker. At about ten every night they start making excuses and peeling off to bed. They don't want to be there really; they want to be back in Cricklewood, achieving.

At one of these meals Zoe suggests it might be a whacky idea if we each tell an embarrassing story about ourselves. 'Who's going to start?'

Dead silence.

'Come on Martin, Old Fruitus!'

I do it, and not just for the sake of esprit de corps; after all something has to happen, or there'll be nothing to write about.

So I tell them the story of how I arrived at Heathrow a whole week early for this very trip. I have their complete attention, as anyone would have in such circumstances. My experience, retrospectively, is a very funny thing to happen to anyone, so I give it my best shot. They receive it in horror.

It's possible that I can detect some appreciation on the *schadenfreude* end of the pleasure scale, but mostly they are just horrified. They are embarrassed by my embarrassing story. They already think I'm a flake for fainting on the plane, but this is precisely the sort of thing no self-respecting high-achieving corporate manager would ever do, and my incompetence makes them acutely uncomfortable. They can't even look at me.

Apart from a strange whinny from Zoe, there is silence after my story. You could hear an ant being disembowelled. I have a sensation – wishful thinking really – that one of them, Doreen, a dromedary of a girl, might be considering uttering some sort of sound, but her mouth is full and, if she ever was, then she changes her mind.

'Anyway, that's one in the eye for all the people who accuse me of being late!' I say heartily. No. They've never been late either.

'Indeedy,' says Zoe.

I will never know how embarrassing their embarrassing stories might have been, because no one chooses to volunteer a story after that.

Not for the rest of the trip, in fact.

The article's dead in the water. I ring *Weekend* and they agree. This sort of thing happens from time to time in journalism. The trouble is, *Weekend* will now identify me with the story's failure. The trip was a failure for Zoe too, and by the grateful looks on their faces when they board the plane home, for the ten middle managers.

But one very good thing comes out of it. On the return trip, I feel no fear at all. It's like that – it comes and goes. By coincidence, Ursula is working on the flight back as well. She smiles at me, but she smiles at everyone. I'm not sure she remembers me. But when we are half an hour away from Heathrow, she comes over to my seat and crouches down.

'I've been thinking,' she says. 'I need someone to pick up Natasha from school, and I like what you said about your au pair. If I paid her a little extra and gave you something towards food each week, do you think she could look after Natasha as well? It's just a thought. Here's my number; maybe we can talk when we get back.'

'I think it might well be possible.'

She goes away and returns a little later to hand me a photograph of a small girl in a too big school blazer, and tie, with a pale, serious face, scowling beneath a hat.

'Weeny,' I say.

'Yes,' she says. She can see I'm hooked. And Ursula smiles the smile that is not for me.

She has go-thither eyes.

Chapter 20   WEENY

I fall for Weeny right from the start. She's so sure of herself; so suspicious of everyone else. She looks at you with a sceptical eye when you try to tease her. She's no pushover.

She keeps herself to herself. You barely know she's here half the time. She isn't gregarious, but neither is she shy. She doesn't fret when her mother goes off for long periods, for different lengths of time every week. She doesn't mind being in the house of a relative stranger. She's her own person and she gets on with her own stuff.

And what stuff! She's always busy doing something in the anonymous spare guestroom, next door to the study. She makes it her own, fills it with teddy bears. She never watches television. You can't *make* her watch television. The other kids line up in front of it, but she's in the room next door, talking to herself. She has so much to do in there. I have no idea what it is. The most fascinating thing about her is what is going on in that head. She won't say.

I like this little loner.

I begin wooing her intensively from the start. I know that I have to play her cool. I know she won't be impressed by clowning. She isn't one of those children who throw themselves bodily at you after one party turn. I talk to her all the time. She's an intellectual, and talk is what she likes best.

She goes to the Catholic school, just up the hill from Mungo's in Brixton. I am amused by Weeny's school because it's so comically strict. All the children are made to line up in their ridiculously cumbersome uniforms, prim and neat, while the mothers hang round the gates in their casual slop, smoking and gossiping.

There is a big brass bell hanging from a wall at the entrance to Weeny's school, one of those many bits of equipment that Catholics love to have around them, enshrined in unknowable rules and protocols.

'Let's ring the bell,' I say.

Weeny's shocked rigid. 'No, don't ring the bell.'

'Yes, let's ring the bell.'

'No, *don't* ring the bell!'

Her whole body is saying don't ring the bell.

'Look, it's just hanging here, let's—'

'Don't ring the bell. Don't ring the bell. *Don't ring the bell*!'

'You don't want me to ring the bell?'

'No.'

As we walk away I can see she is looking at me out of the corner of her eye. Maybe she's starting to think I might be all right.

Every time she enters or leaves this house, I lift her up to the ceiling in the front hallway, until her head tinkles against the glass prisms hanging down from the little chandelier. The unexpected tintinnabulation causes her to jerk her head into her shoulders like a tortoise. I do this with all the children as they come and go, but for Weeny it has become a sacrament. This is all the more gratifying, because she is a rationalist. She can't see the reason for it.

The first time I do it she looks at me with a question mark over her head, but she doesn't say anything because she doesn't know me. After the third time, she says, 'Why do you do that?'

'It's the thing to do,' I say vaguely.

'Hmm.'

You can't fob her off. Her questions are incisive. She is marking the world carefully, and here is behaviour outside the norm. She isn't satisfied with my answer.

Later she is at the side of my desk. 'Why do you do that thing with the light?'

I tell her it is a form of greeting in the land of lights. She's not having that. 'No, why do you do it?' I tell her it has been ordained by a higher authority. I give her a hundred answers, each one different, and still she asks.

In the end I come clean. I tell her I do it because it's a great thing to do, and she has to accept that for the moment, because it's all I know. Even this, I sense, isn't good enough. Eventually, because I do it every time, she stops asking questions. It has become part of the enigmatic business of coming and going, of moving in and out of others people's lives; though I can tell she's still curious.

On her seventh visit, as she is leaving with Ursula, I forget to do it, and she says, 'You didn't jiggle me on the light.'

I jiggle her.

It's a weekday, but it's going to be a late night, because Clive and Sam, Tamara and Rufus are here. They always arrive late, rolling up when it suits them. Then they spend a long time putting off putting Rufus to bed, and eventually, when all that's done, they spend a long time putting off going home.

Rufus has his Clive and Sam routine down to a fine art, unlike Clive and Sam's Rufus routine. Rufus asks Sam for ice cream. She says no, explaining that it's bedtime and therefore not a good time to be eating ice cream. At first, you see, everything is reasonable.

Then Rufus asks her four more times. This is standard practice: (1) in case she hasn't fully considered her answer; (2) in case old age has caused her such brain deterioration that she can't remember her answer; (3) on the off chance that she has undergone a complete personality change and maybe turned into Zippy the free ice cream clown; (4) in case during the time it has taken to check all these factors, the circumstances have altered – for example, bedtime has been cancelled due to an earthquake. All things are possible to a child, which is why they make such untiring and obstinate adversaries.

The next step in Rufus's routine is to go into the room next door, where Clive is phoning some business partner.

'Hold on ...' he says. 'What is it Rufus?'

'Can I have an ice cream, Daddy?'

'Of course, darling.'

Clive, who looks a little like a spaniel at times of emotional indulgence, is the complete pushover he expects others to be for him.

Some time later, after the ice cream, Rufus is put to bed by Sam, read a story, tucked up and kissed good night. As Sam leaves to go downstairs, he asks for a sandwich. No, says Sam, it's far too late for sandwiches. I tell Rufus we have clear rules in this house about not eating at bedtime. Mungo nods in the other bed, but Rufus knows that with guile, he can prise a sandwich out of Clive.

Rufus saves his first major shout until we have settled into dinner. It comes just as we are congratulating ourselves that the boys are asleep.

'What do you want?' Sam calls up.

'I need to tell you something!'

'Go to sleep!'

Ten minutes later he shouts again. Rufus perfected this technique long ago, in the cot. 'Cry for just a minute more and the man will give in,' he used to tell himself. 'He's weaker than her because he's got no theory or method.'

Rufus can hear Clive pushing his chair back. Then he hears Sam telling Clive not to go up. But he is fully expecting this. He can hear Sam telling Clive he is trying it on. He listens while Clive settles down again. This time, Rufus allows only five minutes to pass.

Now the masterstroke. In the old, baby days, he would let out a howl of unknowable despair, followed by a pitiable sob, that together would make the hair prickle on his father's neck. Rufus is too old to look cool doing the howl of unknowable pain any more, but he has devised an effective shorthand for it.

'I feel sick!' he shouts. Pause. 'I feel *sick!*'

That's done it! Clive's on his way up.

'Hello little man, what's the matter with you?'

'Can I have a sandwich?'

Then Mungo has to have a sandwich too, otherwise it's unfair.

But a sandwich isn't enough to put Rufus to sleep. He sees no reason at all why, when we're having fun downstairs, he should be in the boring bed, in the boring darkness, in the boring quiet. All through our meal we can hear the tell-tale sounds of running feet, Indian war whoops and grinding Megapower killer rigs. Halfway through pudding, Rufus comes downstairs complaining that he can't go to sleep. Sam takes him up to our bedroom and lies on the bed with him. At least Mungo and Rufus are quiet now, but Sam has disappeared.

We finish our meal and move to the living room with coffee. Rufus's appearance has made Clive, who is a sentimentalist at heart, reflect on how wonderful the children are and how much our families have changed since we all lived in Brixton.

There have been many changes, but most dramatically to his family. When we first met Clive, he was trying to disentangle himself from a chic household accessory mail order business, that he had once hoped would make his fortune. As it turned out, nobody wanted to buy cast-iron beefeater umbrella stands made in Delhi, even if they could afford the postage.

Martha and I left Brixton when we needed a bigger house. We had weathered our share of break-ins and muggings, but were finally galvanised into action when the Sicilian who lived in the house whose garden adjoined ours at the back was shot in the head by his brother-in-law as a favour to his wife. I was working at home when the shooting happened. There was a bang, though it didn't seem significant until their cat came over the fence into our garden, looking embarrassed. He had never ventured into my cats' territory before.

Clive came into the money about the same time, doing whatever it is he does now, give or take a bit of trumping and coup-mongering here, there, and everywhere. They leapfrogged straight to Dulwich, collecting £200 as they passed Streatham. Since then he and Sam have swanked it up, in comparison to our relatively threadbare existence. They have a leakproof roof, a shiny new kitchen, and two lavishly appointed bathrooms, including one of marble, with a monumental central bath, like a gleaming sepulchre. They have a theatrically laid out lounge and dining area, furnished with carpets made of exotic grass, curtains made of fine silk and sculptures made of junk metal. They have an enormous sofa which sucks you into itself, forgiving all your sins. They have professionals in all the time, doing ever more exciting things to the house.

They even have a gardener; actually, two gardeners. I was formally introduced one afternoon, when I drove over there to collect a child and a hedge cutter: Algernon Farquharson-Spruit, and Jamie; clean, muscular young men in £80 shirts, oozing friendliness. I had been expecting an old Mr Wilberforce character, with honest shoes, a deplorable spitting habit, and birds nesting in the weave of his jacket, but Algernon and Jamie were like no other gardeners I've ever seen. According to their lavish colour brochure, which they fetched from the land cruiser for me, one is a former stockbroker, and the other an ex model; both ex public school, of course.

Old Mr Wilberforce didn't have a company brochure. That would have been bragging in his eyes. He hid his light under a bush. He missed out on public school too. In fact it's doubtful if he'd ever seen the inside of a house.

They don't call themselves gardeners, of course. Nothing so old and whiskery. They are landscape designers, or plant consultants. They talk to the plants by walkie-talkie. Already the front garden of Clive and Sam's house had succumbed to a formal make-over with gravel and urns. It looked like a war grave.

The brochure contained an extract from an article about them in a Sunday supplement. 'Farquharson-Spruit, with his rugged good looks and considerable charm, would be a catch for any home-proud woman,' it said, 'were it not that he has plighted his troth already.'

'And who is the lucky Mrs Farquharson-Spruit to be?' I said.

Jamie smiled bashfully. 'I am,' he said.

The coffee is finished. Clive yawns and looks at his watch. 'I'd better go and see what's happened to Sam,' he says, and leaves the room. It's like one of those films where explorers are isolated in a tent in hostile territory, and one by one set off to see if they can find the last person who went out, and none come back.

Martha and I do the washing up. It's good to have friends, though it's nicer to have friends who are there. We've known Clive and Sam long enough to expect this sort of thing. Atrocious behaviour is tolerated, so long as it doesn't infringe the Geneva Convention.

We haven't seen anything of any of them now for a good forty minutes, and Martha and I have run out of things to do downstairs. We go up. Their daughter Tamara is asleep in Amelia's room. Rufus, Sam and Clive are all asleep on our bed.

Chapter 21 DIY

Kitchens used to be shambolic places smelling of damp dog, where you dropped your guard, threw your boots off and shut out the unforgiving world. No longer. Now they are status symbols. Our kitchen still smells of damp dog though, not that we have one.

Wendy's kitchen smells of luxury liners and new paint. It's quite something. Martha and I have been invited to Wendy's flat, with some other neighbours, for the official launch of the new kitchen with wine and doritos. We admire the humming worktops, open and close cupboards and gasp at the pullout larder unit.

'It's fantastic,' says Martha. 'I do envy you.'

'Well, I envy you your lovely big house,' says Wendy.

'The reason we don't have a lovely kitchen is *because* we have a lovely big house,' I say.

'Among other reasons,' says Martha.

There is only one thing that could make Wendy happier than a dream kitchen, and that's a dream kitchen which carries the endorsement of Amanda Loveday. Amanda is the wife of a speculator in industrial property, who lives in one of the big detached houses on the opposite side of the street. Officially Amanda is an interior designer, but in practice she spends her days spending Graeme Loveday's money. She is expert at it. She has the perfect house, the perfect car and coat; the correct cat. She has the latest nose.

But Amanda's endorsement, like the smile of God, is bestowed only rarely on mortals. She doesn't waste time delivering her verdict.

'Of course this is very lovely and must make you feel very special,

Wendy my dear,' she says, 'but I just wonder why you went for such an old-fashioned concept, now that *unfitted* kitchens are currently in vogue? Very brave, if I may say so, to favour the relentless tyranny of wall-to-wall units; judicious use of built-in pieces is to be expected, but the occasional feature would have relaxed the eye, don't you think? A *batterie de cuisine* here, an end-grain chopping block there ... How about an exposed bread crock? Or an antique dresser? Where for example, can you display your family china? Your fruit of the season? Do you have a hot cupboard for fermented milk of Caucasian origin ...?'

That's the gist of it, give or take a *batterie de cuisine*. It's like watching a seal cub being clubbed.

Martha wants a new kitchen so much it drives me to despair. Unlike Wendy she loves cooking, and she's good at it. A new kitchen is the single improvement that would make her happiest. I've talked about doing it myself and even drawn up some plans, but Martha is sceptical. It's a big project, requiring many new skills. I haven't yet finished half-panelling the bathroom with tongue and groove, and boxing in the bath, with a cupboard space at the end for cleaning things. She's seen how long it's taken me. I'm laying a rubber floor now, and there's a walk-in upstairs cupboard to build after that.

Women want so many things, but ironically, it was me who wanted a big house. Not that it was difficult to persuade Martha. It's great that it's big, but it has big drawbacks too.

You can never quite call a big house your own; it's too big. It's like saying you own a country. One room maybe, you can control; a flat, perhaps ... but a house with six bedrooms? No chance. It gets overrun.

My study is on the middle floor, so I'm conscious of most major disruptions in the house, and don't have far to go to sort them out. It also means I'm constantly on call. Amelia has a habit of calling 'Dad!' from somewhere distant, making me drop what I'm doing and leave my desk and come out on to the landing and shout up to see what she wants, at which point she says, 'It doesn't matter!' This infuriates me.

Though I am in charge of this house, it's too big to control. You can sort something out at the top – an unreasonable noise for example – but then you have to run to the bottom – to stall an argument, say. Just as you fix that, you will hear the unreasonable noise start up again upstairs.

I have a big study too, but again the word big is misleading. Though it is big, it is also full. People say, 'Oh look, you've got a big room all to yourself,' and then they put things in it that they don't want in their rooms any more: pool tables and speak-your weight machines. Before long it isn't big in any usable sense any longer. We have a cellar and a garage where junk can be put, but nobody but me can walk that far. So I sit here all day looking at the stuff that nobody wants to look at. I am a victim of study dumping.

We were drawn to the houses in this street as soon as we saw them. They looked as though they had been battered by many feet in the past and might hold out for a bit more. First we looked at one for sale further down the road, but it reeked of sadness. It seemed fine until we came to a room upstairs, at first sight as ordinary as any other room. Then the owner said: 'This is where my brother died. Cancer.'

That did it. I could never imagine my children living there now, their teddy bears infused with ineluctable sorrow. It's quite possible something similar has happened in this house. It is 110 years old after all, and tragedy is commonplace. All the same, I don't want to be told about it. I don't want to be told, just as I have finished painting a bedroom Summer Blush, that this is where a maths teacher hung himself from the door lintel. It would be haunted then, even if it wasn't before. I am told that a music hall artiste once lived here; I wouldn't mind knowing that she died here, but that she bled to death in the bath? I'd rather not know that.

I'd rather not know Hubert Pinkney lived here either, the most unavoidable of the house's former residents, yet also, paradoxically, one of the most elusive. He owned the house before us, and for a long time after we moved in, most of the post delivered here was for him, which was irritating. Freelance writers live for post. Having things arrive in substantial envelopes with your name on the front is proof of existence in intangible times, even bills. I've had a lot from the Inland Revenue recently. My policy is to put them in the pile under Jack and leave them to marinade in guilt and resentment until they are ready.

Having no post at all, not even a bill or a circular, is to be thrown into a disturbing and stateless lacuna. Having a great pile arrive, all of which is addressed to Hubert Pinkney is worse. I have no forwarding address for Hubert Pinkney, to the distress of many loyal banks, building societies, and collectible commemorative medallion companies which persist in writing to him long after they have been told he doesn't live here. Still, five years on, with touching faith, and despite considerable effort to stop it, the Nations Bank of Greensboro, North Carolina, sends him a monthly statement from America, with the same figures: 'Beginning balance – $0.00, Interest charge – $0.00, current payment due – $0.00'.

Others are looking for him too: mysterious others. I was woken at six one morning, shortly after we moved in, by a knock on the door. A surreal trio stood in my porch like characters from a Pirandello play: a smart middle-aged black man with a brief case and a long black coat, a white man in workman's overalls and a little girl of about eight in school uniform.

'Hubert Pinkney?'

'Hasn't lived here for four months.'

'Do you know where he is?'

'No.'

And that was that,

Hubert Pinkney could be a gun runner, or a draper, or a systems analyst. Nobody knows. He could be in Honolulu, Hainault or Hell. Nobody knows. After he signed over the deed (and nobody met him even then), he disappeared, taking the secrets of the plumbing system with him.

He was an avid DIYer though. I wish he hadn't been, because other people's DIY is always worse than your own, and always needs to be overhauled or pulled out before you can do your own stuff. He wired up the spare bedroom with bell wire, and ran a supply cable to the cooker which contains no earth. Death traps. In this respect his presence is like that of a poltergeist. When things collapse unaccountably, I mutter his name.

The house has a garage in the back garden. I don't know why, as there's no way of getting a car into the garden. Another HP mystery.

Martha's campaigning to get rid of it, but of all Hubert Pinkney's legacies, this is the one I approve of. It's ugly, yes, but it's useful. I have many good things in there, including a lot of bits of wood, some scaffolding planks, a long piece of metal of some sort, a garden roller I never use, a rejected fire grate and mantle, seven bikes, including a big, broken European sit-up-and-beg bike I bought for myself, which Peter calls my Dutch lesbian bike, and a compost bin I made myself, that is brim full of a compost mixture which I made to my own method, and which has turned, over a period of three years, into a foul and reeking soup. The garage is the place I most like to go to gaze; just to stand there and gaze into its depths, to resurrect the feeling that each of us can own a little bit of infinity.

I don't know if this is just me, or if this is common to all men, but I can gaze for a long time without moving, oblivious to what's going on around me. Children walk round me, hand me orange peel, and I don't see them.

Children don't like the garage because it's dark; women don't like it because it's there. Children will only go in there on tip toes, with their elbows tight by their sides, expecting, any minute, something to leap out of one of the heaps of junk and get them.

For me the garage is the place for solitude and contemplation. In there I can mentally insulate myself against the *sturm und dräng*, like a fakir slowing his heartbeat. I stand there like Ramases, impassive, looking out across my desert. It is my sanctuary.

Anyway, I am loath to start pulling it down because it is made of asbestos cement. I imagine it will take teams of white hooded men and possibly a helicopter. Our budget doesn't run to that.

Also, I have plans to make it my permanent workshop. Yes, I've reached *that* stage. DIY takes you over, you see. The initial appeal is simple: to go into the bathroom yourself, break the basin yourself, shout profanities at the basin yourself, and at the end of the day (you also start saying 'at the end of the day') be £120 better off than if you'd called a plumber.

But weeks go by, and next thing you know, you're hooked. You're reading magazines with headlines like 'WOODEN IT BE NICE' and 'ALL CISTERNS GO'.

Peter, who thinks the whole thing is aberrant, says that, like home computing, DIY is sex substitution, appealing to the man of middling years and reflexes, looking for more reliable erections than those he can summon physically, upon which to rest his masculine reputation. This sort don't just thrill his wife, he can show them off to his friends as well.

Martha is deferring her excitement on the new erections. She says she doesn't know if she'll live long enough to experience the thrill. She's only interested in finished results, not in the process. It frustrates her in IKEA when I won't let her buy anything. 'Look at this!' I say. 'Just ten pieces of wood basically. The drawers aren't even dovetailed! I could knock that up in six weeks!'

There is intrinsic moral virtue in woodwork that is pleasing to the devotee, a loving articulateness in its language. The sense of veracity you feel bringing two pieces of wood together in your first properly cut joint is hard to describe to anyone who hasn't done it. Unlike in writing, there's no room for interpretation: for the joint to have *integrity*, for the *bond* to work, the surfaces of its component pieces must be *true*. This is only proper in a fair and moral universe. Play by the rules and you will have it: your first joint – conjoined, replete, beautiful; like sex, but forever. Or at least until someone sits on it the wrong way.

I spend long enough in the local 'IT YOUR ELF' shop, with its brown- overalled men venturing opinions on my caster requirements, but I'm lost in the DIY superstores. They are aircraft hangars, full of stuff, like my garage writ vast, and gleaming. They are so big some of the first ones were called Texas, so people wouldn't confuse them with Berkshire. A man can walk for ten minutes in one of these and still be in the wire wool department, pushing a trolley in which there is a ladder, a hot water tank and a garden shed. You could buy a whole house in there, if you could balance it. I can spend three hours in B&Q on a Sunday morning, to Martha's annoyance, ogling dowel jigs. There are 101 different kinds of saw and I want them all. I have even looked at a sewage masticator with a roving eye.

My descent into DIY has coincided with an invitation to visit the new home of Tony and Janet, our fellow puffers from the NCT class, who have moved recently from Derek Avenue, Sutton, to Kelvin Gardens, Croydon ('Handy for B&Q'), which Tony is slowly turning into an MDF palace. Tony is undeniably a DIY whiz, and I'm keen to tap his knowledge, though he has built so many things about the house it's a bit daunting.

Socially they are not easy. They have a habit of segregating according to sex. Janet talks exclusively to Martha and Tony talks exclusively to me. I like talking to men, but I like to have a choice. I want to talk to Janet, but Tony monopolises me in a corner with something or other he has to show me. Then Janet will take Martha upstairs on the pretext of showing her a baby she keeps up there.

'The men can talk,' she says in that indulgent, smiley, men-will-be-men way that excludes all possibility of me saying, 'No! No! Don't leave me with him! I don't want to see his collection of Tintin ephemera!' On the other hand, how did he construct the really rather handsome cabinet that contains them ...?

While Tony is fetching some hard-to-drink Whisky Collector's Club whisky from a custom-built under-stairs cupboard, I scan the back copies of *Which?* Magazine Special reports lined up on his bookshelf: Channel Tunnel Safety (No. 46), Yogurt (No. 32), Spring Cleaning (No. 45), Scottish Law (No. 24), Electric Plugs (No. 14).

'Amazing reference you've got here, Tony,' I say. 'Is there anything you haven't got covered?'

'Fascinating aren't they?' he says.

'Yes,' I say, gulping his whisky, and wondering if I do really mean it. I can feel myself being pulled into the anorak.

'Sometimes I wonder why you're doing all this DIY,' Martha says to me. 'You've been working on the bathroom two months.'

'You know why. I bet Janet doesn't ask Tony that question.'

'Maybe she should. A lot of it is pretty ugly. They're both on teachers' salaries, so he surely doesn't need to do quite so much. I would have thought they'd like to spend time together doing other things. I wonder what they're avoiding? I wonder what you're avoiding?'

'Avoiding? Don't you want the house to be done up?'

It's not just me and Tony. All over the country, men from all walks of life are doing it, even men of fortune and achievement. Astrophysicists and captains of industry spend their leisure hours constructing their own toilet-roll holders. Why? A sense of achievement yes, but there is a more compelling motive to DIY: it gives you a world you can order and control; not like real life.

You can't mastic the hole in the ozone layer, or build a chipboard rain forest. The world is too confusingly difficult, its problems too intractable. But you can begin to control your home environment, building inwards, walling the nest, re-siting the bird-bath, hanging a hook for the back door key, building a cupboard for the computer, a shelf for the toothbrushes, a cabinet for the DIY magazines, a tool rack to hold each of the tools neatly and reliably in its allotted place, just like God meant tools to be. You suspect you might be turning into a Hobbit, but so long as you have enough MDF, you can shore up the unthinkable.

Chapter 22 PILGER

It's a little-too-formal dinner party, this Easter bank holiday weekend, at the elegant North London flat of Eloise, one of my ghosts. Eloise can giggle like a seven year old, and my fondest memory of her is rolling drunk in the snow with her on a German alp, years ago on a ski press trip, gasping and hysterical with laughter. But if you were to meet Eloise for the first time today, you would think her a very serious person, and for a long time after that, you would suspect her to be humourless. Though it is almost impossible to get her giggling nowadays, her humour emerges in occasional mordant comments, wrung wry by the mangle of her non-indulgent personality. And then again, even as I say it, the word 'non-indulgent' isn't quite right, for I have heard Eloise insist that the only good bath tap is one that can be operated by the feet.

She is single and childless at 43, old enough for most other divergent urges to have been whipped into line to further her overriding ambition. Her career, driven though it is (though briefly diverted by an all-consuming and disastrous two-year amour five years back), has not progressed as far or fast as she would like. She is deputy editor on one of the more intelligent women's glossies. Eloise has commissioned me in the past, but doesn't any longer because she thinks humour is currently unfashionable.

Eloise doesn't hold dinner parties for fun, but to promote, network and ritually establish her place in her professional circle. I tell her off about this, but succeed only in making her anxious. Quite apart from the fact that we are friends, she would not have me along to them, were it not for the fact that I am a journalist too, and she thinks I might gain something, or learn something, by them. She always eyes me suspiciously throughout, as though I might put bread sticks up my nose, or whip out an accordion.

Martha and I, of course, are late. Not very late, but I have been building a partition wall in a bedroom all day, to house a walk-in cupboard, and I am obsessed with pinning the last of the plasterboard before we leave. Then there is the drive to Islington. By the time we arrive, all the guests are settled in the lounge drinking aperitifs. I can tell by the hopeful, diversion-seeking way they look up at us, that the conversation is stilted.

I sit in a spare seat next to a man, introduced to me as John, and we start talking. I tell him about my infatuation with the wall I am building, and how much more rewarding and ultimately useful to mankind is DIY, than journalism, which is what I used to do. He laughs. He seems all right.

'What do you do for a living?' I ask. I know it isn't a very original conversational gambit, but surely that's no reason why the room should fall silent.

'I'm a journalist,' he says.

'Ah, like me. Who do you work for?' There is quite a pause here. Perhaps the furniture has been plugged into the national grid.

'Mostly TV ... but many other papers, the *New Statesman* ...' Eloise is glaring at me.

'Do you specialise in anything?'

After about ten minutes of this it occurs to me from the exaggerated respect he is inspiring in the others, that he must be the guest of honour. I look more closely at his face and sure enough, he does look familiar. As everybody gets up to move into the dining room, Eloise corners me.

'How *could* you,' she says. 'How could you do that to John Pilger?'

'I thought he looked familiar. I couldn't place him.'

'He's a journalistic institution, for God's sake. I *told* you he was coming.'

'Did you? I'm sorry. I'm all wrapped up in dividing walls. I've built a–'

'*Please* don't embarrass me any more.'

But it's too late, because we have already begun an argument about large-scale TV charity fund-raising events, which Pilger says are arbitrary and have more to do with the self-promotion of their participants than a desire to tackle the problems of world poverty. Pilger has been accused of affected piety, but in fact he's merely unendurably reasonable. I agree with him in principle, but I don't think they do any harm and they can do some good.

Unfortunately this is one of those topics which excites extreme sentiments. It doesn't die in the lounge, but follows us to the dining room, and moves like a forest fire across the dinner table, engulfing everybody in hot and intemperate argument. Like the giggling of hysterical children, it is impossible to quell, and despite Eloise's efforts, we all roar at each other furiously until 11.30, when, red-eyed, she leaves the table and runs upstairs.

'So that was the great John Pilger!' says Martha.

'Oh really? Which one was he?'

It's good to have common adversaries (we were on the same side in the argument), and it was a stimulating evening; much more spontaneous than most of Eloise's stage-managed dinners. We're in a taxi homebound, both slightly drunk and comfortable in the back.

'That was a terrible *faux pas* though.'

'I know.' I gaze out of the taxi window. The streets outside are wet and empty. 'But it's not really my world. I was never convinced of the sexiness of news. I was a reluctant ambulance chaser. I only went into journalism because it required less words than other forms of writing.'

'You have a clear idea what you aren't, but you need to decide sooner or later what you are. You're 45, after all.'

'Sometimes I feel I'm standing by the tracks, watching my life going past. I've got to climb back on board.'

'Get a grip,' she says and squeezes my hand.

My accountant, Harvey Solomons, appears to me in a dream. I am in a pub with him and he can't stand still. When I say he can't stand still, his legs are a blur, but his large upper body is entirely motionless. His knees jerk, and his feet flit beneath him like marionettes. Sweat beads yaw across his brow. His face is sticky grey.

He's drinking Guinness, not his normal drink. In fact, I don't remember ever seeing him in the pub before, and come to think of it, I don't know where we are. I buy him another. 'You look dodgy, Harvey,' I say. 'What's up?'

'Riverdance!' he says. 'You're never going to believe this.'

I try to sit him down but he won't have it. He tells his story in deep gasps, his legs describing furious arabesques beneath him. There is not a single ripple in the drink in his hand.

He was in Hammersmith, he says, visiting a client. He was walking to the tube station afterwards when a man ran out of Labbatt's Apollo and gripped him intensely by the shoulders. 'You've got to help us,' he said, introducing himself as a member of Riverdance, the famous Irish hopping troupe, which is doing a season at the Apollo. 'You've got to *save the dance*.'

'Why?' asked Harvey.

The man stared at him. 'Because Concepta has *harped on*. There's no time for recriminations now – though God knows there should be. Fact is: show starts in 40 minutes exactly, and there's a hole in the line.'

'But why *me*?'

The man darted a desperate look at the deserted street. 'Because there's nobody else about. Now come on – just the one performance.'

Harvey can't remember agreeing. All he remembers is being pulled by the arm towards a stage door and knowing with rare, awesome certainty, that from this moment on his life would never be the same. 'I've never done the hop before,' he said lamely.

'Don't worry,' said the man. 'It's a piece of cake. Just imagine you're standing to attention in front of the Queen, but the floor is very, *very* hot. That's it really. Once you start, you'll never want to stop. And remember – no head-butting.'

Then, right there in the dressing room, as make-up and costume people fussed around him, the Riverdance man put Harvey through a ten-minute crash course, shouting: 'Hop! Hop! Hoppitty-hop!' except that, being Irish, he shouted: 'Harp! Harp! Harpitty Harp!'

'They don't actually hop you see,' says Harvey. 'They harp. It makes all the difference.'

Harvey's feet seem to be moving faster now over the pub carpet. From the lower half of his body comes a low humming noise, as of a distant generator.

'You'll have a heart attack, Harvey,' I say. 'What on earth made you agree?'

'Listen,' he says. 'It's not often in life you get a break like that.'

There was something else too, a compelling emotion which hit him like a narcotic as he waited in the line-up behind the curtain: something in the death-defying ecstasy of it all, the lines of sleek, robotic Irish girls at either shoulder, the scent of hot tights and talcum powder ... which ignited a flame of Celtic passion in his large accountant's heart that he never knew was there.

And he danced. He danced on that huge stage like a windblown child. At first he could sense resentment among the cast. He was after all the only 47-year-old, 17 stone Jewish accountant who couldn't dance in the line up. But when the other dancers realised he was giving his all for them, fighting for breath, pounding the stage, though his legs felt like vermicelli, their attitude softened. During solo numbers, when he sat in a heap of sweat backstage, the chorus girls gave him hot tea and encouragement.

'What happened to Concepta?' Harvey asked in one of these brief respites.

'Harped on,' they said. There were tears in their eyes.

'Look,' said one, 'when we finished rehearsing this afternoon, Concepta didn't. She just kept harping on. We pushed her into the escape lane. We threw the harping net over her. But she wriggled free. We followed her in the tour bus as best we could, but we lost her at a red light in Acton.'

'For good?' said Harvey.

'Yes. It happens. They get trapped in the motion. They harp faster and faster until they reach a point where it's impossible to stop. Who knows where she is now? They'll find her in a couple of weeks, or what's left of her, in Hartlepool or St Just, depending which way the spin has taken her; by the side of some road; a small puddle of Irish butter.'

The cue light came on. Harvey struggled to his feet. 'This one's for Concepta,' he said. 'For Concepta!' they cried, and they took the stage.

Harvey grips my arm. Static crackles in my hair. 'Do you know,' he says, 'when it was all over, I felt I was saying goodbye to the family I'd never had.'

'But you do have a family,' I say. 'Your family dotes on you.'

'Maybe,' he says. 'But I never had a family of whirling Irish girls and – you know – colcannon blowing in my ears – you know – the dattle at-a doottle at-a diddl-at a dom – you know? – a-daddle-dattle at-a-dattle dillyittlat-a dillyat-a dattle-at-a dom ... oh God, my feet are killing me!'

But he won't sit down.

'I can't,' he says, 'not any more.' He hovers there like a large Jewish hummingbird. It's painful to see a man putting so much effort into just standing still.

'Anyway,' he says, 'can't stand around here any more – floor's too hot.'

And he whirs across the room and through the door, like a man on a travelator. Briefly, his face reappears in the doorway.

'Tell you what,' he shouts, 'it's one in the eye for the bastards who turned me down for Five Guys Named Mo!'

For a moment I can hear his feet whirring away down the Balls Pond Road. So that's where we are. He's left his briefcase behind.

I wake up thinking about my overdue accounts. Two years overdue. Though I loathe the thought of going through all those tedious files, I have to bite the bullet. I ring Harvey.

'Ah, Mr Plimmer,' he says with sadistic glee. 'To what do I owe this rare pleasure.'

'I was thinking it's time I did my accounts.'

'But what's the rush? It's only been two years. Don't worry: it's never too late to be grilled alive. But let me ask you one thing: what happened to provoke such a rare show of conscientiousness?'

'You'd never believe me if I told you.'

Chapter 23 STORY

Ursula is on a long-haul somewhere, which means Weeny stays the night and I get to read to her. It's my treat. I don't read to Mungo often because Martha usually wants to put him to bed, as she doesn't see the children during the day.

Martha wants me to pay more attention to Amelia. So do I, but Amelia is holding me at arm's length. There seems nothing I can do about this. The harder I try to reach her, the more she blocks me. This is painful, and hard to express in any way other than irritability. That makes Amelia defensive. Apart from the occasional homework, which she begrudgingly lets me help her with, our main communication is me telling her off. 'Yeah, yeah,' she says.

It wasn't that long ago I stopped reading to Amelia, always a book just above her own reading level. It was a fantastic thing to do, but suddenly it didn't seem appropriate any more. Things stop of their own accord sometimes.

'Ah, you only like them when they're small,' says Martha.

'That's not true. I *adore* them when they're small. That's the difference. I love something extra in them, which goes. They are utterly dependent and yet utterly self-contained. As Peter says, they're still in the egg. They're not really of this world. There's none of that uncomfortable duality you get in teenagers.'

Amelia will be 13 in a couple of weeks – a real teenager. She was my Weeny once, but she became complicated. Not less interesting, or less loved, but there is that whiff of adult compromise. All I can do is wait for her to come round to me, and hope it doesn't take long.

Weeny's where it's at right now. She's my connection with the root. She's complete. In some ways, life doesn't get better.

Most of the time I'm easier with Weeny than I am with my own children. I feel sad about this, but I know why it is, and I see the same thing in relationships between grandparents and their grandchildren. I'm liberated from the onus of moral supervision. I'm not obliged to count the number of sweets she's eaten, or worry about how she is expressing herself. I see mischievousness as entertaining, lapses of manners endearing. I'm not looking for faults to correct. I can enjoy her childishness.

We've done Dr Seuss already tonight. We've been to Poo-Boken, where the blue-uniformed Poogle-Horn Players, who serenade the Prince, have to balance their huge orange poogle horns while riding spindly one-wheeled bikes down the Poogle-Horn stairs. Weeny, with her rational mind, is sceptical about the practicalities of this. 'But how do they balance?' she says.

She's more at home in the *House at Pooh Corner*. In fact she's right *there* at Pooh Corner, deep in the imaginary snow, in her imaginary boots, looking for Eeyore. We are sitting on the bed laughing at Pooh, just as my father and I sat on the bed and laughed at Pooh. We are both links in the chain of life, and no less importantly, in the chain of Pooh.

Putting children to bed is one of the rare adult pleasures, a respite of wriggling and nonsense in a world which is too straight and serious by half. I'm good at it too. After three children, I can do all the voices in *The House at Pooh Corner*, I know the words to 'My Baby Has Gone Down the Plughole', and I can make a stuffed sock look as though it's trying to climb up my arm.

I see in the paper that fewer and fewer parents are reading to their children. People are mad.

Weeny has a new teacher, Mr Monaghan, who started at the beginning of the Summer term. I don't know much about him, but from what Weeny says, he's set to become a champion liner-upper. On this basis, I don't like him at all, even before I've seen him. When I pick Weeny up on Europa's day off, and see him for the first time at the head of his miniature platoon in the playground, I *know* I don't like him. He doesn't like me either; I know that too.

He eyes me suspiciously as I approach across the playground. He is a meticulous man and during his first few days he has painstakingly committed the faces of all the collectors to memory. He has Europa's face matched up for Weeny. He isn't just suspicious of me for security's sake; there is resentment in his frown. He wants to keep Weeny for himself. Well, I can understand that. I will try to be compassionate in my dealings with him.

Normally Weeny walks forward and takes my hand, but he has one of his hands, Christ-like, on her head. She's staring glassily ahead.

'I've come to pick up Weeny,' I tell him. '... Natasha.'

He turns imperiously to Weeny.

'Is this right, Natasha? Do you know this man?'

Weeny looks at me with a distracted look, a distant smile on her face, and shakes her head. For a second, one unwary eyebrow on Mr Monaghan's face registers exultant, house-leaping triumph. I imagine he is trying to decide what to say next. This has probably never happened to him before, and he will be savouring the moment, for not only will it vindicate his intensive shepherd regime, but he will get to keep Weeny.

'Only joking,' she says.

I show Weeny the soft toy I have bought for Rocket's fourth birthday. It's Woody, the character from *Toy Story*.

'It's a shame you didn't buy him the one with the string,' she says, 'which you pull and he says something.'

'Ah,' I say piously, 'the string one says one thing only, but in your imagination you can make this one say anything you want.'

'Ah,' she says, 'the string one says the thing he says when you pull the string, *and* you can make him say anything you want.'

Often I feel that Weeny and I are equals; I just happen to be bigger and have possession of the car keys.

Martha and I are at the house of one of her work colleagues. Another guest, a man, is talking about another dinner he attended recently. The point of his story is his embarrassment at not being able to think up an excuse on the spur of the moment.

He says his hostess left the room to put her four-year-old daughter to bed, but came down almost immediately, saying: 'Well, you're the lucky one. She wants you to read to her.'

'Of course I said no,' he says, 'but I couldn't think of a reasonable-sounding excuse ...'

'That's because you weren't being reasonable,' I say. 'She *asked* for you. That's like turning down a lottery prize.'

'You'd have gone up?' he says.

I tell him that a man whose one talent is making a stuffed sock look as though it is trying to climb up his arm, doesn't throw up audience opportunities.

'You're naive,' he says.

'You're daft,' I say.

Then another man chips in. 'He's absolutely right. I wouldn't have done it either. It could compromise you.'

'Yes,' says the first. 'With the climate like it is, you can't take risks.'

I am suddenly furious. I tell myself to keep quiet, but I don't listen. 'Oh I see your problem. You're potential paedophiles.'

'Look you don't—'

'Don't worry; there are thousands of them about, just like you; millions and millions of them. In fact, I'm one myself. You see, the danger of potential paedophiles is that they look just like you and me. They sound the same, smell the same, and they do all the same things—'

'You're being ridiculous—'

'But you'll be relieved to know that 99.999 per cent of us aren't actually paedophiles at all. And the sooner everyone realises that the better. Then maybe we'll realise that there are much more deserving things to be afraid of than four-year-olds!'

'I was only suggesting caution—'

'You're making a climate of suspicion that damages ordinary relationships between adults and children. It's not children's innocence that's at stake in this fucking witch-hunt, it's ours.'

'Martin ...?' says Martha.

'Well. Life's too short and the kids need a story.'

The man who couldn't read the little girl a story is the saddest story I've heard all year. It preys on me. As I've pointed out, I am a big man. I am overwhelmingly powerful compared to my five-year-old friend, cynical too, with sexual needs, and experienced in the devious and deadly ways of the adult world. Why am I not dangerous? Because of her trust – that's why. That's the magic. I need her gift as much as she needs my protection.

Chapter 24   IT

It will get you in the end. Like all insidious diseases, it starts in a small way. You see the light's broken plug and you think, I can mend that. But, to use a woodworking idiom, this is just the thin end of the wedge.

You mend it. Behold: the light works! You've Done *It* Yourself. And now that the light's working again, you see that the little cupboard next to it needs urgent attention. So you buy a book and take the cupboard apart, clean it out and re-glue the joints. After 100 hours of intensive effort, you have a beautiful little cupboard, but then you look at the room and realise that all the other furniture is looking shabby in comparison. You'd be a fool not to take this opportunity to add wall lights. Better buy a book on wiring. Before you know it, six months has been spent within the same four walls. There are tools and trestles littered in every corner, and you resent your wife begging you for sexual attention. Here is the first law of *It:* When one *It* is done, all the other *It* that needs doing is thrown into relief. There's an awful lot of it.

This is the scourge of *It*. It should be on the list of afflictions, with CJD and HIV. Doctors should be trained to spot the symptoms: night chiselling, pointless shelving, missing fingers, planed knees ... Ironically, the better I become at it, the more *It* I can identify that needs attention. Things which are not visible to the casual house-user – to Martha and the kids – are haunting me and me alone, begging for attention.

And what have I got to show for it? Certainly nothing I can safely show Amanda Loveday.

What a clever marketing strategy! And now DIY has become so popular the culture is spreading to other areas of leisure activity. We find ourselves, with Howard and Beth, at Tiger Lil's Mongolian Cook Pot, in Clapham, which has a DIY gimmick. Customers prepare their own meals, combining raw ingredients, sauces and seasonings at whim and handing them to muscular bandana-wound wok-men wielding giant ladles, who, with much drama, clanging noise, and sheets of flame, singe them together in an unspeakable food ball, then dump them in and around their plate.

It seemed a great idea when Howard suggested it. It appealed to our sense of novelty and also vanity, but if we'd stopped to think about it, we'd have realised how absurd it is.

The four of us get into line and wend our way through the raw ingredients section. It is impossible not to overdo it. We can't stop ourselves. We heap raw squid rings on bak choy, raw turkey parts on tofu, Pelion on Ossa, nude meat bits on raw cabbage parts. The inscrutable wok-men pass no judgement, merely encouraging us to add extra sauces and flavourings to our food, even as it goes to its death in the fire. Paying to make your own meal is bad enough, eating it is an ordeal.

'My mouth feels like a domestic science experiment,' says Beth, gulping water. 'In Ulan Bator.'

We feel foolish. The wok men, the drinks waiters and the wind dried sausage all seem to be laughing at us. The endless gonging of the wokpots make us want to behead somebody.

'We could have cooked this badly at home,' says Martha, 'for a quarter of the price.'

Normally we go to restaurants to eat something that has been cooked by someone who can do it, not by some incompetent who has just walked in off the street. Funny how that didn't occur to us until now. And we have no comeback. We have nobody to blame but ourselves.

Peter is incredulous at the objects in Tony's living room. He's never been here before. Bread dough picture frames, an inch-high rocking chair, a brass plaque which says 'I AM THE CAPTAIN OF THIS SHIP AND I HAVE MY WIFE'S PERMISSION TO SAY SO'.

Peter picks up a granite pebble with a face painted on. 'He's sick,' he says.

'Shhh!'

Tony has gone out to his shed to find a router for me to borrow. Peter happened to be visiting me this afternoon, so I brought him along. I wish I hadn't. I have justified my DIY obsession to Peter on the basis that it represents extreme practicality. He has all the evidence he needs here to have my defence thrown out of court.

'You know what this is—'

'Keep your voice down.'

'This is *craft*. This man is seriously disturbed.'

'It's probably Janet's hobby.'

'It's sex substitution.'

'It's better than reading the paper all day.'

'No, it's not.' He's looking at a poorly carved love spoon hanging from a leather thong on the wall. 'Unusable,' he says. 'You know what craft is?'

'Shhh!'

'Craft is DIY for people who've finished all the DIY in the house but can't stop. They have to go on making things, even though there's nothing left to make. So they make deviant things; things that have slipped the moorings of rationality; they put uncomplementary materials together and they spawn mutant offspring – look ...' With difficulty, he picks up a large table lamp whose base has been covered with seashells.

Tony comes into the room holding a router. He looks surprised to see Peter holding the lamp. 'I see you've noticed the lamp,' he says. 'It took two years' holidays in Norfolk to collect enough shells of the colour and size I wanted.'

'It's a triumph of glue over nature,' says Peter.

'Would you like some tea?'

I frown at Peter, who I see is still rubbernecking the room. 'What's that?' he says, pointing to an oblong board lying close to the ceiling and painted the same colour. I've never noticed it before.

'I'm glad you've spotted that,' says Tony, 'though it's meant to be imperceptible.' He walks to the window and pulls back the curtain drape. There is an electrical switch there, which he presses. A motor whirs somewhere inside the ceiling void and the board starts to descend slowly. It is apparent now that there is a thin cable attached to each corner. Slowly the surface of the board comes into view. There is a half-finished jigsaw puzzle on it – a cow by a barn.

'Christmas puzzle ...' I say.

'You see,' says Tony triumphantly. 'Now, without it being an inconvenience, you have it on hand to do whenever you're in the mood!'

When Tony turns round to operate his switch again, Peter mutters behind his hand: 'We've got to get out of here.'

Chapter 25 UMBRELLA

For her third birthday Amelia asked for an umbrella. For her fourth she asked for a cheque book. Even as I smiled at her new-found sophistication, I missed the Umbrella Girl.

That fat-legged thing in the sticky-out dress running round indoors with her umbrella up was phased out. A skinnier, more knowing little girl was taking her place. And the Umbrella Girl? I've never seen her since.

That's the way it goes, year in, year out. Nothing makes you feel so old as being a parent. Each year you watch old versions of your children ruthlessly abandoned. Each new year there are new old acquaintances to toast.

When Amelia turned ten she became a pocket money Tamogotchi hi-fi *Top Of The Pops EastEnders* three-stripe Adidas track-suit Spice Girls girl. To my mind she sacrificed much to become it; giving up carefree girlish individualism for grown-up conformity to peer group pressure. Suddenly what she did appeared to be limited to what her friends approved of. I missed the carefree girl. I suppose one day she'll be prime minister and I will want my Spice Girl back; but there you are.

Children couldn't care less. They're too busy chasing new things. One day, when Amelia was five, she killed off her three invisible friends with casual ruthlessness. I haven't seen them since. A fortnight on, she could barely remember their names. I could. I still can: Mansie, Coatsie, Van Dansie. I miss them all, despite the noise they made. At ten her painting style changed too. The inspired free-form Jackson Pollocks she once turned out, three a minute, in art squalls that raged half an hour, went. In their place were painstaking cartoon mice with identical painstaking whiskers, which she swapped with other girls for other mice.

When Amelia was nine, she held a wild, abandoned birthday party with handstand competitions, door-slamming and much running up and down stairs. The next year she wanted a disco, and invited only children of her age or older, some of whom she barely knew (one had breasts for heaven's sake!), and they self-consciously watched each other dance. I know which party I preferred. In fact, the parties I throw are more like the first one, and I'm 45.

'Daddy?' Mungo asks me, 'when will I be older?' Soon enough son, soon enough.

I've got three children, so I've seen a lot of lives flash before my eyes. I should be used to it by now, but it gets worse.

Am I the only person who feels like this? Children never look back: not until they are irrevocably adult anyway. Even other adults don't seem to care that much. Some seem keener for their children to grow up than their children: they push them forward. I was a bit like that with Lowell. Every new development was a novelty and I was impatient for change. I didn't realise then, how fleeting childhood is, how when it goes, it goes forever.

I pushed Lowell so hard his hair is starting to recede. I swore I'd savour the growing-up process with Amelia, but she would have none of it. From the moment she arrived, yelling impatiently, I realised it was out of my control. Suddenly it was impossible to imagine a world without her. Nothing would ever be the same again. And this moment, already, was slipping away.

No sooner had Amelia arrived than she changed. One day she was a baby: the next she wasn't. One day she crawled: the next she walked. One day she couldn't speak: the next she couldn't stop. At four years old she took up all the space in the bathroom – roaring orders. 'Don't grow up,' I told her. 'Stay here awhile. It's *nice* here.'

But she wouldn't listen. She was too busy. Before I can say 'pierced ears' she'll be off clubbing. We accelerate into the future, her and me. Every passing moment of her childhood is the last that will ever be like that again. I've counted the changes. But watching the child leave her, as I am doing now, is the hardest of all. Because I know I don't have long left. We kiss our children goodbye and we never see them again.

Mungo now: there's hope there. He doesn't seem in a hurry to grow up. In fact he's not in a hurry to do anything. The other day, while idly firing carrot pellets across the kitchen with a spud gun, he said: 'This would be a good way to wake lions.'

I admire the boy. I know from hard experience that comedy writers sweat blood to come up with as fine a concept.

'Stay *exactly* as you are,' I told him, 'and when you grow up you'll be a comic genius.'

Experience tells me that one day he'll put comic genius behind him, just as Amelia put her Jackson Pollock phase behind her. That's growing up, and that, as Amelia would say, is cool. Though I adore my new adolescent (even with her horrible trainers), part of my heart will always be with the Umbrella Girl.

A three-second gap in the guitar wall. The singer shouts *'Will you fuck me for blow?'* The front room is dark. Smells like teen spirit in there: smells like testosterone and girl-steam and sweat. It needs to be wrung out. I daren't go in there.

There are boys here. I don't like boys.

Amelia's 13th birthday party. Unlucky for some – unlucky for us, the old folks perched on the sofa in the cordoned-off back room, with the TV on as though we might actually be watching it, mentally clinging to each other, enduring our massive superfluity. We are like exhibits in an old folks diorama ('slow-moving, proscriptive ...' the label would say), illuminated by ordinary light, displayed here for the carefree young to gawp at from the darkly delirious world, for the three seconds their attention span allows them before yanking them back to the teen fug. We are as alien to them as a pair of nesting tables.

Amelia's friend Jolie pops her head in, smiles and says 'Hello!' in a sing-song voice. Her hair's metallic red and she's wearing a T-shirt with the words 'FUCK YOU, YOU FUCK'.

'Hello Jolie,' I say. 'Fuck you, you fuck.'

Nonplussed. Her mouth is open in the Oh-my-God position.

'It's all right Jolie, I'm only reading your T-shirt.'

This insouciant, yet casually vicious teen culture is speckled with slogans of sex, drugs and violence. They are flirting with corruption, but do they comprehend it? Do they even read the words, or are they just patterns, cool or uncool as the case may be; yes or no, in or out, boo or hiss? Jolie's head vanishes; back to the teen-fug.

'Do you think you should do another round?' says Martha.

'Do you think so?'

'Yes I do.'

I sigh and get up. A party of doom-faced, black clad goths arrives, squeaking with excitement. A mother delivers six girls, all clutching Coca-Cola bottles, which I later discover contain vodka. A crowd of boys make their own way here, then hang around outside on the pavement. It's my job to tell them not to do that, and not to do other things they want to do too. It's an unenviable job. I herd a bunch of them in, even though the house is full. A framed picture leaves the hall wall with a crash of glass.

Upstairs, in the one bedroom we have managed to carpet, a boy is sitting drenched in mud from the waist down. It's a cream carpet. 'You never told me you had a pond in the garden,' he says.

In the garden a fat boy, rolling drunk, sits on a table, egged on in his ludicrous drunken gabble, by two giggling girls with nose rings. There is a large crowd of kids smoking in the shadows by the garage. I half expect them to defy me when I tell them to stop it, but they apologise brightly, as though my request were the most reasonable thing in the world, and light up again as soon as I go indoors.

I love parties, but I've never been to a party before, where my function was to tell people not to do things. I am the anti-party. It's depressing. I feel like the Ghost of Christmas Past: wrong time, wrong place, wrong season. I see exactly why you might want to set fire to a line of hair mousse along somebody else's dad's kitchen floor. It's obvious: it's daring, spectacular, and funny. But when a youth of 13 does it in your own kitchen, it's irresponsible, dangerous, and dumb.

I return irritably to Martha. The back room, with its lights on, is gloomy. All we can do is wait for it all to go away. After a while two boys join us. One is wearing a 'Boy George Knew My Father' T-shirt. He wants to know if he can read our *Independent*. The other boy wants to know if he can have an avocado. Kids today!

Chapter 26 CUCKOO

You keep an open heart: you must expect to be hurt once in a while. You keep an open house: you must expect the occasional cuckoo.

'Any friend of Anna's is a friend of mine,' I told Toby the actor when he rang – stupidly, as it turned out, but then even the most level-headed of us can be tempted to make an irresponsibly dramatic gesture.

By now it's early June and I still have no profitable work to be getting on with. Instead I've agreed to play host to the friend of the daughter of the man who once owned the house whose front door window I smashed last Christmas. Perhaps this is payback time. Maybe I can assuage my guilt about the affair and make things right again.

He arrives two days early: an intense, flop-haired man with the face of one who has suffered much before a mirror. He wears dark shabby clothes and black canvas shoes which smell of decomposing dishcloths and which, every night, he leaves on the landing, and which, every night, I transfer to the garden with fire tongs.

Toby is well-spoken and briefly personable, but his attention soon wanders from the petty conversation of people like us, who are not in the thrall of his own high calling. One day he will be a celebrity, he implies loudly, but for now he is struggling. He has come to London to showcase his one-man play, *Winston the Warrior*, at an Edinburgh Festival preview. Anna gave him our number apparently.

'I must to my room,' he declares archly. 'I have but four days to infuse my characters.'

'Four days?' I said. 'On the phone you said two.'

'Alas, they've scheduled a tech. rehearsal for tomorrow. And the scenery has to be sorted.' He shifts into actorly mode: 'I have nothing to offer you but blood, toil, tears and sweat. By the way, I'm a vegan.' Indulging us with a lavish smile, he vanishes upstairs.

We don't see much of him, but his presence is oppressive. In the evenings, Winston Churchill, Theodore Roosevelt, Lord Haw Haw and some other characters with big boots sing 'We'll Meet Again', tell each other to fight on beaches and make troop deployment noises in the spare room.

Occasionally I run upstairs with a vegan snack Martha has prepared. One time, when I open his door, he scowls at me and says: 'Were you born ignorant or did you remove your brain yourself!?' I freeze, open-mouthed. 'Heckler put-down. Like it?'

For four nights we lie awake listening to Hitler shouting for more *lebensraum*. During the day, the actor sleeps till noon (in his clothes, by the look of them), then goes out. In the afternoons, when he isn't here, things are delivered for him: a large overcoat, camouflage netting, an air-raid siren and an eight-foot resin statue of Winston Churchill himself, which takes the driver and myself forty minutes to get inside the house. It won't fit up the stairs, so we manhandle it into the living room. 'That'll be sixty quid,' says the driver.

Martha doesn't like the statue. Doesn't like it at all. This has gone too far. This man is no friend of hers, she says. Come to think of it, Anna is no friend of hers either. She hasn't even met her! I suggest a hot bath. She goes but comes back instantly.

'I can't have a bath,' she says. 'Stalin's in the bath, demanding increased tank production.' Every evening Martha and Winston watch TV with grim expressions. Upstairs, war rages.

On the day of the performance the actor asks if he can borrow £20 to have Winston delivered to the theatre. I've had enough. I refuse. That's why we aren't invited to the performance. We sit at home with Winston, who didn't make it because of my intransigence.

We are about to go to bed when Toby turns up, morbidly drunk, with six people.

'The play's a dog!' he announces dramatically. 'But these people ...' he waves his arm vaguely at the figures behind him, 'are my friends. They also happen to be my entire audience!'

It would be churlish to deny him at such a low point. It is a moment for compassion. So I uncork my commiserations and a few bottles of wine. One of the people Toby has brought back with him, and who spends the next hours eating and drinking in our house, I discover to be his father. I ask how far he has travelled to see the show.

'Putney,' he says.

'Putney? Then why didn't your son stay with you?'

He looks at me as though I have insulted his intelligence. 'I wouldn't have him in my house.'

By 10 a.m. the next day, Toby is packed and halfway out of the door, chewing a chicken leg from our fridge, and bright as a new idea. It is as though Winston Churchill had never existed. 'Au revoir then!' he says, edging off. I notice the neck of one of my wine bottles protruding from his bag.

'But ... what about Winston?' I call after him.

'I've thought about that. I've decided to put it all behind me.' He carries on down the path.

'No! I mean the statue! And Toby – what about my £60 ...?' He doesn't stop walking.

'Oh, er... I'll send you a cheque. I'm sure I have your address.'

Part III

SUMMER

Chapter 27 FISH

I dream I am in a fishmonger's shop before a sumptuous display of large whole fish laid out on a sloping marble slab. I am trying to decide which fish to buy. The fishmonger's wife is a grotesque, plump woman, all apron, with pink sausagey arms, big wet lips and a sly eye. She has a manner of talking as though she is sharing a secret.

'I'll show you something,' she says, and she bends her red lips to a large cod lying on the slab. Gently, very gently, not taking her eye off me, she breathes into the fish's mouth. After a while the tail quivers; then flips, and then the whole silvery body undulates slowly. The fish writhes awake, and rises from the table into the air, where it starts swimming slowly around the room, as though the air were water.

'That's incredible,' I say.

She winks. 'He's such a handsome fish, that one,' she says. 'I was moved to breathe the life.'

The other fish lie on the slab, stark and dead, with their stomachs removed.

'Why him and not the other ones?' I ask.

'Some are blessed and some are not,' she says.

The good and sometimes bad thing about being freelance is that your circumstances can change very quickly without warning.

I am lying on my side in the walk-in cupboard I have built upstairs, pondering intractable *It* problems. First of all the lighting circuit I fitted in the cupboard has stopped working. I've checked the bulbs and the connections in the fittings and found them to be in order, so now I have the prospect of climbing into the filthy loft space to fiddle about with connection boxes. I can't face that, so I'm pondering the second problem instead, which is even more intractable. The built-in shelving I have designed and constructed has a rectangular space at the bottom to accommodate six plastic drawers I bought at Muji. When I came to fit the plastic drawers I found that they were now an eighth of an inch wider than when I first measured them. This may not sound like much, but it means the drawers won't go in. Here at the cutting edge of DIY we work to very fine tolerances. For two hours I have pondered possible solutions, but I still haven't worked out what to do.

The telephone rings. Could this be a clarion call from the Seraphim announcing good news to the toilers of the land? Or Martha ringing to tell me to take a shoulder of pork out of the deep freeze, make sure to hang the coloured wash out to dry in the garden and reminding me I must deliver Mungo to a birthday party this afternoon, as Europa won't know the way?

It is the seraph after all. It is the *Evening Standard*. They tell me Mark Stein, their TV reviewer, is taking time off and may decide he'll leave the job altogether. Would I like to try my hand at it? It's not something which suits every writer and it's not as easy as it sounds. The brief is to deliver five 1100-word articles a week between Monday to Friday, the daily deadline being 7.30 a.m. Each day's article is to review two or three programmes transmitted the previous night. They will pay me £1000 a week and if I'm good enough to be still doing it in a few weeks' time, there might be a permanent position available, for which I would certainly be considered.

All right.

A thousand pounds a week! They picture me at a prairie desk in a furrowed study, phones on hold, tomes open at relevant passages, assistants creeping in with newspapers, sandwiches and scribbled updates of this and that, airline tickets in the letter rack, computers fluttering in extremis, trying to keep pace with my brilliant mind. If they could see me as I am, in my sawdusty socks and my old jeans with the knee coming out, a still-bleeding chisel injury on one hand and a head full of implacable wood, they might take the job elsewhere.

It's been a long time since I've been able to savour such a feeling. Mostly, at the moment, I feel relief. Here is proper, good work, and regular too. I'm scared too of course, but this answers so many problems, one of the most important of which is that it will make Martha happy. It may not always look like it, but pleasing Martha is one of my main priorities. Unfortunately it so often clashes with the others.

I ring Martha. She's overjoyed. She's whooping at her secretary. She's happier than I am.

I turn my back on the cupboard. I have to do something delicious now. I have to make fishcakes for Martha to eat tonight. I have to make fishcakes because Martha loves my fishcakes. We'll eat fishcakes tonight and then we'll make love: proper love, with kissing.

Two Jehovah's Witnesses on the doorstep. Two earnest black women, one of about 50, the other, who could be her daughter, maybe 27. They are always so earnest, so black, so kind, so clean and smartly turned out, so keen to save my lily-livered cynical soul. And always wearing hats. What have I ever done for them? What will I do? I will disappoint them and then they will smile at me and leave with polite, good-natured resignation.

'Do you agree that the world today is like this?' the older woman says, unravelling a roll of paper in her hand. It is a composite picture of many things: guns, cigarettes, drug syringes, a bottle of liquor, men in balaclavas, people with grim faces, or faces distorted by anguish, and over all, a mushrooming nuclear cloud.

'Well it's pretty bleak,' I say. 'But it's not all bad, look.' I point at a couple of people who appear to be having it off in the corner.

They both turn their heads to look at the poster, then as one, turn back to me. Their faces don't register anything but kindness. Now the younger woman is unrolling a poster. 'But God's eternal kingdom will look like this!'

The picture is a sunny mountain scene with a flowering meadow in the foreground, in which an idealised family sit next to a babbling stream, bathed in benevolent sunshine. I notice that the father is wearing a suit and playing a guitar. The mother is earnestly singing the father's song. There are about seven children of mixed gender in the meadow, of various ages and with various yellow, black and coffee complexions. Some are playing ball, some laughing, one is helping another with a project of some sort and one – a baby – is rolling on the grass with a tiger. A mixture of other animals, including a fawn, are gambolling in the meadow, and an abundance of birds and butterflies fly about among the trees and flowers.

'No.'

'What do you mean, no?'

'That's not God's eternal kingdom. I've been there.'

'You've been to God's eternal kingdom?'

'No, I've been *there*. It's Switzerland.'

'No, you don't...'

'Except for the tigers – they're not so tame in Switzerland; in fact they can be quite a nuisance – no, that's a joke. Sorry. But everything else is pretty accurate.'

They look confused now, but I can't help it. Who wants to live a life of virtue only to end up in Switzerland, where if you stand still long enough someone will carve a heart on you, and where deputations of citizens will arrive at your door to tell you off if your firewood isn't stacked in alphabetical order, and you have to do army training every year, and build a nuclear shelter in the cellar, and lowly paid Italian origamists will sneak into your chalet at night to fold the last sheet of your toilet paper in a neat little triangle, set the *gut nacht* mat by the bed, and put a milk chocolate on your pillow? Who wants that unto eternity?

'*Nein Dank*,' I say. 'Don't get me wrong, Switzerland is very nice to visit, but for all its charms, I prefer the eternal kingdom of the Muslims, where you lie around on gold-weft couches all day in a glade of thornless lote trees, eating bananas and drinking wine, and where every man has, oh 70 or 100 – there's some confusion how many exactly, but who's counting? – 70 or 100 lustrous wide-eyed virgins, to do as he wants with.'

The two women smile their kindly smiles at me and move off to try next door. I feel mean now, so I thank their backs profusely for coming. They must prefer the misanthropes who tell them to piss off to the clever-dicks who bang on about Switzerland and Muslims and virgins.

'Go on then,' says Martha, 'say golly Moses.'

'*What?*'

'Golly Moses – say it.'

We're lying in bed, looking up at the ceiling.

'What do you mean?'

'You always say golly Moses just before you go to sleep when you're in a good mood and you've had an eventful day.'

'I never say golly Moses!'

'Yes you do. You always do.'

'Golly Moses.'

Chapter 28 PROFESSIONAL

Five deadlines a week is a gruelling pace. Writing is difficult enough as it is. I don't know why I ever started doing it. Writing is a relentless procession of choices. With every word you select there are a thousand ways in which to alter not just the present sense, but the sense of everything yet to come. It's the worst possible profession for the indecisive.

Not everyone finds it difficult, but I was never good at streamlining the work process and concentrating on priorities, the most urgent one of which, in journalism, is usually speed. I'm always tempted to write around a subject to see if there's a more interesting way.

In the old typewriter days, you were obliged to write in a linear stream – the way the writing appears on the paper. You could have one or two stabs at it, but each time, once the annotations became illegible, you'd have to type the whole thing out again. There was a limit to the number of times you could do this before your fingers fell off.

Word processors make writing harder because they turn it from a linear process to a sculpting process. This doesn't mean you can have a naked woman in the study. It means you fiddle with your work for ever, then fiddle with the fiddlings. Anything's possible. You change the order, then you re-order the changes. For ever.

Other writers (I've seen them doing it) tap away, tap, tap, tap, making snap decisions, snap, snap, snap, as they go, defining the territory, like generals on the march, with barely a second thought for the consequences. They know exactly what they want to say before they say it. I canter off bravely in one direction, then get lost.

And then I have a cup of tea and do one of the 1001 things a writer has to do around the house – mowing the lawn, organising the sock drawer, thinking about sex of course, and enjoying the writer's favourite fetish: stationery. The arrival of a new Viking catalogue in the post is a moment of delirious joy. I am lost in its pages, fantasizing about pencil sharpeners, colour printable inkjet labels and paper, paper: orgies of paper. The attraction is the hope, however delusional, of organisation in a disorganised world; the promise of products which can do for material things what the writer tries to do with ideas: categorise, label, sort, highlight, format, render splash-proof and make safe yet easily accessible unto eternity.

You might think this is strange, yet other freelance writers are as hooked as me. Though he would never admit to a weakness for stationery, Peter has suspiciously penetrating insights into the Viking mail order catalogue. He has a theory about I. Helford, the company 'Chairman' who is pictured on every other page, pointing woodenly at rubber stamps, smiling enigmatically. Pelvic floor? No.

'Dead,' says Peter. 'He died years ago, but it's a closely guarded secret. They can't let the news out for fear company morale would plummet. How would they be able to guarantee same day delivery on orders over £30? They keep his body preserved in some warehouse somewhere, and dust it down for every catalogue shoot, dressed in a suit, and strapped to a filing cabinet. He's the El Cid of the stationery world.'

I'm getting through this job by the skin of my teeth. I'm watching a lot of television as well. It's been an eye-opener. I never realised TV was so good. But this too, is a distraction. Life has more meaning than it had before, though less mystery. Best of all is the approval it brings, particularly from Martha; the sense that I'm part of the working world – part of the *contributing* world.

Even so, I sometimes envy people who sell computer hard drives. The Samsung EIDE 20.4 GB hard disk, for example. It has a rotational speed of 5400 rpm and a seek time of 9.5 milliseconds, connector type: 40 pin. There's no beating about the bush here, no decisions to be made, no nuance or variations in tone to devise, no hidden meanings to hint at, no sub-text to infer, no infinitesimal possibilities of interpretation to take into account. Either it has a 9.5 millisecond seek time or it hasn't.

The best thing about being unendurably overloaded with work, apart from the cash it brings in, is that it has sent my DIY fixation packing. First of all I stopped thinking about all the things in the house that needed doing; then I stopped caring. I no longer care about the half-finished walk-in cupboard, the unplumbed second bathroom or the peeling window frame. When the downstairs doors beg me to give them their knobs back, I pretend not to hear.

I have entered a new phase. And with it, a certain chirpy stroppiness has set in, an expression of my right, now I am so busy at a proper job, to decline the occasional household chore. Let somebody else sort it out. When Martha asks me to fix the vacuum cleaner, I say, 'Nature abhors a vacuum; why should I care?' I am a free man!

But my new TV review writing schedule is not the only reason I have managed to rid myself of the scourge of *It*. There have been three other significant occurrences, all of them traumatic in varying degrees, though now that I have survived them all, I feel lighter-headed than I have in months.

The first was a DIY dream. That in itself, is not unusual. I've had lots of DIY dreams. They hijacked the slot formerly reserved for sex dreams and are as single-minded and as graphic. They involve me tooling a perfect dovetail, or routing a pristine rabbet, then gloating over it for the rest of the night.

But this was no ordinary DIY dream. This was a DIY nightmare. This was an invention scenario, in which I was putting a shelf up in a carrier bag. It was such a beautiful concept – so practical, so felicitous – which would enable the transportation of two distinctly separate and inviolable objects in one bag at the same time. But there was a snag. I managed to fashion the shelf all right, out of a sort of MDF, but try as I would, I couldn't work out the brackets. Eventually, after an eon of frantic effort, I cracked the problem by utilising a material as yet unknown to man and a special kind of soft saw I had to invent myself. It was only when the shelf was finished that I realised there was no way of getting into the bottom compartment. I woke up flailing.

The second reason why I am hanging up my power planer is that we are engaging a real builder to do the heavy work at the back end of the kitchen. Once, at the height of my DIY frenzy, I had fancied that

I myself would pull out the old brick chimney, prop up the house, take out the loadbearing wall, install a steel joist, demolish the silly toilet beyond, open up the back external wall, fit French doors, turn a side door into a window and dig up and level the kitchen floor. But reality has hit home. These are serious building jobs and I am a writer. I would be more gainfully employed writing articles to generate cash to pay for professionals. After months without doorknobs, Martha is emphatic on this point and I acknowledge the truth in what she says. It pains me to admit I can't do everything, nevertheless release from the tyranny of *It* has brought huge relief. To finance the work we have remortgaged the house, a traumatic and mind-cauterising process too tedious to relate. Enough to say that, with the help of the Coventry Building Society, we've increased our mortgage from a lifetime debt to something longer than a lifetime debt. It's all over bar the repayments.

My life hasn't become any simpler though, for now I have the task of showing builders round the house. They arrive at different times to the appointments they have arranged. When they bang the door I am always in the middle of something important. I am watching a home decorating programme for the colour-blind, in which interior designers sneak into somebody's house while they're out and paint their kitchen custard and pastel green. Or a gripping examination of the sex life of the dwarf Siberian Hamster. That's my programme for today.

David Attenborough is my lyrical guide, gently romanticising the urine attractants, the blatant tail lifting, the elephant seal porn. Sex, he says, is a means of 'transcending mortality'. How endearing is this animalistic behaviour, seen through his loving filter. The deep serenade of the female right whale turns male whale heads five miles away, the booby bird signifies her willingness to mate by dropping some token nest material on her darling's attractive blue feet, the female something or other (I miss the name because the doorbell is ringing) chooses her mate by examining his droppings like a conscientious customs official.

I can barely tear myself away, for suddenly I am spirited to the Russian Steppes, to an improbably complicated *mise en scène* in which a female dwarf Siberian hamster is preparing herself for her night of passion in her underground boudoir and the camera tracks up through the tunnels to where David Attenborough sits, like Mowgli, in a red Siberian sunset, among her waiting suitors. The bell rings again. I switch off the video.

The builder uses Alvin Stardust stage entrance techniques. He is standing with his back to me as I open the door, emphatically poking at my brickwork with his car key. One full second later, he pretends to suddenly realise I have opened the door and swings his open and trustworthy face round to me with an expression of amiable surprise, as though to say he had become so absorbed by the structural detail of my porch that he had forgotten he had actually rung the bell. So help him guv, here he is, right at the beginning, caught out being keen!

I know instinctively that anyone with an open and trustworthy face is as shifty as hell and this knowledge, as he pokes around my house, measures and squints and hums and hahs, says 'Nice old houses these', showers the fabric with good intentions, pats the children on the head, winks at the au pair, makes me fetch the stepladder from the garage, peers into the only room I've actually finished and says how nice it will look when it's done, borrows my pencil to write with, borrows an old envelope to write on, diagnoses imminently dangerous faults which I haven't yet considered, stands in the flower bed gazing predatorily at the roof, condemns the work of all previous builders and relates the painful history of his back problem, before disappearing from my life forever, wipes all constructive thoughts of hamster sex from my mind. We won't transcend mortality at this rate.

Most builders never send an estimate. I don't know why. Can't write? Can't do sums? Can't find the envelope? Dropped a paving slab on their head? Probably it's a mixture of all of these. Whatever, once they've looked round the place, most of them feel they've done enough already. Why spoil a perfect impression? The few estimates which are submitted are recklessly optimistic.

So then Martha arranges for more builders to come. She rings me to tell me to drop everything: Stan, or Vic, or Bill and Ben are on their way. I am locked into a cyclical game of grown-up make-believe: the

Builder's Estimate Game. It's impossible. I'm trying to be a professional writer here. I'm doing a full-time job; plus, I'm supervising a whole yammer of children, not to mention a sizeable au pair. Right now I should be curled up with the hamsters; instead I'm following Mr Shifty round and round my own house, carrying a stepladder and two cups of tea, talking with forced amiability about skips and scaffold hire, three-man days and cash upfront and what-the-VAT-man-never-sees, for a pretend building project that he knows full well, due to the fact that he can't write, do sums, may or may not have dropped a paving slab on his head and anyway isn't really paying attention, he has no intention of ever carrying out.

Finally, when all the when all's said and dones have been all said and done and we have come to the end of all the at the end of the days, we shake on it, whatever it is, and I never see him again. I bet John Pilger doesn't have to put up with this.

The third and most affecting reason why I abandoned *It* is that Amelia has shunned my DIY talents. I don't know why. I have built her some lovely modern bedroom fittings. I have built her beautiful white alcove shelves fully 5' 11" in span, strengthened with hidden metal strips to prevent them sagging and to obviate the need for central supports, their lips faced with bull-nose routed two-inch timber strips to make them appear thick. I made the bottom shelf deeper to take her television set, curving the front in a groovy wave shape. Under this I built three deep floor-drawers with sub-compartments, fitting flush and pulling out on rubber wheels. I built her a curved desk painted with silver Hammerite, taking up an inside corner of the room, and over her radiator, I made a silver half pear-drop shelf. I fitted two sets of lights, one for the sitting area and one for the bed area, with two-way switching, so she can turn them on and off either at the door, or beside her bed. The two-way switching was incredibly difficult.

Amelia has ignored the cool, clean lines of my design and has covered everything with stuck-on coloured feathers, decals, trinkets, pink things, piles of *Kerrang!* magazines, angel wings, cryptic notes from friends on bits of heart-shaped paper and shrines to Limp Bizkit and Barbie doll. It's like an anarchist craft shoppe in there.

On one wall, in large collage letters, she has put the slogan: 'Why does life have 2B such a bitch?' How can a girl who has any item of clothing she wants from Topshop, a monthly standing order to top up her own personal bank account, a fully furnished room of her own, a TV, Minidisc and hi-fi, not to mention Unconditional Love, think life is a bitch? What has it done to her?

'What has life done to you?' I ask.

'What do you mean?' This is her stock response to any question from me.

'Why have you put that slogan on the wall?'

'I just think it's cool.'

It's cool, but she doesn't know why.

On the remaining free wall of Amelia's bedroom, I have fixed a large, framed, four-foot by six-foot pinboard for her notes and posters. This just annoys her. By designating a place for her to pin her stuff, I have transgressed her right to pin stuff wherever she wants.

All this has taken me weeks. I have been anxious to make a quality job of it, because there is no satisfaction otherwise, and it would look cheap. The next step is to build a stunning curvy wardrobe to match the shelf lines, which would incorporate additional shelving down the outer side, next to her bed.

'Dad,' she says, 'can't I just have some normal furniture?'

'What do you mean?'

'You know, like a chest of drawers or something, that doesn't have to be made.'

'What do you mean?'

'Can't we just go to, like IKEA? Like normal people?'

I have grown accustomed to the eyes of beautiful women glazing over when I talk about the speed gains, convenience and strength of sensibly applied biscuit jointing, but this really hurts.

Life's a bitch.

Chapter 29 BILLY

So here we are at IKEA, like normal people. We have traded DIY for BUY. We are on Planet Flatpack, ready to talk furniture. 'Take us to your leader. We are Martin, Martha, Amelia and Mungo the humans. We come in peace.'

'I am Peter the practical hi-fi rack and this is Dick the handy storage solution. We come in pieces.'

Notice how people who've been shopping at IKEA are embarrassed to tell you the names of the things they've bought. It's un-British. It disturbs us that our shelving system is called Billy; that our non-allergenic polyester duvet answers to Nora. Over-familiarity with furniture makes us uneasy. We are a formal race, after all.

Attitudes are different in Sweden, where there aren't many people, but there is a lot of wood. Wood is a friend to the Swede; it has to be. A primordial sense of kinship between man and material survives today, especially during the cold, dayless Swedish winter, when people are snowed in with little but furniture for company: Emil the chair, Lilian the place mat, Ringo the likeable stool. To the Swede, a bookshelf is not just a conjunction of timber sections, it is an emotional expression of the tree from which it sprang. It is a spirit, a *being*: it is a Billy.

Martha and Amelia couldn't care less what the solutions to their furnishing needs happen to be called, so long as they are cheap and chic. In fact they're irritated by my reading the names out, and have said as much. A pity because so much effort has obviously gone into it. Clearly IKEA employs a team of creative professionals in its Naming Department, whose job is to nail the word which most precisely expresses the personality of each new product. It's not hard to imagine the hours of debate which must go on in such an office, as nuance is weighed against nuance. 'Say Gabriel, where do you stand on the vanity unit: Ånn or Ingeborg?'

'I do not have an opinion. I am a shelf.'

And so on through the long winter.

No doubt even as you read this, managers of IKEA stores across the country are writing letters of protest with their funny foreshortened wooden pencils. They are pointing out that, had I bothered to read their catalogue, I would know that IKEA is a rational, progressive company; that Sweden is a scientifically advanced nation which leads the world in the development of composite particleboards and the managed farming of sustainable forestry ...

Maybe so, but you only need to look at these product names to see that IKEA is a company torn between its dark, primeval Scandinavian roots and its shiny cosmopolitan future. On one side stand the traditionalists, who like to characterise items as mythic Scandinavian spirits (like Smidd and Snåcka, the rough-and-tumble doorknob pixies); on the other, the progressives, who favour blander modern, Anglo-international personalities (Bang the mug and Micky the mirror). It's my guess the Naming Department sees some bitter in-fighting.

The traditionalist's work is marked by poetic felicity. It strives to say something about the material nature of the object, for example, the Klunk tumbler, the Storkrake tubular steel table leg, the Observatör TV swivel. Though rooted in Swedish, traditionalist names often have an onomatopoeic universality. The Våffler tea towel says much about the condition of damp cotton, the Ört galvanised tub makes you just itch to fill the thing up with buttermilk, the Skogsblåbär baby bag is a classic of the genre.

Traditionalists tend to be men, middle-aged or older, who have drifted into the job from the folk professions – zither tuning and the like. They have a beard often, a pipe with a bendy stem, leather rucksacks and walking sticks carved out of laughing pine. They may have made the odd piece of furniture themselves in their time.

Yet their narrowness of perspective caused problems in an IKEA bent on global expansion. They burdened the Lighting Department with a huddle of sad Swedish light names. Glimt, Lack, Fade 2 and Smog may sound effervescent in the grim context of an everlasting Scandinavian winter, but they do not sparkle here in the south. What do Californians make of a lamp called Sediment?

It is this weakness that prompted IKEA to recruit a younger element to the Naming Department. Fresh-faced agnostics were taken on, straight from the new particleboard polytechnics, heads bursting with abstract ideas learned on trendy training modules like The Dada of Furniture Names. Of course the progressives had no patience with the old guard. They were unschooled in life; 'ideas people' in love with modernity; not in awe of the products. They came to work in plastic shoes and yellow clothing decorated with contrasting oblong patterns. It was they who came up with the jolly shelf gang, Billy, Boris, Ralph and Jonathan – an immediate hit across the globe.

In their hubris the progressives made errors. Most worrying was a tendency towards irreverent experimental surrealism, evident in Fungi the kettle, Spurt the mug, the wardrobe Bra, and a trio of storage crates called Papp, Nob and Muck. Customers began to think they had wandered into a Britart installation. It was particularly strange coming from a nation which speaks English better than we do.

It had to stop. The traditionalists didn't need much encouragement to stage an aggressive comeback and old namers were prised out of retirement bungalows in the far Norrbotten to swell the ranks. They are in fighting mood. Those quieter Swedish characteristics which we applauded in Komplement and Rationell (the furniture of the modern day peace broker), have been replaced with a creeping neopaganism. Most disturbing is Gröndal, a name conceived in a spate of corporate *berserkgangr* (battle madness): a buffet counter which seems to imply it will obscenely eat your babies. What next? Gröndal's mother?

Amelia is oblivious to it all. I am aware by her happy trill, as I assemble her new Anebodas chest of drawers (ridiculing how pathetically easy it is to put together), just how delighted she is. She is stretched out on her new Orgryte sofa, unabused by troubling connotations of swingers' evenings in Uppsala, where those who are able to survive the twin chrono-biological yearnings for uninhibited sexual experimentation and suicide, turn inevitably to furniture making.

Names are important.

Never trust alliterative builders: Ray the Roofer, Declan the Decorator, Odd Job John (not forgetting, of course, Paul the Plumber). It's too pat. When they arrive they are heroes with hammers, buoyed up with optimism and the promise of better things, demanding thousand quid wads up front, grinding the inside of your house to dust and despair then, three weeks into the job, they disappear for long, empty days.

We don't know this yet.

Bert the builder is our man, recommended by Cheryl the Char who cleans for Clive and Sam. Bert the builder has an open and honest face. Bert the builder has the grand scheme, the big picture. Bert has the vision that will shape the heart of our home, the dream kitchen made real with bricks and mortar, old-fashioned skill and hard, honest toil.

For a moment I believe it. For just an instant, maybe I do.

'A finished job – that's what you'll get,' says Bert the builder when he comes to size up the job. His estimate, which he scribbles decisively in blunt pencil in the margin of the Ho Fun section of a Chinese takeaway menu, and presses into my hand then and there, is half as much as the next lowest I receive. It covers the substantial work in the kitchen as well as the laying of a concrete floor in the cellar, fixing felt on the flat part of the roof and plumbing in the new upstairs bathroom. As a special consideration to the lady of the house, he will fix the downstairs doorknobs for free. Materials will be paid for by me, as and when they are needed.

'All that end wall,' he says, waving across our kitchen with a vague but generous hand movement, 'will be finished. That patio door: finished. The winder: fin-ished! Plasterwork ...' he stretches his hands out with a gesture so wide it includes Surrey, '...finished. Finished. *Fin-Ished!*'

I buy it. What I should be doing is paying attention to the tell-tale tremor in his voice, the almost messianic passion which can be detected there. I don't know it yet, but this *finished* by which he sets such store, and which makes his dewlaps tremble like a mendicant shouting a hosanna, is not a feasible objective in his mind; not seriously to be regarded as something normally achievable in the real world. It is a Holy Grail, the builder's equivalent of the cup containing the blood of Christ at the crucifixion, the pursuit of which is mystical and heroic. And like the Grail, this precious *finished*, if glimpsed at all, vanishes tantalisingly away again unless the seeker is of pure heart. I don't at this stage have any information on Bert's purity of heart.

There's just one thing: he has to start on Tuesday. It's the only way he can fit us in. Well, that forces my arm really. I am impressed by his urgency. We've prevaricated long enough over this project already. 'You're on,' I say. 'But you have to understand, this has to be a smooth operation. I can't be constantly disturbed. I have an extremely important writing job on at the moment.'

'Oh is that so?' he says.

If it wasn't for Bert, I might still have a nice house.

I have until Tuesday to move the entire kitchen into the dining room. I set up the poor wounded oven in this new and incongruous environment. It feels odd. We pile packets of food on to a table. I spend an entire weekend emptying the cellar and squashing its contents into the garage. I set up the dishwasher in the garden.

The cats normally go out via the kitchen, but as cats won't voluntarily go anywhere near men with wheelbarrows, I fit a cat-flap in the door connecting the dining room to the garden. The cat-flap will be a new challenge in their lives. I am hoping for the best. This job is a significant act for me: it is the last piece of DIY I will ever do in my life. I have entered the era of professional specialist help.

Life's not going to be easy over the next couple of weeks. It's going to be hell. In fact it's already hell. But it can't be helped. As Bert the builder points out: you can't make an omelette without breaking eggs.

'You can't make an omelette without breaking eggs,' he says.

'True enough, Bert,' I say, and I smile roundly back at him. We're like mates. We're going through this together. We know it's going to be tough, but we're in for the long haul and we're going to pull through.

Bert the builder starts work on Tuesday morning as promised, with partner Frankie and a sullen young chap called Des, who is the labouring muscle. They arrive bristling with hope and hammers and the promise of better things. By lunchtime they have knocked down three walls, dug a large hole in the kitchen floor and jacked up the ceiling with rusty scaffolding. And now here comes the really hot weather: ideal for dust. Builders, like visiting grandchildren, bring hot weather with them.

And they sing all the time; not a song as such, but rather an amalgam of songs, segued into one long song string. It starts when they arrive in the morning and finishes when they leave in the afternoon. The words vary but the tune is constant. Bert leads, hopping from song to song, fitting them seamlessly into that one catch-all melody, while Frankie, an intense, dreamy fellow who works on things in corners of rooms, drones an instant reprise.

'A-wonchoo come 'ome Bill Bailey, wonchoo come 'ome' ('come 'ome', Frankie echoes eerily in the background), 'Oh it's a longa longa way to Tipperary' ('erary' intones Frankie), 'Just-a one-a cornetto' ('etto'), 'We are Siamee-eese if you plee-ease' ('ee-eese'), 'A-we're so pretty, oh so pretty a-vacant' ('We're vacant,'), 'A-West End Girls tra-la-la-la' ('la-la') ... It's a small price to pay for a dream kitchen made real with bricks and mortar and hard, honest toil.

Builders are dynamic at the start of a new job. They love a new job. They are full of energy. Knocking things down is much easier than building things up, which is boring and problematic. My dining room is a tip, but never mind. The gutted kitchen looks excitingly big and full of potential. From the direction of the cellar, where Des is toiling single-handedly, sweating like Bruce Willis, comes the sound of heavy industry. 'Des the Destroyer,' Bert calls him.

Then the hammering stops. The singing stops.

'I say! Hullo!' It is the call of the builder, echoing up the stairs. 'I say!' The call cuts through the dust and the heat to my study, where I have shut myself away, trying to write about a documentary on Dame Vera Lynn. I will hear that call many times over the next few weeks and in time, of course, I will come to dread the sound even more than I dread the wall-shaking crashes and the generic singing, but now I run downstairs eagerly to see how I can help.

They have stopped work and are standing in the garden, talking and passing wind among themselves. I notice they have carefully laid a pile of planks on top of the flowerbed. 'Hold it, Bert,' I say. 'That's a flowerbed.'

'Oh is that so?' he says.

Builders can't see flowers. They could easily put their plank on the path or on the grass but they don't; they put it on the flowers. Flowers do not exist for builders. If you applied to go to a college for builders and your interviewer held up a picture of a flower and said 'What's that?' and you said 'flower', you wouldn't get in.

'I need £800 in cash,' says Bert. 'Now. For wages and sand and cement,'

'Right now? I have a very urgent piece to finish on Dame Vera Lynn.'

'Oh is that so?'

There's nothing else for it but to get in the car and go to the bank. I withdraw £800, come back and hand it to Bert.

'No need to count it,' says Bert (we're mates). 'I'm sure it's all mis.'

'Mis?'

'Miserable.'

'Miserable?'

'Miserable fucker.' Pause. 'Pukka. And another thing. I've got no van.' He points to the road where his grimy white van was parked yesterday, but isn't today. 'It broke down.'

'So?'

'I need sand and cement.'

'So?'

'So you'll have to go.' There is a gap here in which many thoughts go through my mind. 'Can't work without sand and cement, can we?'

So I go down to the builders' merchants and I buy sand and cement and I load it into the boot of Martha's company car, which settles down on its axles like a baby with a very full nappy. Dame Vera will just have to whistle.

And so it goes. Day follows day. Frankie and Des hammer out the back wall of the house. The sun hammers in. Some days they have the van, some days they don't. There are frequent infusions of £500, sometimes £800; always required instantly, whatever I am doing, or this or that won't be able to take place. £500 or there'll be no skip, £100 or no lintels.

Always they sing: 'You are my sunshine' ('sunshine'), 'If I-a had a hammer' ('a hammer'), 'A-will the real Slim Shady a-please stand up' ('a-please stand up'), 'Oh-you can get it in the Y-M-C-A' ('C-A'), 'A-you're my Barbie girl-a' ('And I'm your Barbie boy').

And my whole family, me, her, the two kids, the great lumping teenager, the guest children, the increasingly sullen au pair; all the dusty lot of us are cooking and eating in the dining room, overdosing on Indian takeaways, washing up in the bath ... Only now the hot water has broken down. Bert says it's no problem. He'll fix it for us — for free. The boiler blows up. It is all going to be worth it, isn't it?

Chapter 30 RUG

And so the old orders are shaken and ravaged.

It's one thing to install the Staywell draughtproof cat-flap, it's quite another to get a cat to use it. Jack finds it a natural thing to bang his head against apparently immovable objects, so he masters it quickly.

Simpson watches Jack operate the cat-flap without curiosity. Simpson is a Luddite. She won't consider attempting it. Lying on the other side of the door making a noise like a pilchard, only makes her uneasy. I know what she's thinking. She's thinking why should she risk getting her tail snapped off by the new-fangled thing? Why run the gauntlet of builders' boots? Why bother to queue up for a cat-flap at all when there's a perfectly good luxury toilet right there in the study?

She's referring here to my hand-made pure-wool Scandinavian-design Sixties-look op-art rug. She has decided that this will be her new toilet. She's acquired a taste for luxury defecation. She thinks she's Ivana bloody Trump.

The rug was made by me a long time ago, when I was young and single. Ever since I saw Claudia Cardinale being seduced on a bearskin rug in *The Pink Panther* by David Niven (with the aid of Henry Mancini), I wanted a naked woman rug of my own. I bought a pattern, canvas backing and a hundredweight of finest wool, and after six months of myopic evenings with a latch hook, like Queen Matilda in her bower, there it was: a beautiful, luxurious, sensual thing no woman could resist. All I needed now was Claudia Cardinale, but the years went by and she never once lay on it. Neither, as it happens, did Simpson. Recent circumstances, as we know, have caused Simpson to re-evaluate the rug. I'm only thankful Claudia Cardinale hasn't had a similar change of heart.

I've washed the rug twice and that's no mean feat. It's huge. It had to be manhandled in the bath, and it brought the washing line down. By soaking it in vicious floral disinfectants for an hour, I have imbued it with the scent of Alpine Breeze. It is almost as bad as having a cat lavatory in your study, and effective, I would guess, at repulsing naked women too. Not that the rug has ever been a great success in the pulling stakes. I have yet to come across a woman who has liked it, let alone wanted to lay naked upon it. Martha has never deigned to touch it – not even with a foot. When she comes into the study she skirts it carefully, as though it were a snake pit. So the loss, once and for all, of its pretension to seductive magic, doesn't signify any great sacrifice, though it does mark the end of a dream.

I'm alert now to Simpson's every twitch. I spring from my desk to shoo her away if she goes anywhere near the rug. There's no more I could do to keep her off it, short of setting fire to it.

Jack's my boy. While downstairs making tea, I watch him operate the cat-flap as suavely as Luke Skywalker disembarking a space pod. This is gratifying. Seconds later though, I see him rolling on his back on my pansies, like a lion in clover. Why on earth should he want to do that? That's what grass is for. I bang on the window and shout out: 'On the grass!' (which cats don't understand). He gives me the 'Who the fuck are you?' look.

When I go back upstairs, Simpson, Alpine breezes whipping round her ankles, is doing a dump on the rug. I manhandle the whole miserable creation into the garden and burn it.

Oddly enough, now that it's gone I don't miss it. No, I can't say that entirely. It was, after all, the biggest, and most enduring thing I have ever made, and if I was pressed I would have to admit that its passing has left a small and incongruous notion of emptiness in the box room of my soul. Yet I can also see that it had begun to look passé, and I did keep tripping up on it on my way to the dictionary shelf. Besides, it is healthy and refreshing to shed elements of the past, particularly hairy ones. I know nobody else will miss it, except maybe

Howard, who one afternoon, overcome by the vivacity of my conversation, fell asleep on it for two hours.

In a way Peter will miss it too, for though he despised the rug utterly, he relished it as evidence of my true petit-bourgeois nature. He saw it as clear proof of a craftist tendency at work in my psyche. He couldn't walk past it without asking me when I was going to start my sea-shell bedside lamp, and the removal of this opportunity will disappoint him. I have to consider that Simpson's apparently gross vandalism may actually have been an act of good taste, possibly even one of compassion. My main concern now, though, is: where will she strike next?

The dust blows in. The dust blows out.

We cannot sleep. There is grit between the sheets. We toss and turn with worry. There is grit in Martha's lovely thick hair.

It feels as if the family is fractured; all its cohesiveness has gone. A house without a kitchen is a house without a heartbeat. Everyone looks distracted. Our home no longer feels like it belongs to us. It is an alien place, a refugee camp, where the inexplicable and the unfamiliar are only to be expected.

Until Bert plumbs in the second bathroom we are all of us dependent on one toilet, which is perpetually clogged up. Someone – I don't know who – is dumping toilet paper in it. I don't know why. Every day I find the bowl filled to the brim with clean white paper, wads of it. I am forever attacking the toilet with chemicals and plungers to get it clear. At the corner shop, to which I am obliged to return twice a week for fresh toilet rolls, they shake their heads, suspecting an incurable bowel problem. I have questioned each child individually, taken them to the bathroom, shown them the problem and pointed out the waste and undesirability. They all deny it. I don't trust Weeny and Mungo. They sense the gravitas in my voice and morph into wide-eyed, open-mouthed alien creatures from the planet Gosh!, an effect so extreme it looks fake. I have even, with great difficulty, broached the subject with Europa, who just giggled.

That natural sanctuary, the bath, is full of dirty plates. Dirty plates are never in short supply. The children have been told to put them there and they do, walking away feeling virtuous, leaving a mess of crockery and remainder food. I'd almost prefer them to leave the plates scattered round the house. Every time you want to wash, you must first wash up.

When Lowell isn't out with his Brixton mates, he's shut in upstairs. He only emerges to raid the fridge. From his room the pounding thud of hardcore house comes clanging down the stairwell, to do battle on the first floor landing with the pounding thud of house hardcore clanging up from the kitchen. Where they meet is where my study is: the epicentre of bedlam. I sit in this vortex, this whorl of sound, with the sensation of floating on clamour. I shut my door tight, but it keeps on being opened.

The children are dispossessed. They no longer feel secure downstairs. The living room, which used to be Mungo and Amelia's afternoon den, is full of furniture and boxes full of things, making it impossible to watch the TV. Amelia has her own little TV in her room. As she won't let Mungo in there, he slopes into the study and watches whatever videotape I happen to be reviewing. He was never bothered about what he watched, so long as the TV was on. Once when he was off school with a cold, he watched the horse racing all day.

Today we watch a documentary about the inner workings of the White House. I am transfixed by an interview with a senator, who has hair of an integrity I have never seen before. It's like Disney hair. I don't know how he can speak at all, let alone so seriously, knowing that's on his head.

'Look at that Mungo,' I say. 'That man's hair is solid.'

'It's an omelette,' says Mungo.

He's right: it is an omelette, an eight-egger; a little greyer than is conventional perhaps, but undeniably an omelette. Mungo has the eye.

Dust has curdled Europa; made her sullen. During her time off, she is either in Lowell's room, with the door firmly shut, or she is out shopping, buying stuff which bores her long before she reaches home. She doesn't bother to unpack it. For Europa the point of shopping is shopping – not merchandise. She no longer sleeps in the au pair's room, preferring to use it as a personal storeroom for her unopened shopping bags. Let's face it, there isn't room for her to sleep in the au pair's room. This irritates Martha, though there is a lostness about Europa which makes me feel sorry for her.

'There must be a hole in her life,' I say, 'for her to need so much shopping to fill it.'

'It must be a very big hole because she's almost filled the house already.'

'She's got a problem, obviously.'

'She has got a problem, but she's also got two bedrooms. *I* don't have two bedrooms to put my stuff in. Look at this.'

We peer fearfully round the doorpost into Europa's abandoned, yet crowded room, like those people in films whose house has been hijacked by poltergeists. The carpet is no longer visible to the naked eye. We daren't look in Lowell's room.

Martha thinks Europa has a cushy number, especially since she has been subcontracting out the cleaning part of her work to Bernard. She pays him £10 a week. The arrangement worked well enough at first, although he became distressed when Europa shunned his conversation. She meant it when she said she didn't like French people. Bernard should stop trying, but it is obviously too horrible for him to consider that her behaviour is anything but an aberration, and every time she enters the room, he tries again with a new topic, watching her with the expression of an eager, yet neglected Labrador.

As soon as Bert began his *builderkrieg*, a paralysing bewilderment settled on Bernard like a pall. His house-cleaning skills are rudimentary (he maintains, and probably believes, that there are no such things as dustpans in France, and no need for them either) so a house in which a dust storm is taking place is way out of his league. He doesn't know what to do. He flails about downstairs for a while, then makes a coffee for me and brings it up to the study. Then he fails to go away again: this is his work avoidance technique. He stands for a bit, making light conversation, then pulls a chair up by my desk and lights one of his unfiltered cigarettes. After a respectful minute or two, to make sure there is no hint of demurral from me, he pulls out his most recent copy of *Aghast!* Magazine. He wouldn't get away with this with most employees, but it doesn't bother me. He makes the odd rueful comment, and occasionally passes me his magazine, so that I can better appreciate a finely rendered spread of intestines, or suitcase of arms. I don't shoo him away because actually, I find his company rather pleasant, especially when he brings with him some of the *pâté de foie gras* that his mother sends him from Angoulême.

I always ask him the same question: 'How are you finding London, Bernard? Exciting?' In the four months he has lived next door, he hasn't left Streatham once. I believe my study is the furthest he has travelled in his exploration of the city.

'I do not like London. It is so dull.'

'Why don't you go up to town on the bus: look around, maybe take in a show, or a club?'

'I do not like to do that.'

Bernard can convince himself quite easily that two hours sitting with me in the study is more or less equivalent to cleaning a house. Europa wouldn't know any different. Martha, on the other hand, can see only dust, and is very unhappy about the arrangement. 'It's not working,' she says. 'He's not cleaning.'

'He's trying to clean,' I say. 'Though how anyone can clean when everything's so dirty, I don't know.'

'So he's not cleaning?'

'Would you really be able to tell if he wasn't? Anyway the vacuum cleaner's broken.'

The dust blows in, we toss and turn.

Martha is vexed. Bedlam is not a good place to come home to after a stressful day at work. I've noticed that she has taken to wearing pyjamas of the most unerotic variety in bed, heavy things in unresponsive burgundy. From past experience I know that this is evidence of a bad state of mind.

This is what women do in times of perturbation: dress up in heavy and off-putting clothes, which they get from a secret draw. In the secret drawer they keep pop socks, track suits, uni-slippers, sleep sacks, woollen hats from the Third World with tassels, whole body TV couch cocoon duvet gowns, ear-warmers, enormous underwear and thick pastel coloured tights ... All women have a perturbation drawer and they go to it at times of heavy periods, when they have crashed the car, or have accidentally become pregnant. Here are clothes to keep the world at bay, hands-off clothes which convey the message that life isn't all about sex and gaiety and carefree abandonment. And if you don't watch your step, it might never be again.

Here too are dungarees: the most off-putting clothes of all. There is no faster way of removing the sexual allure of women than dungarees. Dungarees are an all-in-one manifold repulsion outfit, which work on many levels. They turn women into gross children, with disturbing connotations of boiler men. On the Three Little Pigs they are à la mode; on women they are sacks. They disguise all hints of shapeliness. Everything that men hold dear – breasts, waists, hips, bottoms even – disappears inside their voluminous denim bucket. This is stealth clothing, designed to evade all male sexual directional aids.

You never see your wife in dungarees before you're married. She doesn't warn you about them; doesn't prepare you in any way. Then suddenly, three months in, on an otherwise normal day, a psychotic Appalachian backwoodsmen walks out of your bedroom, just like that.

'What's the matter?' she says. 'You've gone white as a sheet.'

'Nothing ... It's just that you look like one of the Three Little Pigs.'

You are, of course, choosing the mildest option open to you, in an effort to be nice. Your consideration is wasted. You might just as well have told her straight out that she looked like a psychotic Appalachian backwoodsman. For now that she thinks you think she looks like one of the Three Little Pigs, she looks more like a psychotic Appalachian backwoodsman than ever.

Now, I'm not saying Martha is wearing dungarees to bed, though it's a close call. I sense, by her aura of lumpiness, that there may be more than one layer of perturbation clothing in play here, so it is always possible she has dungarees on underneath.

In this case I sympathise entirely. We are, after all, sleeping in a sandpaper sandwich, so insulation has become a necessity of life. Also we have a strong urge to hide. In fact, for the first time in years I am wearing pyjamas myself – and it's high summer. It's hotter than the Yemen in this bedroom, but we curl up tight in bed like hedgehogs, with our hedgehog clothes on. When Mungo crawls in between us at

4 a.m., like a human blow heater, there is a real risk that one of us will catch fire.

'We must be thankful for small mercies,' I tell Martha.

'And what are they?'

'I'm not doing the work. At least we've got the professionals in.'

'Yes, that is a blessing,' she says.

Chapter 31 **BLUE**

Father Christmas comes to me, personally, in my room, wakes me. Shakes my shoulder gently with his huge hand, cups me in his gentleness. I can't remember my age. I just know Father Christmas comes to me – I see it as clearly as if I am watching *Newsnight* – and he takes me by my trusting hand and leads me through the snow, in all the bountifulness of his generosity, in his great protection.

We leave the reindeer panting in the hoar frost, in the cold which is as cold as magic. My ecstasy is ice-clear and vaulted as the bright, stark sky. Inside his warehouse, on computerised racks, on cranes and fork lifts, lie all the toys in the world, wheeled, unblemished, assembled, batteries included, larger than life, shiny; fragrant of new paint and rubber.

His beard tickles on my cheek. I am not afraid. 'Martin,' (he knows my name) 'take anything you want! Take them and run with them through the world.'

I do. I take everything I've ever wanted. Personally he supervises it. Then: 'We'd better wrap them,' he says, 'otherwise they won't be a surprise,' and winks, rolls them all in red ribbon and bright red wrapping paper.

Then he brings me back home, where I know I will be happy forever, and he stacks all the presents at the foot of my bed.

Then I wake up. There are no toys in my bedroom; none at all. What's more it is the middle of July. And I am not a boy. I am 45; my hair is falling out. A deep and beautiful sadness overcomes me, like the pure white snow of a Christmas dream.

The only person in this house not wearing a haunted look is Weeny, who behaves exactly as normal. She has never watched TV anyway, so that doesn't bother her. She plays by herself in her favourite place – the spare bedroom next to my study – just as before, arranging and re-arranging teddy bears round the edge of the room, each with his own plastic plate and knife and fork. I can hear her telling them what to do and what not to do. She is independent and I love her for it.

But I worry about Weeny. I worry that her mother will stop her coming here. Ursula has exacting standards, I can see that just by looking at her. I can see she is a woman who does not tolerate dirt or chaos. There is no dust on aeroplanes, which is probably why she likes them. And there is never a speck of it on Ursula. When she calls in the evenings to collect Weeny, she stands there on my doorstep with her shoes together, glinting, her little winged hat perched ready for flight, her blouse collars spiked and glowing, like the Persilled peaks of matching mountains, the street light behind her casting a nimbus around her uniformed figure, crisp and pristine and utterly desirable. She is a neat parcel, unwrappable, yet unopenable. She doesn't have my name written on her.

I know too, by the way she sniffs the air like a police dog and by the quick, sharp little frown which follows, that she has spotted the bloom on my clothes, the rubble in my hair; that she can see through my pretend insouciance and my view-blocking body moves in the doorway, into the dirt and chaos beyond.

Ursula wouldn't tolerate Bert the builder for an instant. She would have only clean builders. They would take their shoes off at the door, keep all their dust in a special bag, go to the toilet in their own bucket and wash their bricks every night before they went home. If they didn't, she'd drop them without a second thought. She is super-efficient. She progresses through life choosing and rejecting people according to her needs, with no thought for the discarded. For the time being at least, she has chosen me.

I know too, without having to ask, that her flat is spotless, her husband probably sterilised. Her drains smell of pine forests. These nights, when Weeny gets home from the pick-up, the little girl must leave a trail like a runaway powder puff through her flat.

This afternoon I have to write an article about Saturday afternoon TV programming, but I have also cooked up an exciting and unusual activity for Mungo and Weeny to do. I thought it would be fun for them to dye the plain wooden chair which we bought at IKEA for Mungo's room. I have set the chair up on some paving slabs at the bottom of the garden, decanted some blue wood dye into an old container and come up with two usable brushes.

It's gratifying that the children, when they arrive home from school with Europa, are wildly excited at the prospect, though I take great pains to explain how careful and responsible they must be. I dress them in old clothes – I can't stress the importance of wearing old clothes enough to them – and I explain to them how they must only lay their brushes down on newspaper. They are desperate to get started, but I make them wait while I demonstrate how to use the brushes properly.

'When you put the brush in and out of the pot,' I say, carefully picking up the container of blue dye, 'do it very carefully and slowly. Think very carefully about what you are doing, because if you don't ... are you listening to me because this is very important? If you don't take care, this blue dye will make a terrible mess.' Then I spill it all down my front.

Neither of them laugh, or look surprised, for this is no less than what they expect will happen if you pick up a container of liquid. It happens to them all the time. They are just pleased, given the preamble, that in this instance it didn't happen to either of them. It is unfortunate that I am the only one who is not wearing old clothes.

I pour out some more dye, leave them to it, and get changed. Then I scuttle into my study with a videotape of *Blind Date*, a programme that makes you want to be a Muslim fundamentalist. Here's Giselle from Middlesex: squirrel-coloured hair, electric red shirt, no neck, looking for a husband. And Ruth from Surrey, in acid tangerine. R. Cilla's in Blind Lime. I am in the full glare of light entertainment here. And now I am being bludgeoned by innuendo: 'I would sit you on the Aga and show you how to put a bun in the oven.' It is the worst kind of smut: it's light smut. 'I'd tune you up, make you spark and pump your pressure right up ...'

Mungo comes in. 'The paint has gone on Weeny,' he says. I remove the brush from his hand and run down to the garden. Frankie is standing there, holding the other brush, looking sheepish. Weeny beams up at me. Her face is covered with blue spots. Nobody could accuse me of not being ambitious where children and dyestuffs are concerned.

'Frankie?'

'I was giving a hand to the kiddies you see,' says Frankie, 'but the brush is – you know – flicky.'

There is no time to wash up all the plates that are in the bath. I pile them in the basin and on to the floor and put the two children in hot water to soak. It's not as easy as I hope it will be. It's not easy at all. Weeny is undaunted by the prospect, but as soon as I look at that precious up-tilted face, I realise that there is no way I can scrub at it, or do anything with enough force to make an impression; it would be sacrilege. Dabbing with the corner of a soapy flannel is as far as I'm prepared to go. Anyway, the dye has settled into her limpid skin like a tattoo. It won't budge.

'Well, Weeny,' I say. 'You'll just have to tell Mummy you've got some blue freckles now to go with your brown ones.'

And I'll just have to write my TV piece in the night. For some reason that is my most productive time.

'There's been a little mishap,' I tell Ursula when she arrives to pick up Weeny. 'Nothing to worry about,' and I hold out my hands in supplication. I have forgotten that they are bright blue. Ursula's eyebrows shoot up. She looks down at then Weeny. Her mouth opens. I explain what happened. I put the blame firmly on the builder. I tell her the blue will grow out. That doesn't seem to go down well. She takes a deep breath.

'Martin,' she says. 'Mr Monaghan tells me that the school pick-up is often late on a Tuesday. He says that last Tuesday he timed it and the person was 25 minutes late.'

This throws me, this sudden switch to Mr Monaghan. This is Weeny's teacher. I, of course, am the person. Every Tuesday on Europa's day off, I pick up Mungo from his school and then Weeny from the Catholic school round the corner.

'Mr Monaghan says Natasha is often the last child in the playground.'

Mr Monaghan, Mr Monaghan. I hate that man. Mr Monaghan is the perfect teacher. Pious. On time. Neat. Neat in word and deed. Neat in jacket. Exemplary. He is exemplary. I hate that word: exemplary. I hate Mr Monaghan's exemplary jacket.

'It's very difficult on a Tuesday,' I tell her. 'Weeny and Mungo's schools come out within five minutes of each other and it's impossible to get to both on time – even more impossible if I don't have the car.'

I know she understands me perfectly. I know she knows that everything I have chosen to tell her is the truth. But I also know that she can see, by my demeanour, by the condition of my house, by my bright blue hands, that timing is not my strong point.

She smiles widely: that instant smile that I hope is true, but know is not; that is part and parcel of her uniform, her professional carapace; signifying nothing.

'Perhaps Martin ...' she says, 'perhaps in future you could arrange to pick Natasha up first, as they are stricter at St Joseph's, and Mungo is that little bit older.'

'Well, yes of course. I will. Yes. I'll make sure I'm on time in future.' I am pathetically grateful for any straw she offers me. She's in control. She's very clear about that. She has the power that comes from knowing her own mind; she intends that I know it too.

She is not grateful to me. She takes my contribution to Weeny's care as her due. She pays her bit to the au pair, issues formal declarations of thanks and goes her way without looking back. I don't care. I want Weeny. Ursula knows I need her more than she needs me.

Chapter 32   TOY

It's a difficult day. It's Tuesday, Europa's day off. She's at the swimming pool and who can blame her? She has made a beeline to the least dusty place in Streatham. Martha has taken the car to work, so I am doing the school pickups by bus, always a bit dodgy, particularly when there is Weeny's teacher to worry about too. I determine to get to Weeny's school first and on time. Thankfully, though it seems touch and go when the 159 bus stops at Streatham Bus Garage to change drivers, I make it (give or take a minute or two).

As always, I have the temptation, when I see little Weeny in her too big regulation tie and hat and blazer, corralled with her mute class mates beneath Mr Monaghan's suffer-the-little-children good shepherd hands, to say something grossly insulting about the Pope. I resist the urge.

'You grassed me up, Mr Monaghan.'

That eyebrow – the left one, moves up a notch.

Like Ursula, he too is clear. Exemplarily clear. 'Teachers have a very difficult job to do and they cannot stand around all day waiting for parents and carers who may or may not arrive to pick up their children.' There is a dose of irony in the word 'carers'.

In Mungo's school playground, when we get there, is a reception committee. Two supplicants, Sean and Toby, petition me to be allowed to come back home with Mungo to play dust games at our house. These three are now close-knit friends. Their best thing is to lie together on the living room carpet all afternoon playing Nintendo and watching TV, with breaks for tea and for Toby to demonstrate World Wrestling Foundation throws on Sean, who cries. Their mothers nod approval.

It's difficult, but two extra little boys surely can't complicate life much more than it already is. I agree.

'*Yes!*'

They dump three book bags and three sandwich boxes into my arms and tumble after me, their euphoria faltering only when they notice I am walking in the wrong direction.

'Haven't you got the car ...?'

'No. Bus.'

'Tnohw!'

I can't see this through though. Once on the bus, the more I think about it, the more I can't face cooking supper. Mungo and Weeny are easy, but cooking for Toby and Sean is like looking after exotic animals at the zoo. Right now I can't stomach the job of rummaging through the jumbled food packages piled on our dining room table and in boxes underneath, trying to find two such mutually exclusive things as red meat for Toby and Quorn for Sean. I try talking my way out of it using metaphysics. I point out that as meat and Quorn are, in material, ethical and gustatory terms, antithetical, they cancel each other out; therefore Sean and Toby could achieve the same effect by not eating anything at all.

Toby considers the hypothesis for a second or two, then says: 'I think I'd rather eat.'

So there's only one thing left really. 'Only one thing for it boys: plan McD.'

'*Yes!*'

Plan McD. Sure-fire winner. So we hop off the bus in Streatham and here we are in McDonalds, where adults don't have to do a thing except pay the bill.

Fast food is the curse of the slow classes. It is one of the ironies of our age that movers and shakers like Clive, who have hectic schedules and no time to spare, spend two and a half hours over lunch at The Ivy, while those with all the time in the world – the unemployed, the desperate, the preternaturally docile, the wounded mothers with pale children and plastic bags, the pairs of brittle girls with jutting chins and grievances, the people damned with tiny brains and trainers the size and shape of cross-Channel ferries – eat fast food.

Fast food is exactly what the name implies. One second it's there: the next it's in the toilet. Usually you don't notice it going through. It's quite possible, if the attention is momentarily distracted by an interesting breadfruit plant, to eat part of the polystyrene container by mistake. You *can* taste the food, if you wilfully restrain it with the teeth, though this is not recommended.

The most comforting thing about McDonalds, particularly to those adults whose home is being shredded by men with sledgehammers, is that they are all reliably the same. This is strange considering they are the product of a culture which honours individualism above all. The only spark of individual expression I have ever seen in a McDonald's was a handwritten NO ROLLER SKATES notice taped to the door of the one in Charing Cross, which was itself an attempt to curb the individualism of others. I have never seen a sign, by the way, which so made me want to roller skate in a restaurant.

The interesting thing about McDonald's is that though all of us middle-class people hate them without reserve, and insist that we are too superior to go in them, we know them intimately: the smell of warm cardboard, the nickname food, the *wipeable aesthetic* of the decor, all those people with buckets and bins doing things while you eat. 'Why can't we all relax a bit?' you think. 'It's my lunch hour.' But relaxation isn't the point.

Getting the hell out of there is the point. The interior colours have been chosen carefully with this end in mind. From the scarlet and yellow of the logo to the maroon of the uniform: everything clashes. It's designed to stop people feeling so comfortable they might want to stay. But we do stay, because we have nowhere better to go.

We go to McDonalds *despite* the food and despite Ronald McDonald too, who looks like a serial killer from a 70s B movie (wearing a mutated variation on the dungaree, I notice). Children even tolerate him. They are only interested in one thing: *the toy*. The toy which comes with the Happy Meal is McDonald's greatest triumph, the reason for its unstoppable success. If you could just go in and *buy* the toy you would, but you can't. You have to buy food in order to get the toy. The toy is the point of McDonald's. It is McDonald's very clever trick. It means every parent in the country *is forced* to go in there and sit among all the slow people and eat fast food at least once a month.

'The toy! The toy!' they shout. 'What have you got! What have I got!'

'Eat some food too.'

People who oppose McDonald's often say: 'Britain has a great tradition of bad food; why should we put up with bad American food?' Ask them this: when was the last time they got a free articulated duck with their pie and chips?

Chapter 33   DESPAIR

The singing stops. The hammering stops.

'I say? Hullo!'

It's the call of the builder. I am coming to dread the sound.

'A little snag.'

'Snag?'

'We're going to have to knock a hole through into the dining room.'

Long pause.

'To get the joist in, yeah? The joist's too long. It has to go in sideways, see and we can't turn it sideways in that position unless we pass one end – right? – through the wall there, into the dining room.'

He waits while I digest this. I look at the too wide beam, at the too narrow kitchen, at the ground zero decor, the dust ...

'You can't make an omelette without cracking eggs.'

I snap. 'I don't want an omelette, Bert. If I'd wanted an omelette I'd have engaged a chef. What I want is the back end of my house held up – with bricks preferably. I don't know about you, Bert, but I just don't think an omelette is up to the job.'

'Not a plain omelette anyway,' he says.

The summer holidays are here. Now children demand attention 24/7. Now life is easier for them and harder for parents. When the children aren't supping heartily on my time, energy and forbearance, they are nibbling at my conscience. I have so little time to spare for them and they have so many exploding needs. I've told Mungo to go to Europa first with his urgent questions, but they're too hard for her.

'Dad, Dad!'

'Hmm.'

'Dad! *Dad!*'

'Yes, Mungo. Yes. Slow down.'

'Dad! A man is walking down the street and a dinosaur comes along and bites him! What if?'

'Ah. Well ...'

And then I lurch back into the real world of TV reviewing and a game show in which they try to stop a man running down an alley by hitting him with enormous inflatable bananas.

Meanwhile out there, the fleeting euphoria of the English summer skitters by. Martha and I are denied its benefits. Ironically we should be getting on well now, as our trials are not of my making, thank God, but we are both under a lot of strain and our moments together have sometimes been snappy. It would be great to get away, share a few soft moments in the sun. Tranquillity is what we crave.

But we are etiolated creatures, staring out from our nuclear winter at the carefree taken-for-granted summer enjoyment of others. Out there tea-cups clink in sunshine; tennis balls plock. Out there the countryside hums with heat. Villages wait for us, as yet undiscovered behind folds of hills, preserved as in amber, dust motes, butterfly wings intact. Ducks broil on rippleless ponds. People set out picnics, fend off bees/ moths/ants/farmers rendered enormous by the greenhouse effect, run shrieking from surprise showers, play wheelbarrow on the barrow down; with Rosie, drink cider. Out there the slo-cooker of the English sun works sublime enchantments. Secretaries strip in parks, moved by the aphrodisiac aroma of freshly cut grass. Out there on languorous evenings, women kick off their shoes and run barefoot across cooling lawns: the English equivalent to going topless on the Copacabana.

Out there, too, is Howard, somewhere. Every summer he goes off in his van for six weeks, to get his head together, or whatever it is ex-hippies do in the country. It's a mystery and he wants to keep it that way. He never gives much away and his air of smug exclusiveness is irritating.

Why should I care if he wants to play the yokel? We haven't seen much of him lately, as building sites offend his refined ex-hippy sensibilities. He can't understand why we're having anything done.

He says the kitchen was fine before. I've met up with him once or twice at the Marrakech Coffee House, and he and Beth popped in briefly before they left for the country, to drop off the dope run kit. This is a folder containing door keys, a timetable and instructions mapped out with Howard's usual logistic thoroughness. I am one of a roster of eight friends, each with their own folder kit, charged with watering the dope plants in his attic while he is away.

So just now, when Howard would be such a welcome distraction, he's off doing his folkie thing, whatever that is, roasting hogs on the beacon or annoying English Heritage people at Stonehenge. I know in the past it has involved meadowy-type folk festivals with the Albion Band and once, in his younger days, he was arrested at Henley with some Class War punks for throwing potatoes at Hoorays. He gets around. Though a city boy by birth (he was brought up in Manchester), he is a rural ritualist by inclination. He'll set his sails for any hey-nonny-nonny that's going. He loves the theatre of British folk history. I told him that perhaps this year, now that he is retired, he should give it a miss. He was shocked.

'No way!' he said. 'It's my holiday!'

There are photo albums in his flat which I have always resisted the temptation to investigate, but today, having done the tedious round of his indoor farm with the watering can, and relishing the novel sensation of being in a house other than my own, I linger. I sit in an armchair and open a volume, beguiled by my own nosiness. Sure enough, here is Howard, a blurry wraith from summers past, at some esoteric ceremony – Norfolk perhaps – loudly singing cuckoo, or something, knees (though not in frame), garlanded (I'll bet) with horseshoes. There he is – mooning? – on the crag with ... Druids? Northumberland, looks like. I'm enjoying this.

Now he is with some bishop person, distributing lardy cakes to the poor – that sort of thing – at Bream's Eaves, or Thwing, and what's that? Hooping the Rabbit looks like (must be The Lophams!) in traditional goatskin and clackers ... what look like clackers anyway. Here now, in frozen dance, is Howard, high I should think, on magic mushrooms, and behind him, unmistakably, Morris Men: quaint superannuations, half man, half hanky; in real life, quantity surveyors to a man. It's a scream. And there is Beth, beautiful, lying under a tree on a bank of moss in dappled sunlight, naked.

The photograph is more than I need to see. Feeling suddenly creepy, I replace the photo album and return a small pile of papers to the shelf in front of it. The top paper I can't help seeing too, as it is now in my hand. It is a letter from an IVF clinic in South London detailing procedures for a course of hormone injections.

Other people's lives are fascinating precisely because they are theirs. This information Howard and Beth have chosen not to reveal. But I know it now. I feel like a thief. I lock their house and go home. Martha is mourning the downstairs doorknobs again. Her sense of loss is sharpened by the fact that she was trapped in the dining room all the while I was at Howard's.

'I couldn't make the kids hear me; they were making such a noise upstairs,' she says, when I get her out.

'Why didn't you use the pliers?'

'I couldn't find the pliers.'

'Surely you could find something else in there to grip the spindle with?'

'That's just it: the spindle fell through the other side.' Her voice is agitated. 'And anyway, why the hell should I!'

'Well, if you want the door open ...'

'Why can't I open it with a doorknob? I don't understand. We've got doorknobs. Why can't they be on the doors?'

'It's not that simple. We have to get special screws ... Anyway, Bert has promised to do it.'

'Then why doesn't he do it? Why doesn't he just do it? Why don't you make him do it? I'm sick of talking about doorknobs! I've been talking about doorknobs for months and it's driving me mad!'

'We can't have everything at once.'

'Look, I just think it would be nice to have doorknobs on the doors. Like other people. We've had our turn being without doorknobs. It's someone else's turn now. All I want is to be able to open my dining room door without first having to look for a pair of pliers. Does that sound unreasonable?'

Not really; not put like that.

Builders are delicate creatures. More delicate than poets. Half-way into a job they are overcome by Builder's Despair. They look around and see the world in chaos and this distresses them. They become mournful. Their lintels sag. Their singing stops. This is worse than the singing. I would give them a hug if I didn't think they might misconstrue it. And if I didn't hate them.

Their vision, once so robust, wilts. It is the prospect of the painstaking work of building, after which they are so misleadingly named, which engenders such despair. They did the smashing down with verve, they hauled me out of my study to drain me of money and force me to drive to the yard to buy them extra cement, and they insisted at the eleventh hour that I move all the kitchen equipment from one end of the dining room (currently a makeshift kitchen) to the other, so that they could knock an expedient hole through into the kitchen (currently a makeshift gravel pit), and they have knocked the hole through with great conviction and certitude of what is right and what must be done and they have done it despite the fact that my entire family – wife, cats, children – is living here beneath their sledgehammers, subsisting on a diet of takeaway dust curry.

And in doing it they have opened up a vent into the house, whereby great gusts of grit are now being admitted; there is grit in our underwear, grit in our teeth, grit in our jalfrezi; turning our home into a grit palace of the old Punjab.

And we tell each other this can't go on much longer; it can't get any worse; we must have reached the bottom of the grit heap, and from now on things can only improve and life will slowly but steadily consolidate in some as yet unimaginable manner towards civilised calm and cleanliness. And it is at this point, this very point, that Bert goes down with Builder's Despair. I can see it writ large on his open, trustworthy builder's face.

Downstairs I can hear Builder Bert's formerly robust song-cycle fade to an eerie wail: 'O-wo-the-okey-cokey ...' ('cokey'), and then die out altogether. Silence hangs with the dust in the void that was once our kitchen. I daren't go down. I dread to find Bert and Frankie slouched motionless on the floor, staring glassy-eyed, mouths open in the primeval listening position, hoping against hope for the arrival of rescuers.

Chapter 34 BREAK

Returning from ferrying Mungo and Weeny to Sam and Clive's, there's a message on the answer phone from my friend Eithne: 'What on earth is the matter with you? You sound like a man who's fallen down a well and is too proud to ask for assistance, and might at any moment lose his footing and plunge another hundred feet into the abyss. Just calling to see how you are.'

That's how I am.

I need a break. Uniquely, everybody agrees I need a break. The 7.30 a.m. deadlines, five of them every week, are taking it out of me. Other writers, I know, would not find them so daunting, but my writing is so laborious that I often work through the night. When I lived in Brixton the compensation for doing that was the V formation of Canada geese that flew over my house each dawn, on its daily migration from Brixton's Brockwell Park pond to its day pond in St James's Park. To the fashion-conscious goose, Brixton is the new Canada.

I would hear the geese before I saw them and their fusspot honking always cheered me up. Then, if I'd finished, I'd go to bed for a delicious hour.

We don't get geese in Streatham, though the occasional fox screeches outside the window at 2 a.m., like a child being murdered. On rare nights, a couple of times a year, a maintenance unit on the railway is a welcome distraction in the small hours, repairing the track or collecting snails, whatever it is they do. It first impinges on my consciousness as a faint and incongruous industrial clamour: a clanging of metal, foremen shouting directions, pneumatics pishing, engines heaving and whirring. It is as though a foundry has been set up in secret somewhere among the back gardens and has suddenly been launched into production.

The sound increases in intensity as the unit creeps up the track. I can't make much out from my window because of undergrowth in the cutting, but as it passes the foot of my garden I see flashes from arc lights, grotesque shadows flicked up in the trees, and sometimes a glimpse of part of a slow-moving, mysteriously functional metal juggernaut, inching through the dark with its antennae out, like a deep sea submersible. The sensation of alien but purposeful activity is eerily comforting.

Most nights though it's just me here, and purposeful activity has to be imagined. When I do get to bed I toss and turn in the heat. Lately I've been dreaming I can't go to sleep. Sometimes it wakes me up.

It's August, the time of year journalists call the Silly Season, because there is so little important news to report. The nine to five world has slowed down, or else gone to Lanzarote. Politics, the law, intractable Europolicy debates, and certain intercity train services have ground to a halt; movers and shakers lie prone on beaches; celebrities have evaporated; wars are unofficially suspended; serial stranglers are taking a breather.

This is the time when newspapers, desperate for material, raid editorial spikes and resuscitate stories that were rejected the first time round. Consequently the Silly Season editions are a lot more interesting than normal. For example, in Brightlingsea, Essex, mother of two Noleen Barthurst has been abandoned by her husband after a ghost wearing jackboots scratched 'Warren Leave Noleen' on the bedhead. In Germany farm crops are being ravaged by unprecedented numbers of wild boar (the only effective deterrent found so far, says a farmer, is the amplified music of Jennifer Lopez). In Ripley they've developed an extended shelf-life bagel. There's a spate of frenzied wife-swapping in Lincolnshire and Maningtree has an aardvark reportedly able to troat to the tune of Handel's 'Hence Iris Hence Away'.

The irony of my situation in these news dog days, when eager, ambitious journalists sit twiddling their thumbs at their Fleet Street desks, praying for riots, is that I, the slowest and least motivated writer in the land, who has in addition a house-full of sighing builders and neglected children to contend with, am working round the clock. And because everyone, apart from burglars and the insane, goes to Lanzarote at this time of year, there's no one around to read it either. I need a break.

At last Friday evening comes, and I have no more deadlines until 7.30 Monday morning, so we are going to dinner at Peter and Candice's in Brixton. The prospect has lightened our mood, but when we get to their house the atmosphere turns out to be gloomier than an episode of *EastEnders*. They are so absorbed in their intractable relationship problems that they barely notice we've arrived. There is nobody else there to talk to, apart from Rocket, who is refusing to go to bed and is shuffling miserably between Peter and Candice in turn, seeking a solution to his overwhelming tiredness problem that doesn't involve going to sleep. It's making us all weary.

Peter is tense and distracted, Candice is tightly humourless, the food is foul. The food is foul because neither of them has bothered to work out what might be nice to eat and neither of them has bothered to taste it while it was being made. And they still aren't tasting it – obviously – because they keep putting the stuff into their mouths. They don't know what it is they're eating and they don't care.

Whatever it is – and I think it might be chicken breast (or muscle) – it must have needed three men in the slaughterhouse to hold it down. It's hard, white and chew-resistant, and tastes of boiled down balloons. It's so tough the broccoli has wilted. It has the mass and texture of something you might use to put under the wheel of a van to stop it rolling down a hill.

'Mmmm,' says Martha, 'what's this?'

'Chicken,' says Candice.

'Yes?'

'And sauce.'

I take solace in wine. The conversation is morose and tentative. Rocket starts whining and Candice gives him a plate of chicken off-cuts. He is extravagantly sick.

Exhausted now, he may be persuaded to sleep on the kitchen couch. Peter points a whisky bottle at me and I follow him into the living room. Martha watches us go, enviously.

Peter fills two glasses, flicks through his old records and pulls out an album by the Holy Modal Rounders. He is wilfully choosing music that is incompatible with Candice's ears. This is blatant anti-woman music from some anarchic American backwater where you are not allowed to play an instrument which doesn't squeak or rasp, or sing in a way that isn't a whine or a croak, and there is a house rule banning rehearsals. I notice he has lined up Pere Ubu's *Datapanik in the Year Zero* for later, and, representing the world of experimental jazz, *Sounds Like Bromley,* by Billy Jenkins' Voice of God Collective. The only thing women fear more than experimental jazz is cellulite.

As the Rounders rattle into 'Euphoria' – 'I put my hat on my head/My feet on the ground/I'm going in town/I'm gonna mess around/I'm gonna drink that gin/Getting outa hand/I'm a red hot daddy in the Promised Land' – we settle ourselves on the sofa of despair and sink into its whisky-flavoured depths, buffered from the real world in the kitchen next door by our noise. I ask him how things stand between him and Candice.

'Very bad,' he says.

Candice is having an affair, or a past affair has been revealed, I'm not sure which – he doesn't want to do more than hint at it. Anyway, I sense this bothers him less than the knowledge that Candice is slipping through his fingers. His marriage is crumbling about him and there is nothing he can do about it. He's a rabbit caught in the headlights, unable to move a muscle. I suggest this or that, but he is without hope – clueless. He is a rabbit – albeit an unusually witty and erudite rabbit – which in an uncharacteristically assertive moment persuaded an eagle to marry it.

'Are you rowing?'

'No, not at all. It's much worse than that. It's creepy. I can't make her row any more – I can't even do that. She keeps giving me talks: "as I see it" talks. She wants us to talk about the relationship all the time, wants us to be adult about it, face up to "new realities" and recognise why we have "changed". The underlying assumption is that it's not working.

'She says she's trying to be fair. Ironically I think she is. In her way she's trying to be nice to me. She's trying to explain something ghastly. She's made up her mind it's over, but can't quite bring herself to say it. She wants it to come out of our "discussions" – a sort of consensus we arrive at maturely, then shake hands and go our separate ways.'

'What do you say?'

'I've got nothing to say, except "Let's not do this". She's the one with something to say; I know what it is and I don't want to hear it. I'm not co-operating and so I have to listen to all her psychobabble. She keeps talking about the need for "closure".'

'Isn't that what the families of murder victims get when the killer's executed?'

'Exactly! It's like listening to some sort of death counsellor. It's as though I'm dead and neither of us will get any release until I'm properly buried. Closure for God's sake!'

'She should come and talk to Bert.'

'You know we have quite a nice life. We don't have an awful lot in material terms but we've got the boys and they're great; they're the best thing in the world. There's no reason for us to be as unhappy as she claims we are. She's talking us to death. I feel like I'm in the interrogation room at Colditz and if I let my concentration slip for a second, the wrong information will come out and it will all be over. It's all crap. I haven't got time for all this: I'll be 50 next year.'

He refills our glasses, sighs, hums vacantly along to a couple of bars of the Rounders' 'That Belly I Idolize', examines the back of his hand intently, sighs again, then says: 'When someone's talking to you face to face – you know, intently – which eye do you look at?'

By the time we leave, Martha and I are both grim. Two-and-a-half hours talking to Candice while Peter and I were sealed inside our cocoon of horrid music has made her brittle. At least I am warmed by the whisky. She drives.

'She's leaving him,' I say.

'I know.'

'She's being horrible to him.'

'I know. But he's hopeless.'

'He's not entirely hopeless.'

'He is hopeless. He should get up off his backside and fight back: sort it out. He is *entirely* hopeless.'

'You shouldn't say that.'

'Why?'

'Because it doesn't help.'

'But that's what he has to face up to. He's got to stop being hopeless and start earning some money.'

'He's been going to auditions.'

'But he can't act.'

'No. But he's trying.'

'He should give it up for a bad lot and find something else; work as a barman – anything's better than this *nothing*.'

'Maybe it's our fault he's like he is.'

'How could it be our fault?'

'Because we're always saying he's hopeless. Everybody says he's hopeless. We've typecast him.'

'That's probably the closest he'll ever get to the actor's experience.'

'Don't you think if we all stopped saying he was hopeless, maybe he'd stop being hopeless?'

'Don't be ridiculous. Maybe if he stopped reading the paper all day and spent his time sorting things out instead.'

'He's not a sorting out sort of person.'

'That's ridiculous.'

'He's incapable of it: just like you're incapable of playing the ... zither.' She tuts with exasperation. 'You're branding him just like Candice brands him. The fact is, she doesn't understand him. She doesn't even know him. She sees only the things he's bad at – homemaking, wage earning ... being glamorous. Admittedly he's bad at some major things, but she doesn't see one per cent of all the things he is good at. She can't see them.'

'What is he good at?'

'Well, being witty and clever and cynical, er idiosyncratic, and ... gloomy, and liking appalling music ...'

'It's no good. He has to sort his life out. There's too much at stake.'

'You're wrong. He can't. He's Peter Rabbit.'

'What?'

'He's Peter Rabbit and Candice is Mr McGregor, the eagle.'

'You're drunk.'

'I think you'll find I'm correct.'

We're both tetchy now. And hungry. We talk about buying chips, but neither of us has any cash.

When we get home the world falls apart. Martha wants to get into the dining room to find something to eat but once again the door pliers have disappeared from the place they are supposed to be.

'I just *wish* you'd sort this out,' she says.

'*You* sort it out!' I'm already halfway up the stairs. I have in mind a twenty-minute soak in a hot bath, but the bath I cleaned out before we left this evening has been refilled with fresh dirty crockery by Lowell and Europa. The flannel is covered with spaghetti hoops.

I know I am losing my temper because I have that exhilarating release from convention that indulging anger momentarily delivers. I grab a handful of dirty crockery from the bath and I take the stairs two at a time. I push into Lowell's room and crash the plates down on his bed. I am shouting all sorts of stuff: 'Here's your washing up! Why should I do it! You live like a pig!' There's no chance of his waking up, I know that. I can see Europa's eyes peeping out next to him, and I know she is doing that funny little half smile beneath the bedclothes.

Immediately I regret it. I know I will have to apologise. This isn't the right time (it's 2.30 a.m.) or the right moment to ball Lowell out. And whatever he did wrong tonight, it's no worse than many things he has done in the past which I never bothered to punish. More significantly, Lowell has been a much more considerate son in recent months. He no longer turns his music up to full volume when he leaves his room at the top of the house, so he can hear it while making toast in the kitchen. He's changing fast. He has turned himself round by his own efforts. He is caring, funny and capable. He has coped admirably with the peculiar upbringing that was lumped on him. He had a tough time of it, and it was my fault he was put in that position. And he has never blamed me for that. He has transcended it. I am proud of him.

His eyes open.

Another thing has changed apparently: he wakes up now when you shout at him.

'Dad,' he says. 'You need a break.'

Chapter 35 DOORKNOBS

'I think we need a break from each other,' Martha says.

It's exactly what I've been thinking, but I hate to hear her say it. We were going to spend this Saturday and Sunday morning at her father's, but instead I drop Martha and the kids off at his house in Salisbury and head off by myself.

So, unexpectedly, just after midday, I am alone, heading nowhere at 90 mph, with the roof open and rowdy, lid-banging Texan polka music roaring out of the stereo. I am playing Brave Combo, not just for fun, but to demonstrate spiritual solidarity with Peter, whose discovery they were. Peter saw a Brave Combo CD transform a friend's father's wake into an ecstatic lurching barn dance. The magic is not lost on me, for I am singing at the top of my voice: 'Who stole the kish-ka!? Who stole the kish-ka!? Who stole the kish-ka!? *Someone call the cops!*' Out the way, Norbert Dentressangle!

I made sure before setting out from Streatham, as Lowell and Europa are also away for the weekend, to fix the Staywell draughtproof cat-flap in the open position with a piece of string, in the small hope that if left in this inviting mode, Simpson might just find it in her heart (and if, in fact, cats do have hearts), to use it. I also sprinkled pepper on the few pansies in my garden to have escaped Bert the builder's attentions, in order to stop Jack lying on them. It is a curious fact that though Jack and Bert may at first glance look very different from each other, they have much in common. Apart from crushing pansies, neither of them, to my knowledge, has ever built anything. This puts them, in evolutionary terms, at roughly the same level. When Jack and Bert die they could find themselves sharing a bunk allocation in the Afterlife, and they will shake hands in a puzzled way.

I'm not sure where I got the pepper tip, but I think it was from *The Plain Truth*, an American evangelical magazine which is delivered occasionally to my door, and which holds the answers to most of life's burning questions, such as 'Why doesn't God do something?' and 'What is Scandinavia?' I'm waiting for it to tackle the what if? of a dinosaur coming along and biting a man who is walking down a street. If it can keep Jack off the pansies it must know that.

Nowhere, Gloucestershire – that's where I am. I turn off the main road and come to a stop in the soft green countryside. I don't know where exactly, but I don't care, and there's a little bed and breakfast here with a golden green garden that fits my need exactly: The Habanero. I don't know why it's called that and I resist the temptation to ask, because I suspect the mystery might have more value than the answer. Twenty-seven years in journalism have given me a nose for stories which are better for not having any questions asked.

I have brought along my book, *The Underground Empire: Where Crime and Governments Embrace*, by James Mills, which has been eyeing me resentfully from the bedside table all year. It is my intention to spend the rest of the day indulging the hedonism of reading, and I do just that, sinking into a canvas chair in the sunny garden. Every hour or so I go to the house to order another pot of tea, because tea is one of the best things in the world, better if it is made by someone else, better still if served in white China. In the gently suspended animation of a summer afternoon, tea is a libation to tranquillity, as essential to this mood of becalmed euphoria as Brave Combo was to the excitement of the morning flight.

The book is heady stuff. I'd like to know how Alberto Sicilia-Falcon deals with cats. I suppose anyone clever enough to control one of the world's largest narcotics empires would have cracked the cat-flap problem long ago. According to the author James Mills, Sicilia-Falcon shot people who didn't obey house rules. No one dared muck about with his pansies.

When the cops finally came to arrest Sicilia-Falcon, he wrote six zeros on a cheque and handed it to Mexican detective Florentino

Ventura-Gutiérrez with the words: 'Put any number you like in front of the zeros and get the hell out of here.'

Gloucestershire has no underground at all, which makes it the perfect place to escape the crime and grime of South London. In Gloucestershire there are just flowers and birds and sunshine, and a gradual realisation that your urban trousers are making you hot and irritable. This is what causes me to walk three miles to the nearest town, Wotton-under-Edge, on Sunday, to buy a pair of shorts. On the way I pass just one person, an old lady wearing the kind of floppy brimmed white hat that is exclusive to old ladies and real ale enthusiasts.

She has just struggled up the scarp of the Cotswolds at a painfully slow pace, and she seems to me, with my city cynicism, brittle and entirely vulnerable. She hails me as I come close, fully confident that I will stand and pass the time of day with her. Despite being short of breath, her conversation is vigorous and cheerful: 'How lovely to see another hiker!'

Life in Wotton-under-Edge, she tells me, is rather dull. One has to get out for excitement to places like Bristol, where she has seen reflector strips tied to the tails of police horses. 'Fancy that!'

I tell her how hot I am. Ah, she says. There is only one thing to do really, and that's to visit a local cheese farm. On such a day, to walk through a sort of refrigerated cave lined with great wheels of fragrantly exhaling Cheddar, breathing in lungfuls of pure cholesterol, is simply wonderful. 'That's where all the cool dudes go,' she says, and winks.

She tells me she relies on television for outside news, and was amused to see that pop socks, which she uses for tying up her tomatoes, are once again in fashion. She was interested to note an item explaining why cats get stuck up trees: their nails point the wrong way for the descent. And yesterday she described to someone the colour of some clothes she had seen in a television advert and then felt a real Charlie when she got home because she remembered her television set was black and white.

'Oh well,' she says, 'these are the lighter things of life ... I must get going now. I thank God I still can. One must never stop: that really would be the end.'

She is gone, heading indefatigably Eastward. I sweat on down the scarp to Wotton-under-Edge in time to see the few shops which open at all on a Sunday, close for lunch. The town is like an oven: a closed oven. Every shop door is locked, but the pavement displays have been left out to tempt absent criminals. The place is dead. There are no down-and-outs, drunks, beggars, prostitutes, squeegee men or international narcotics criminals. And not a pair of shorts in sight. I can't even find a policeman to bribe: 'Put any number you like in front of the zeros constable and get me a pair of shorts.'

This afternoon it's the cheese farm for me.

I'm still overdressed when I pick up my family on Sunday afternoon, on the way back from Gloucestershire, but I'm significantly refreshed for all that. I'm ready to tackle Bert first thing in the morning with fresh vigour and resolve. The house looks exhausted, the pansies are all slain. Now when Jack pays his regular 5 a.m. visit to my bed and lays across my face purring like a taxi, he smells of pepper.

'Bert, do you think you could make those doorknobs a priority now? Martha's getting anxious...'

'Doorknobs?' He looks furtive.

'The doorknobs on the downstairs doors.'

'There aren't any doorknobs on the downstairs doors. Bloody nuisance.'

'That's just it – you were going to put them on.'

'Me? That's the sort of job you could be doing'

'That may be so, but you said you'd do it. For free. You said you might have some retaining bolts to fit them in your garage.'

'Oh is that so?'

'Yes that is so. You said it would only take you a moment.'

'Nah,' he says, shaking his head. 'Don't remember that.'

But I have the Chinese takeaway menu estimate ready in my pocket and I pull it out and point to the Ho Fun section. 'See here, it says "doorknobs". Quite clearly.'

He examines it laboriously, squinting like an ancient mariner. 'That doesn't say "doorknobs".'

'Yes it does, right there next to "felting the roof".'

'That doesn't say "felting the roof".'

'What does it say then?'

He holds the menu up to the light in his big grey fingers and stares hard at the word 'doorknobs'. 'I don't know what it does say now but I do know what it doesn't say, and I distinctly don't remember it saying anything about doorknobs.'

'And what doesn't "felting the roof" say?' I realise my voice has gone up an octave, which is not good practice when arguing with builders. Nevertheless I seem to have wrongfooted him. He probably forgot about the Chinese menu.

'Look, I don't want us to fall out over this, yeah? But I know I'd never say doorknobs; it's just not a job for a builder see? Is it Frankie? But if I *were* to have said it – if I were to have said doorknobs – in the heat of the moment like – and let's just say for your sake that it might just be that I did, well then I might be prepared to make an exception.'

'Which is?'

'Ah, but it's not that easy. You see, the way this job's going now, all that's come up with the floor and the walls and all – and there's the brickwork coming in too, don't forget – well I just don't know ...'

'So what are you saying?'

'Look, doorknobs isn't a builder's job. This is a job for someone else. But the last thing I want to do is let you down; so what do you say I do it for a drink?'

'You said you'd do it for nothing.'

'Ah yeah, but that was before and, well, you see the problem here. We got the floor, we got the walls ... If you want the job finished ...'

'How much is a drink?'

'Fifty quid?'

'What's that you're drinking? 1925 Chateau D'Yquem?'

But I agree to pay him £50, and feel instantly wretched.

'Well, that's all satisfactory then. I'll get Des to take a look at your doorknobs.'

The next day while Bert and Frankie are out at lunch, Des comes up from the cellar and goes off 'for an early one'. I never see him again.

Chapter 36 **FLEA**

Clive and Sam and their two kids return to their Dulwich mansion from a few days in France to find it buzzing with giant fleas. Their new Swedish au pair, Rut, reports for duty at the same moment. Clive rings me.

'The joint's jumping,' he says. 'It's like a Lindy hop.'

'Surely you don't get fleas in Dulwich?'

'Not your common or garden flea. These are the size of Chinook helicopters.'

'Everything's bigger and better in Dulwich.'

'You've never seen anything like this.'

'Perhaps that's where the name comes from: "*Dull-Itch*".'

'Look, you've got to help us. The kids are like livebait and Sam's gone frantic. We have to decamp.'

'Can't you just get the pest control people in?'

'We have, but these mothers really are big. They say they're going to have to use a stronger than usual pesticide – specially imported from Iraq, I believe. They're advising us to evacuate the house for a few days.'

'Well, you can't come here, we've got builders.'

'I'm sure whatever you've got there is luxury compared to this. Put the kettle on, we're on our way.'

I go down to tell Martha. 'Clive and Sam are coming over.'

'What? Now? Where are their kids?'

'They're coming too. And their new au pair. They've got fleas and they're coming to stay for a few days.'

'No they're not. That's ridiculous! How can they? Well I suppose the children can all move into one room. They'll just have to make do with the children's beds. Have they eaten?'

Martha's not a free spirit, not impetuous. She's conservative by nature. Her first reaction to an alarming development is to be appalled, usually in a manner that suggests she is being profoundly insulted. Yet her outlook is positive and her manner flexible, and almost immediately, when under pressure, she'll seek the merits of a situation and adapt to it. I admire that in her. I love it. Already she's plotting how to sleep and feed 11 people.

Clive and Sam arrive as though expecting a hearty welcome. Their new au pair, Rut, is as tall and skinny as a Tertial floor lamp, and as shiny. Her dark hair is cut in a precise sphere and has a doll-like satin sheen. She's dressed in bright red plastic shoes, drainpipe trousers of startling orange and a crocus yellow top. I ask Europa to take her upstairs and burrow out a longish space for her in her old room. I ask Clive if he got her from IKEA.

'Yes, she's a flat-pack au pair. Folds up like a deckchair. I assembled her myself. My God, what is going on here? Your house is a tip!'

Clive has an ability, no matter what he is told, not to know anything about anything that is going on in anybody else's life. 'You having some work done?' He can instantly spot that something is different though, when he brings his super powers of perception into play.

'Yes we have builders in. That's why our children have been coming over to your house so many afternoons. It also explains why we've been talking about builders so much lately.'

Clive's blinkered world view is to do with his gargantuan self-belief. Like all my male friends, Clive lives inside his own head, though unlike Peter and Howard, he holds most of what is not in it in contempt. He has no appetite at all for the prosaic. It doesn't exist for him. Bus services, school timetables, shopping requirements, local government regulations, aromatherapy practitioners – in fact most of the activity of the majority of the population – exist on a level that is beneath his attention. He is a man of high ideas, epic notions, firmament-vaulting concepts. He will talk elegantly and enthusiastically about politics, science, business, morality, art or philosophy (while never missing an opportunity to point out his own significant role in the larger picture), but he doesn't have a clue what his daughter might want for her birthday, or what time his son goes to bed. He is in love with his own erudition and he has no compunction in criticising the less mentally agile for not keeping up. He is famous for having once said, with utter scorn: 'Surely everybody knows there are eight types of gluon?'

But he has redeeming qualities, one of which is that he is never less than interesting. A lot of what he says is untrustworthy, particularly when he is talking about his own exploits, though it has happened more than once that a claim he has made about himself in the past, which most have dismissed as being outrageously unconvincing, has subsequently turned out to be true. Most of the time you can't be certain where fantasy and reality meet in his stories; neither can you pin him down on it.

None of us, not even Sam, is sure what it is exactly that he does for a living. He has fingers in many pies, all of which he hints at; none of which he explains. He is a charming and slippery fish and he won't be caught. When cornered he will change the subject and flit away again in a giddy new direction, flirt outrageously, or, if he senses that the net is about to fall, burst into laughter, as though the whole thing had been a joke all along. Often it is a joke. He likes nothing better than to see how far an absurd theory can be built up before its logic can no longer support it, at which point he too collapses with mirth. He is a *bombastio furioso*. His attention is drawn to the grandiose, but also to the gaudy; he can't resist melodrama; he is always up for intellectual adventure, however dubious the premise.

Clive thinks of himself as a pragmatic empiricist, but actually he is a romantic, in love with any exotically apparelled idea that bats an eyelash at him, unable to resist the temptation to pursue it quixotically wherever it leads, until that is, he sees another more attractive idea going the other way.

He can of course be tremendously irritating. Martha treats him like a naughty boy and scolds him. Sam, with whom he has nothing in common, apart from a family and a successful working relationship, laughs in his face, spends his money and only rarely explodes in fury at him.

Clive is unimpressed with the way I have handled Bert. He's appalled I have given him an extra £50 to do something he'd already agreed to do. He's shocked that the work is going so slowly. 'How come you've put up with it so long? Why haven't you put your foot down?'

'Oh ... I don't like putting my foot down.'

'Why ever not?'

'I'm just not a putting the foot down sort of person. If I put my foot down, I wouldn't be me, I'd be you, and I'd hate that to happen.'

It's getting late now and we are all squeezed around a table in the cluttered dining room, drinking wine. The four children have, with difficulty, been packed off to bed. I'm exhausted, but the company is convivial. I'm socially deprived, so it's great to have guests, however awkward and argumentative they may be.

'You've got to either force Bert to fulfil his part of the contract, or else cut your losses and get rid of him. You can't faff about. You're indecisive – that's your problem.'

'I know I'm indecisive.'

'So change.'

'Why? It's not an accident I'm like this, you know. I chose to be indecisive after a great deal of agonising. It seemed to me that people who know exactly what to do are often wrong.'

'Pah!'

'Like you for instance.'

'When have I ever been wrong?'

'Well, when we were on holiday together in Portugal. You were very wrong. We couldn't get the water heater to work in the house, and you said there must be a fault in the electricity substation, which was ten feet up a pole in the garden. It was covered with skull and crossbones symbols. And you found a ladder and a screwdriver and climbed up, and told me not to hold the bottom of the ladder – "just in case", you said.'

'That was for effect. I knew exactly what I was doing.'

'Well, you didn't because then the maid came along and showed us the water heater switch, which we'd overlooked. Anyway ... I almost feel sorry for them.'

'Who?'

'The builders. You may find this scary, but I do sometimes find myself feeling sorry for them.'

'That is scary!'

'They're desolate, and vanquished by their own desolation. They're scared to build, just as I am scared to write. They're scared to put brick on brick because it's the hardest work, and because as soon as they raise their artifice above the level of the plain it attracts criticism.'

'Oh spare me!' says Clive. 'The fleas would have been better than this!'

'Look, I was making a philosophical observation. You're not meant to take it too literally. I wouldn't have trusted you with it if I'd thought you were all going to damn me for it.'

'I didn't damn you,' says Sam.

'You're mad, all the same,' says Clive.

Actually Clive wouldn't know a madman if one came up and bit him. Clive thinks madmen are people who sit at home all day unable to make up their minds about whether or not they should write a book. I think madmen are people who wake in the middle of the night to dabble on the Japanese stock market, are hung up about whether they earn less than the man next door and are so driven they can't sit still for a second and get ulcers. We look at each other's worlds and see plenty of madmen.

Martha is nodding her head slowly, damningly. 'You *are* mad,' she says. The words sting me.

'Well, maybe *you* should deal with slippery Bert from now on, Martha. Ah, but you can't, because you're at work. Well I work too – very hard at the moment, and I have no choice. Maybe next time Bert calls up the stairs asking for £500 and needing me to fetch something from the builder's yard because his van's down again – and by the way, could I tell him the positions I want the radiators in, and did I realise the guttering needs replacing? – maybe he could pop in to see you at work instead – "She's in an important meeting, but just walk right in, she'll stop whatever she's doing and deal with all your requirements in a clear-headed, but firm manner" – and I'll send the kids along to shout in the background, and Europa with something she doesn't know how to deal with, and we'll get you a private line too, so you can talk to the Barclaycard sales force and all the utility and phone companies whose codes of conduct don't allow them to ring people at work because it's so intrusive ... Sure it's hard coming home after a working day to a wrecked house, but I'm in the wrecked house 24 hours. And I'm trying to work too. Give me some credit!'

Clive looks pained: 'Look, I wasn't suggesting ...'

'Ah Clive, why don't you break off from taking over the world one day and come and sort Bert out. Come on your busiest day. Your contribution would be more than welcome.'

We study our food for a while.

Then Clive coughs. 'Talking of Portugal,' he says, 'what are your holiday plans this year? Sam and I have been looking at brochures of fantastic villas in Mallorca. We were thinking of trying to get a last-minute booking for a couple of weeks. Why don't you and Martha and the kids join us? The two families together again? We should definitely do it this year, while we can. God knows how much longer the girls are going to want to come on holiday with us.'

I haven't considered that, and though it pains me to admit it, Clive's got a point.

Chapter 37 FINISHED

Bert has started disappearing for longer and longer chunks of each day, popping out on ill-defined errands or all-day breakfasts, leaving Frankie working obsessively on something obscure and desperate – God knows what – humming a tune that no-one is calling.

Frankie looks bleak. Without Bert he's lost. He's in Bert's thrall. He's a hanger on with a serious toilet-paper habit. Yes, I know he's the culprit now, because on the days when Europa takes the children over to Sam and Clive's for the afternoon and there are just the two of us in the house, the toilet bowl continues to fill up with paper. Not only is Frankie against the flowers, he's out to destroy the trees too. Already I'm missing Des. He did at least finish something; he did at least lay the cellar floor.

When I corner Frankie and question him about Bert's absence and the building plan, he mumbles, runs out of words, then looks as though he is going to cry. Two days go by with no sign of Bert. Frankie is ... tinkering with bricks by the back door. But then:

'I say? Hullo!'

It's the call of the builder carrying up the stairs! Bert is back! I am almost pleased to see him. God willing, he is here to complete the work!

'I say! Hullo! Ah there you are. We need another £700 in cash now – to finish the job.'

'*Another* £700? We started going over the estimate price two weeks ago, when we had to get the extra skip.'

'Ah, but there's been other extras.'

'What other extras?'

'Like, ah, like the skip see, and the extra cement.'

'The skip was only £100. And I paid for the extra cement.'

'Is that so? And another thing.'

Not another thing. *Please don't let there be another thing.*

'There's a little snag on the plastering.'

'What snag?'

'You see, Pete my plasterer can't come after all because he's in Lanzarote. So I've got Paul to come instead.'

'Well, that should be OK ...'

'And of course he'll be an extra £500.'

'An extra £500? Why?'

'Well, Pete was cheap see and Paul is ... not so cheap ... But he's good, Paul. Very good.'

'Does that mean Pete was bad?'

'No no. Pete bad? No. Pete's the dog's bollocks. But Paul's ...'

He scans his vocabulary for a superior metaphor. Defeated, he changes tack. 'Heh Frankie?'

'Huh?'

'Paul, yeah? If you got Paul see, all this here ...' Bert shuffles round in the rubble, patting the blasted walls, 'all this would be finished. And all this (pat pat) too. You'd have a finished job here – *if* we got Paul in. He'd do up there and along there. It would be so finished. A finished job. *Fin-ished.*'

'Yes I understand what you're saying, but if Paul's going to cost an extra £500, and as you've still got lots of stuff to do, we might as well wait for Pete to come back from Lanzarote.'

'No no. You see, by the time Pete came back he'd cost £500 extra too.'

'Why?'

'Extras. All those extras: the skip, the extra cement ...'

And so we go round in circles. I bring up the subject of the roof repair and the upstairs bathroom floor, neither of which he has started yet. I have the Chinese menu in my hand again. My trump card.

'We did the cellar,' says Bert.

'Yes, Des did a good job there, but see here on your list, it says: "Felting the roof, bathroom flooring."'

'No no no.' He takes it from me. '"Felting the roof, weather permitting." You've read it wrong.'

I look at the smudged and ham-fisted pencil lines on the menu and actually, it could be saying anything. It would never be admissible in a court of law. 'You should have been a lawyer Bert,' I say. 'Bert the Barrister.' He looks at me with the smile of the uncomprehending.

A tougher mood comes over me. Something has to be done. This situation could continue for ever, with Bert and Frankie making occasional visits to demand money, then clearing off again, to return when it runs out, while me and my miserable family subsist in the dining room. I'm not putting up with it any longer. I am getting angry enough to put my foot down. The feeling is novel and not unpleasant.

I do a deal. I do give Bert more money, but I make him compromise on the amount, which I will pay him only when the job is finished, and I tell him I'll reserve the decision on the plastering. Secretly I have decided to find my own plasterer and get shot of Bert as soon as the brickwork is finished and the extra cement is dry. I don't tell him that of course. The news might break him. Frankie and he might lay down on what remains of my kitchen floor in a state of terminal builder's ennui. Then I'd have to pay for a funeral skip.

I tell Bert that from now on there will be no more trips to the builders' yard for me and that I expect faster progress from him. Also, it is very important that I be disturbed as little as possible, as I have a very important and difficult work project on.

'I hope you don't mind me asking,' says Bert, 'but what exactly is it you do for a living?'

'I write ... humorous articles.'

Unspoken comments are putting their hands up behind Bert's eyes. 'Oh is that so?'

With the imposition of my new structure on their lives, Bert and Frankie begin to look almost cheerful again. We celebrate with a cup of tea. 'By the way,' I say, 'why is Frankie building a ziggurat in the garden?'

I have noticed for the first time that Frankie, during Bert's absences, has constructed six monolithic platforms of consecutively increasing size, extending like tank traps into the heart of the herbaceous border. It dawns on me that these are my new kitchen steps.

I am still feeling tough. I asked for kitchen steps, I say, not a podium for a Nuremberg rally. I am not likely to want to address the masses of Streatham from my kitchen door, even if I could get them to come. Frankie gives a terrible sigh and taking a great sledgehammer, smashes the edifice to rubble.

This is probably a mistake on my part. The steps constituted the only structure that Bert and Frankie have succeeded in building so far, and a substantial one at that. If the worst had come to the worst (this house being in the state it is), they could have supported a family of six, sleeping in parallel rows.

A snake is eating a bird's egg four times larger than its head. It's like watching a human swallow a chair. It's a videotape of a children's programme. Mungo, Weeny and I are doing research in the study this morning, with packets of crisps and orange squash. The phone rings.

'Hello Peter. What are you up to?'

'I'm painting the hall.'

'What colour?'

'Midsummer Night's Cream.'

'No!'

'Yes. That's its name.'

'Have you tried The Beige of Reason?'

Pause.

'Candice has told me to get out.'

'No? For good?'

'She says it's the end.'

'Is it?'

'I think it might be. I don't know. ... The Far Vermilions.'

'Yes! How do you feel about it?'

'There's not much I can do about it really. But we're rowing again – with a vengeance.'

'That's good ... Is it?'

'... Mischief Black.'

'Ah! Hotel White.'

'She said she couldn't stand me moping around any more and that I must go. Today.'

'You mustn't go if you don't want to.'

'I have to. There's no life for me here any more. There's no warmth. It's ... The Lime Of Your Life.'

'Old Yeller.'

'Graham Greene.'

'... Elizbeth Barrett Browning.'

'Rouge Elephant!'

Pause.

'How do you feel about her?'

'I know this sounds crazy to you; I still love her.'

'Yet you're going to leave her – just like that?'

'I suppose so.'

'Why are you painting the hall?'

'She'll never love me. I know that. She's too wrapped up in her ... you know, plans – whatever they are. I'm going to be 50 next year. I know: Elegy Gray ... Er, War and Puce.'

'I suppose it's hard for a woman to love a man who spends his afternoons reciting literary paint blends.'

'Yes! I suppose.'

'What about the kids?'

'They'll stay here for now. I just have to hope she doesn't take it in her head to go back to Australia.'

'And where are you going to go?'

'I thought I'd come and stay with you. I'll come over when I've finished this.'

'You can't ... you can't just leave ... Peter, why are you painting the hall?'

'I want to do something for her before I leave. Krapp's Last Taupe.'

Knowing I am going to sack him before the job is finished, I can no longer look Bert in the eye. Now *I* am Mr Shifty with the open, trustworthy face. It has to be said that since we had our talk, the kitchen does seem to be moving forward. The ceiling and support joist has been clad in plasterboard and the new brickwork is taking shape. Whatever Bert does now though, even if he were to build a silver gazebo overlooking the fishpond by way of compensation, he will never redeem himself in my eyes. He's been Bobbing me about for too long. He was removed from the *Useful* category in my mental filing cabinet long ago, and re-filed in *Tossers*, with a cross reference to *Odious*. If by some incredible stroke of fortune, Florentino Ventura-Gutiérrez's gun were to go off in Streatham today, and Bert were to eat it, I wouldn't shed many tears.

The singing has revived too, and though I should probably regard this tedious ululation as a clarion of good omen, it now bears a tone of menace. This is because of a disturbing nightmare I had the night before last, in which multiple grinning Berts, dressed in cowboy hats and strumming plywood guitars, converged on me slowly, singing 'Maresydoats and doesydoats and liddlelambsydivy ...' This trite piece of wordplay (Mares eat oats/And does eat oats/And little lambs eat ivy) makes my blood run cold, for it is the one thing that is certain to pop up in my head whenever I am suffering acute pain or anxiety, repeating endlessly. It is my mental *fatal error* sequence, programmed to play whenever the system goes down, an interior version of the Muzak that takes over the TV when terrorists shoot the anchor man. Once, in hospital suffering acute peritonitis, Maresydoats and doesydoats looped through my head for days. It's a sobering enough thought, that instead of some soaring John Barry arrangement playing in the background when I die, Maresydoats and doesydoats will repeat to the bitter end; appalling to think Bert might be accompanying on guitar and vocals.

I try to arrange my working day so I don't see him. When he's in the house I barricade myself in the study and absorb myself in watching video cassettes of review programmes. I cling to my work. I live through TV. Up here in the study, despite the chaos all around me, I can pretend I am in control, entertaining Jilly Goulden, TV wine queen, with a bottle of TV wine. The wine looks good, but Jilly is glorious, in a magnificent tartan dress with ailerons; twitching intensely as she anticipates the taste, like a racehorse waiting for the off; rolling the grape across her tongue; saying 'creamy little wretch, isn't it?', without caring. It's going to be impossible to write about Jillie without bringing oral sex into it.

On my way home from a trip to the Marrakech Café one day, I spot Bert coming the other way and rather than face his gratuitous bonhomie, I duck behind a hedge. It has come to this: I am 45 years old and I am hiding in someone else's garden from Bert the builder.

But eventually, at last, I am free. I wait until Bert has completed the brickwork and levelled the floor, re-felted the flat part of the roof and made free generally with tubes of Mastic, the builder's Band Aid, and then I confront him with my *fait accomplis*. I tell him that I've made other arrangements for the plastering, that I'll fit the doorknobs myself and that I've had second thoughts about the upstairs bathroom floor after all.

'The bathroom floor isn't one of ours,' he says reflexively.

'No it's not. And neither is the plastering any more. It's over. We can call it a day; rip up the Chinese menu.'

'So are we ... is it ... finished?'

'Yes, Bert, finished. *Finished!*'

I have to restrain my joy. He looks hurt, confused, misunderstood. He is spinning in space, trowel in hand. His open, trustworthy face has crumpled into a well-would-you-believe-it rictus. He counts the last payment out slowly, note by note.

I'm not going to be kicked around by builders any more. I'm free. I will never again have to look into Bert's open and honest face. I am released from Frankie's toilet-paper habit. I buy, fit and glaze the patio doors myself. It is the last bit of DIY I will ever do in my life.

Enter Mick the plasterer, recommended by Tony: Scottish, retired, open to the odd job.

I like Mick because he isn't alliterative. He's 60, short and incomprehensible. He doesn't look me in the eye. He doesn't have an open honest face. In fact he looks treacherous. After Bert, I'm drawn to him immediately.

I can't understand what he's saying. He doesn't speak English as we know it. He speaks Plasterer's English, a language caked with aggregations of gunk, spoken through layers of render (render – that's some word to be heard coming out of the mouth of a plasterer), of great blurted words that are going off even as they hit the air, forming unsympathetic knobs and lumps as they collide with the ear. He's not a man at all. He's probably a sort of dog. A terrier of some kind, small and possibly evil.

For a long time he says nothing. He looks around the site and sniffs the walls suspiciously, like a man who can't believe what he sees. He taps the beam that's holding up the back of our house and shakes his head, tutting. A sceptical dog. Then he barks at me. 'Rharrharrhar' he says. 'Rharrharrhar,' and 'Cornercops'.

He's going to plaster the whole lot for £500 all in. I shake his plasterer's paw.

Unlike Bert, Mick fulfils his part of the bargain with sensational skill. He works by himself, like a devil, all day long. He fills up the wounds of our home, smooths our anxiety, transforms Bert's crude hackings into porcelain. He brings his own sandwiches and watches the walls while he eats – he's not going to risk them wrinkling while his back is turned. He's not a romantic like Bert and Frankie, with their song medleys and ineffable sadness. He's in for the kill. He's out to win. The enemy is gravity and you can't rest for a second, or it will bring you down.

Exactly one week after he arrives, he's finished. We still have a long way to go of course, but we have a kitchen space with a floor and walls and a back end that looks out on the garden. Mick is a man of few words and mighty deeds. I want to kiss him but I know he would probably bite me. I give him a bottle of whisky instead and he almost – perhaps I'm kidding myself – smiles. 'Rharrharrhar,' he says.

Things are looking up. In fact they look pretty damned good. Suddenly the house feels like a fresh and exciting project, and though my writing work is difficult, I've managed to survive as a TV reviewer six weeks on the trot. Furthermore, and simultaneously, I have managed to steer this house and its precious cargo through Bert's treacherous shallows, I have convincingly put my foot down, and the blue spots on Weeny's face are starting to fade. Last but not least, my dreams have returned to normal. Last night I dreamt of a naked woman blowing up a balloon.

But at 3 a.m. when the aggregate train goes by, making the house quiver like a horse scenting blood, and I wake to the sound of Martha's scent bottles shivering against each other on the dresser top, I recall, with an answering shiver, that the back of the house is now held up by Bert.

Chapter 38 CELEBRATION

The *Evening Standard* has forwarded three readers' letters. This is indescribably exciting. I force myself to make tea before allowing myself to sit down to read them. The first writer is deeply offended that I should compare a senator's hair to an omelette, the second says I am the voice of all small voiceless nations and the third, a long-term fan of the singer Cher, says I am an arsewipe of the worst kind and don't deserve to live. On balance I am pleased.

My job makes every Friday evening a little jewel. This Friday is particularly precious. Corks are popping in the kitchen, a sound it must have doubted ever hearing again. I certainly did. Clive and Sam are here, and Peter. In fact Peter is here all the time now, a lugubrious addition to the household, though fortunately his mood hasn't affected his wit, which is bitter-sharp. For all his gloom, it's good to see him unfettered by Candice's shrill pettinesses. He moved in as Clive and Sam moved out. They had been loud and demanding and the void they left is, for the moment at least, space enough to contain Peter's desolate irony. Peter's children are staying the night too and, uncontrollable as ever, are leading Mungo and Rufus on a hue and cry through our raw, echoing, plaster-pink, born-again kitchen void. 'Shuttup!' we shout, adding to it.

It's good to see them all in a relaxed setting. No – it's great to see them. I've been living like a hermit, albeit a hermit with many children. Good to see Martha relaxing too. Not counting time spent sleeping, we have barely passed an unstressed hour together. We've shouted snatches of instructions at each every morning and evening, before being yanked away again by our individual schedules, like two people on different spurs of a calypso roundabout.

Tonight I can cope with any amount of chaos. The champagne has already bewitched, and besides, my soul is at ease. This morning I sent off the last TV review I will write for two weeks, and tomorrow Martha and I, and Clive and Sam and the four kids will be in Mallorca. I am not sure exactly what the champagne is for: the cessation of work, the imminence of holiday fun, or the absence – the blessed absence – of Bert the builder. Whatever it is, it's making me deliriously happy.

'I'm not at all hungry.' Clive kicks off the dinner in his normal thoughtless way. 'I had an enormous lunch with very important clients at the Oxo Tower.' We are all so used to Clive's bluntness that nobody raises an eyebrow, not even Martha, who has spent two hours cooking our meal tonight.

'Guess what I had.' You can't stop him.

'Cow pie?' says Martha.

'Spatchcock Poussin! Anyway, tell me how the TV column is going, Martin.'

I'm touched that he is making the effort. 'Still going, which is something.'

'What do the *Standard* think? Will they give you the job?'

'They rang me once, about four weeks ago, to tell me it was along the right lines. Otherwise not a peep.'

'You'd think they'd want to talk to you all the time,' says Sam.

'Just because they're communicators doesn't mean they can talk.'

'So you've no idea if anyone likes it?'

'None at all. Though I am lucky, at the moment, to have a supportive friend in the house, who reads me a passage from Nancy Banks Smith's *Guardian* TV review every day, pointing out how brilliantly she's described the same programmes I have reviewed. As she's funniest writer in the country, that's very helpful.' Peter doesn't look contrite.

'And only today I got a letter from a reader saying I was an arsewipe of the worst kind.'

'Is there a good kind of arsewipe?' says Clive.

'There's good and bad in everything,' says Peter.

'Describe a good arse-wipe.'

'Don't,' says Sam.

'It's difficult, though quilting might be a differentiating factor. I can certainly describe the worst kind.'

'Don't.'

'All that needs to be said, is that the paper is candy pink. They don't come worse than that.'

There is general agreement here. I pretend to be offended. 'Not the candy pink! I can't be that bad.'

'Certainly not,' says Clive. 'I see you more as a lemon-yellow one-ply man.'

'A toast...!' Peter waves his glass in the air vaguely, 'to absent friends.'

'Candice?'

'Surely no one would call Candice and me friends. No, I was thinking more of Bert.'

To Bert. Long may he be not here.

We play a round of Epitaphs. Clive suggests *He put his foot down* for me, and for Peter: *He would have been 50 next year*. This makes us all feel sorry for Peter, as he'll be alone here for two weeks when we go away tomorrow. Lowell and Europa will be gone too, to Lowell's mother in Somerset. I've asked Peter to water the plant pots in the garden – that's one annual problem taken care of. I've also asked him to keep an eye on Jack. The tabby hasn't been looking himself lately. It could be the heat, but he seems less active and I think he's losing weight.

There is a long debate about who will sleep where in the villa. Sam has brought the Vintage Holidays brochure to show us our house. There is a picture of a large villa reposing in sunshine on its own verandah, by its own pool, in its own garden, in a valley of fields rolled out under the hills; remote, carefree, dreamy. Another cork pops. The world is full of promise.

Chapter 39 CONFESSION

Schoolboy dread assails me. Anna's on the phone, daughter of the man who once owned the house whose front door window I smashed last Christmas. I am found out! She will be furious/upset/vengeful! And why now of all times? – I'm just off on my holiday. It's early Saturday morning, and the car's loaded ready with all the necessary holiday equipment. I was just waiting here on the doorstep for Martha and the kids to bring out the unnecessary things, which they insist must come too.

But Anna's merely friendly. She is going through her address book, bidding goodbye to people. I probably don't know, she says, but she got married a couple of weeks ago to Peanut, a lawyer – real name Ben – and they are moving to Ottawa in a couple of weeks, where he is to take up a job with a law practice.

I tell her how happy I am she has found her Peanut and I wish her well. Then, after some light pleasantries, we lapse into awkwardness. This is the point where, in normal circumstances, I would say goodbye, but the truth is, I am having difficulty ending the conversation. It has occurred to me that this is the perfect opportunity to come clean to Anna. I have been tempted to tell her the truth many times during the last eight months, in order to exorcise the door incident, which lives on, in my mind at least. I tried to forget about it, but found I couldn't. Lying isn't the easy option that honest people often try to make it out to be. It bothers me that I lied to Anna's father, and that I allowed Anna to apologise to me so wholeheartedly, when in fact I was guilty.

I have been wondering if it would be possible to put things straight, and now, suddenly, fortuitously perhaps, here she is on the phone; furthermore, she is about to leave my life for a long time. It seems like fate is showing me a way out.

My lie was not so many shades removed from white, surely. And the sin which prompted it was not a huge one. Anyone, given similar circumstances, memory loss and alcohol consumption, might easily have done the same thing. I behaved in a silly way. Nobody got hurt. Probably Anna has forgotten about it already. Probably the only damage done, apart from to the door itself, was to my archaic sense of honour. Nevertheless, here is a unique opportunity to set the record straight.

'So that's that,' says Anna. Clearly she'd like me to get off the phone now, so she can get on and phone the rest of her friends. But I'm stuck to the handset.

'Um ...' I say.

'Yes, that's what everyone says. That's the trouble with final announcements: people think there should be something uniquely memorable to say, but they can never think of anything and what they do say always sounds banal. I've had an hour of it already this morning.'

'But I do have something important to say,' I say, amazed at my words, even as they emerge. 'Remember that incident at Christmas when someone smashed the front door glass at your former house in Kensington, and your father phoned me to ask if I'd done it?'

'Yes I do, and believe me I can never apologise enough for that.'

'Thank you. Well, it was me after all.'

It takes a moment to sink in. 'Aha,' she says. 'Good God. Yes, that *is* uniquely memorable.'

'Yes.'

Anna's response is not as positive as it at first sounds, though I don't realise that instantly. Immense relief floods me for five seconds. Then she starts to speak, carefully, deliberately. I couldn't be more surprised by what she says next if she told me my lie had grown tentacles and was terrorising the North Atlantic shipping lanes.

The fact is, my lie sparked a family argument so bitter that Anna hasn't talked to her father since. When he told her he had rung me about it she was profoundly embarrassed and it led to a series of rows.

There was a fraught investigation into the mystery. Her father suggested the culprit may have been one of her close friends; someone who might have heard her mention my name; someone bearing a grudge perhaps. The fact that an innocent man – myself – had been deliberately implicated, was despicable in his opinion. Anna resented his suspicions, for she was loyal to her friends, and besides, none of them had ever met me.

People were interrogated, accusations laid. The most likely culprit was a close college friend of Anna's called Simon, who had been enthusiastically experimenting with cocaine at the time of the incident, and couldn't be sure, when questioned, whether he had done it or not. Finally condemned by Anna, whom he secretly loved, he entered a vicious spiral of degeneration, eventually becoming an actor.

Meanwhile Anna's boyfriend at the time, an intense young man called Adam, who was given to moody reflection and the writing of poetry, perceiving something deeply suspicious about the incident, but uncertain what it was, jumped to the conclusion that she was two-timing him with Simon. Adam wouldn't be persuaded otherwise, and in what Anna admits may actually have been an excuse for a gesture of melodramatic masochism, shot himself with a revolver his mother kept in her dressing table drawer in the family home at Crouch End. He had placed the barrel of the gun in his mouth, but (whether through nerves or lack of resolve is not clear) fudged the shot, succeeding only in blowing a hole in his cheek and removing part of his upper jaw. Their relationship was not strong enough to survive the trauma, which terminated one afternoon during the hospital visiting hour, when Adam's sister accused Anna of being a 'killer whore' and threw a vase of flowers at her.

Adam's mother was subsequently charged with possessing a gun without a licence and (in what might turn out to be a lucky spin-off for national security, Anna generously concedes), due to a discovery that she was also a fund-raiser for a dubious Irish charity, is now under investigation by MI5.

By this time Anna was disorientated and distressed. Her world had been shattered. At the time of the incident she had been on the verge of taking up a junior position in her father's publishing company, but the ramifications of it all caused her to reconsider the wisdom of that, and she took a job instead in the library of a London university, which turned out to be not what she wanted at all. Her mother has never got over the family rift following what she calls 'that wretched door business', and has taken to drink.

A reckless night at a weekend party with Peanut, an old face from her university, left Anna pregnant, and when Peanut proposed marriage, he seemed to her to be offering a solution to a variety of problems. Peanut was never her first choice; in fact she had always thought him rather a bore, but he was reliable, had reasonable prospects, and was incapable of doing anything crazy. Plus the idea of starting afresh in a new country appealed to her, though she isn't at all sure about Ottawa.

'So there it is,' she says. 'Absolutely fucking marvellous.'

My family is sitting in the car, watching me balefully. I'm going to have to try to put all this behind me.

Chapter 40 HOLIDAY

Never again, we said. We were three families that first year. Peter and Candice came with us. It was a reckless idea conceived in a fog of Tesco Rioja and after-dinner bonhomie on a wistful February night. You think that by going on holiday with friends you can escape the tyranny of your family, but find yourself trapped in a larger tyranny. From the start we couldn't agree. One lot wanted Greece, one Italy and one Spain. It took three dinners to settle on France. At the fourth dinner Clive made a late bid for Iceland. I was putting on weight.

Once on holiday, I found myself remembering with nostalgia, the cosy arguments I used to have with just Martha. Consider the mathematics for a minute. Add up the irritating characteristics of any one adult with whom you have to share a bathroom, then multiply them in some sort of compound arithmetical way which is beyond me, by the number of variations of argument sets possible between six adults, and you begin to get an inkling of how myriad are the opportunities for disagreement. Now I had three wives (for the sake of argument), as well as two husbands. I had two booming daughters, four rattling sons, eight divergent opinions, 24 shoes ... no make that 48 shoes, counting spares ... no make that 66 shoes, counting the extra shoes packed by Sam – just in case – of which one, on the stair, waits to trip and kill me, 64 mosquito bites, 82 incipient traumas, 1,001 directions in which to lose children, one ping-pong bat and no tin opener as we know it. And one villa (only).

'Why,' I asked myself, as I primed the eight-seater hire vehicle with a payload of small, rattling, shoeless humans for the day's excursion to the closed folk museum, 'Why, when we have 66 shoes, am I searching for shoes?'

Now here's a good tip: never hire an eight-seater vehicle. It is a bomb waiting to go off. Share children, wives, anything, but not cars. Hire two cars; it may be the only privacy you get. We learn useful lessons all the time. Here's another one: never walk through a town with women. Even taking the kids off by yourself is preferable. A man with children will progress forward, albeit with a bit of tacking. Put a woman in the caravan and he's hobbled; two and he might as well set up his own tablecloth shop right there and then. There are quite a few *nevers* among our rules, and one important *only*: only go with people you love; they won't behave any better, but you will forgive them.

At the end of that first holiday, we said 'never again'. Then we did it again, and again. And again, though this year, of course, only with Clive and Sam. We are suckers for punishment. Noise? We love it.

The most essential requirement is a swimming pool, a necessary safety valve, even if it does jack up the rental. Fortunately for us, Clive has offered to pay two-thirds of the house cost. Generosity is one of his redeeming features (wealth is another). We hire two Hertz Fiestas – our independent escape modules, our lifesavers, even if we do always end up with the wrong children in the back.

It is only fair that Clive and Sam have first choice of bedroom, though we argue about it all the same. Predictably, they choose the vulgar master bedroom overlooking the pool. Martha and I have a smaller room on the other side. The worst thing about it is not its size, for it is romantic in a frilly sort of way, but its closeness to the field at the front, where every night just before dawn, an army of sheep, wearing bells, musters, tended by a dog with a megaphone and some gruff Spanish farmers banging clang pots and whistling through tubes. Sam, who is a light sleeper and is sometimes disturbed too, claims there are no sheep; that it is my snoring which wakes her. This is fiercely debated and never properly resolved.

'Dad,' says Mungo. 'Who invented sheep?'

We have only one major row, in Pollença old town, in whose main square, decorated with floating white ribbons, people dressed as Moors and Christians are noisily re-enacting ancient quarrels. As with most rows, I'm not entirely sure what it's about, except that it's their fault.

Whatever it is though, it does cause the eight of us to climb, for no logical reason, with the obdurate purposefulness of the peeved, up 365 steps from Pollença to a mountain shrine, in arduous festering silence, broken only by sounds of warfare below, and the piteous bleating of resentful children. Then we storm off separately in our blessed Fiestas, only to join up again later on the way home, at some idle bar, leaving open the doors of the cars, in which the boys are already asleep, to drink cervesa by the roadside like real friends do, while the girls watch geckos modelling brooches on the wall.

After four holidays together we know each other pretty well. I know for instance, never to arrange to meet Sam anywhere, because she won't be there. Perhaps she's out bulk-buying shoes. Perhaps she's in the shower still. Who knows? Not there is all I know. I am there though. Alone. I am waiting an hour and a half in the car park, feeling more alone than if I'd gone on holiday by myself.

'Never again,' I said after the first time, when I waited two hours for her in the vast, damp, sad caves of the Gouffre de Padirac, holding Amelia and Tamara's cold little hands. I had gone on ahead with the girls – 'I'll meet you in there!' – I was hopelessly over-optimistic in those days. The girls, who were then six, said: 'Is this still the holiday?'

Sam packs enough clothes to dress a small riot scene – just in case. It's a professional neurosis, though it has its value. When Clive and I discover we have both forgotten our swimming trunks, she is able to fit us out in matching striped numbers in a teeth-hurting orange and blue colour scheme, which were originally intended for a photoshoot featuring Griff Rhys Jones and Mel Smith, but rejected by them, probably on the grounds that they looked too funny. Mine are too large for me and Clive's are too small for him. There is no middle way. Together, we look like synchronised husbands on a budget.

Sam has a habit of unhooking her bikini top and lavishing her breasts on the sun. At Magaluf, where breasts are two-a-penny (sometimes three-a-penny), they wouldn't turn any heads, but in the modest context of our little patio they are an electrifying presence, and since Sam is never wrong on matters of dress, nobody dares protest. I pass many a happy hour trying not to look at them.

Clive, being an intellectual, knows seven languages, and though Spanish is not one of them, he claims it is a simple matter, given that body of knowledge, to master the basics of a new one in a couple of days. He sees no reason why, if he moves his mouth around enough, any Spaniard won't be able to understand what he is saying. But they can't. When shop assistants look blankly at him, he thinks the sensible thing is to repeat it in Russian and then Dutch.

Though he prides himself on his cultural sophistication, and often preaches to his children the importance of a balanced diet and proper nutrition, he doesn't know how to eat. He eats whatever is in the fridge at the moment of his hunger: sardine bits, cold mashed potato, jelly. He puts as much in his mouth as it will hold and swallows. He doesn't know how to defer his gratification. In the world of big business this habit is not a handicap; in fact it may give him an edge in that greed-is-good ethos, where days need to be seized and opportunities grasped the moment they present themselves, or someone else will. For us it presents a recurring problem: by the time we have rounded up all the shoes necessary for a group excursion to a restaurant, Clive is always full up with cold custard, half sausages and cheese rind, and can't even look at the menu. He dreads the menu, and when pressured by Sam, can only dart woebegone glances at it, like a misunderstood spaniel.

Waiters wait for him to order until their knees give way. Sometimes, irritatingly, he'll say 'Oh I'll have anything'. One day we order him a Hawaiian pizza and serves him right.

Occasionally, to get it over with, Clive orders something impulsively, without checking first to see if it's on the menu, or even making a rational deduction as to its feasibility; an arcane item from a menu that exists only inside his head. 'Austrian coffee!' he blurts. 'Shaved Italian ice!' When the waiter looks blank, he tries the order again in Russian.

Meals can be a strain with four children and one Clive.

Despite all this, we adults get on, even when the kids are rowing, which is most of the time, particularly in the evening when they should be in bed but aren't. Just as moths like to fly into naked flames at night, so children like to fight each other. It's one of the laws of nature.

But the adults manage, without obvious signs of boredom, to maintain an agendaless two-week discussion starting with topics like Moral Relativism, or The Agnostic's Yearning for God, moving on to Words on A Menu Which Put You Off the Food (drizzled, coulis, nestling), then Musicians with Instruments Named After Them (Adolphe Sax, John Sousa, Simon Rattle), and finally, Which Son has Got the Biggest Penis? We have the penises to hand but no ruler – thank goodness, for though I deny it hotly, Rufus, though two years younger, does appear to have an inch on Mungo, whose penis, in the lexicon of body language, is but an apostrophe.

Tamara and Amelia are passionate rivals, either fighting like cats or competing in the obsequiousness of their compliments ('Oh Tamara, what lovely arms you've got!'). They maintain a shrill background cacophony, interrupted by what at first are disturbing lacunas of silence: they have discovered underwater swimming. Tip: encourage underwater swimming.

The boys play industriously, if you could call the aimless moving of furniture industrious. They make a train out of stools, which they say is going to London. This is all they want to do. Forget the sunshine, the pool, the view: all little boys want to do on holiday is sit indoors dragging ululating furniture across a stone floor. How long before tour operators cotton on to this? Why build Aqualand? Chairland would be cheaper.

There are regular crashes. Mungo gets the blame, being older and knowing better. He is in the thrall of Rufus who, though only four, is man enough to cope with a flight of 200 steps from the beach on his strong brontosaurus legs, no problem, and has a manner which brooks no disagreement. Shame he dresses as a girl.

Rufus enjoys a licence to misbehave which Mungo, who carries the responsibility of age heavily on his shoulders, has but recently lost. As Mungo watches Rufus hurling fire irons across the living room he is filled with Nostalgia de Chaos. He can't resist joining in. When we confront him, he is obliged to pretend he hadn't. 'It wasn't me!' he protests. 'I was trying to stop him!' Nobody believes him, frankly.

One day we travel to the north coast town of Soller on the little wooden train which climbs slowly northwards out of Palma through the back streets of the city, then across the mid-island plain through hot almond groves and lemon orchards, into cool mountain tunnels smelling of cathedrals, before winding down to Soller on the other side of the island. We find a restaurant and take lunch at a garden table. Wherever possible we eat alfresco, as nature is more absorbent and doesn't echo so much. Amelia has discovered mussels, Tamara, who is squeamish, eats hardly anything; Rufus, who isn't, eats everything. 'Can I have the eyeballs?' he asks, when my grilled fish arrives.

During coffee there is a loud metallic crash, with a knock-on skitter of glass and metal across a tiled floor. Rufus and Mungo have knocked over the restaurant's cigarette machine. I take the furious manager aside.

'It wasn't my lad,' I say. 'He was trying to stop the other one.'

'Never again!' says the manager.

Despite Clive making a great play about the cigarette machine being a hazard, we leave promptly and ignominiously.

Meals with children are a tense affair at first, eaten amid dancing cutlery, on tables dotted with little mountains of sugar, during which the whole point of eating out is negated. Eventually we settle down to more civilised behaviour, but only after we have been broken in. The person to do it is Joan, owner of Ca'n Joan, a plain little café in Carreto Formosa, Puerta Pollença, full of laughing old ladies. Joan works her customers with an adroit blend of force and charm. When Clive says he won't eat anything, she tells him he's ill, pokes him in the ribs, asks him if he is a man at all, and brings him plates of unordered treats. He's a baby in her hands and so too, incredibly, is Rufus. Joan picks Rufus up casually in one arm, as though collecting a pile of dirty plates, and before he can protest, bears him off to the kitchen, where the chef must give him a magic potion, because when he comes out he can only stare at Joan with the eyes of adoration and he doesn't once trash the sugar.

We start to relax. We laugh. Clive remarks how tiresome family duties can be and yet how intensely gratifying are the moments of recompense, the special times which bring emotional belonging. Then he tells Joan in Dutch.

One evening at a monastery perched on a rock high above Felanitx, the children's effervescence is dramatically subdued by a room of votive offerings, where supplicants pin their hopes on the wall: locks of dead hair; photographs of moped crashes; smiling babies with terminal illnesses; yellowing youths in military uniforms. The children are rendered uncannily tranquil and re-emerge into the honey twilight becalmed and glorious.

As holiday euphoria takes over from the demons of the working week, things which once annoyed no longer do so. Happiness arrives when your defences are down; when you admit the unexpected, your preconceptions forgotten in a drawer somewhere with your Filofax, your clothes and a clutch of bills you meant to post at the airport – you're not sure where and you're certainly not going to look now, you're having such a good time.

You feel more real than you have since this time last year: the real you, the real them, the real us, the real nippers arguing in the real sunshine. One night of course you get too real even for yourself, when you catch yourself climbing up the side of the house at 4 a.m., whooping, with no clothes on, full of calvados and pool water, bleeding from the head from an encounter with the pool bottom. Is this the real you? You don't know. But you do know you'd better get back to the slightly less real you before you die, possibly, by the look of her, at Martha's hand.

Days pass without leaving the easy-going verandah, eating meals strung out as long as possible, their edges just about merging; lunches which last all afternoon, all night dinners, breakfasts at noon. We are in a different time zone here. On Martha's birthday we breakfast on cake and Cava, and Sam massages everyone's feet while singing 'Golden Slumbers'. Don't ask how this comes about. 'Not many people at Mummy's party,' notes Mungo.

Other days we make expeditions to Marineland or Aqua-City. We don't eschew the neon disco coconut cocktail strip. Tourist traps are easy and children adore them. We head out in the Fiestas to hunt fiestas. There's always a fiesta somewhere. We find a little smiling town with its ribbons up, fluttering. An accordion act playing in the genteel plaza is followed by a heavy metal band called The Cellophane Heirlooms. We leave at midnight and the town's still jumping. This could never happen in England.

We spend a whole evening at a nomadic hamburger stall in a deserted town. It has all we need: white-hatted chefs, chairs, tables, hanging hams, a tinny music system ... and it becomes, once we walk into its embrace feeling only slightly peckish, an end in itself, delineating its own care-free realm in fairy lights in the middle of an empty car park on the edge of town, like a carnival float adrift. We are happy.

The last night is the best. We drive to a torch-lit festival commemorating a local girl saint in the mountain village of Valdemossa, in which village children toss handfuls of sweets into the crowd from elaborately garlanded donkey carts. The children love it. I wish Weeny was here.

We are so softened up by this time we'd find gladiatorial combat charming. We hang around the village square long after the procession has ended, drinking in the warmth of the night and indulging that small grief you have at the ending of good things, reluctant to drag the sleepwalking children back to the cars.

We survive to say never again again.

Part IV

AUTUMN

Chapter 41 ITHACA

We have arrived home to find that everything has changed in subtle, possibly sinister, and not instantly comprehensible ways. The pot plants are dead, the snails have turned into slugs, Jack is grievously ill ... I half expect to find a bearded lady in our bed. I feel like Odysseus returning to Ithaca.

Peter, Lowell and Europa are all in the house, glowing with health, but outside, the potted bay, the daisy, the orange tree, the camellia ... all the pot plants have died of neglect. The garden is taken over by rude swathes of Love Lies Bleeding. I planted this from a pack of free seeds that came with a gardening magazine months ago. When we left for Mallorca we marvelled that the plants were three feet high; now they are triffids, six feet tall and advancing. Love bleeds all over everything.

Talking to Peter about plants is like trying to communicate in a foreign tongue.

'You let all the pot plants die.'

'Are they not well? I watered them once or twice. I thought it would be enough.'

'I told you in hot weather they needed doing once a day.'

'I think that's probably excessive.'

Even Bert didn't manage to kill the pot plants. Who needs enemies when you've got friends?

'And what have you done to the snails?'

'What snails?'

'That's just it. They've turned into slugs. I don't like slugs.'

There are lots of slugs in the garden. We never had slugs. On reflection, this could be my fault. I may have upset the balance of nature by tipping so many snails on to the railway embankment. These may be opportunist slugs which have spotted a window of opportunity. I don't know why but I feel this is a change for the worse.

It's not just the garden. There's no milk or bread in the kitchen. Nothing to welcome us home. And everything is grubby. I didn't expect special consideration from Lowell and Europa, who have only recently returned from Somerset themselves. In any case they are young, and dirt doesn't exist when you are young, nothing so dirty that you can't blot it out with high volume trance music and drugs. The adults point to invisible dirt on carpets, walls and furniture and say 'how can you live like this?' and the young people humour the old people as best they can. They haven't got long to live now, poor things.

I expected more from Peter though. He hasn't got the excuse of youth. He's going to be 50 next year for God's sake! Yet it is clear that Peter has been living like a tramp who breaks into someone else's house and gradually consumes everything in the fridge and freezer. Eventually, presumably, given enough time and continued isolation, he would drop dead of starvation. Already he has got down to raisins, pickled onions and cream crackers, judging by the packets open on the kitchen side. The only food left in the fridge is a tin of water chestnuts which has survived by virtue of being weird (though it looks as though it has been poked with a stick), and a large bowl half-filled with lasagne, which Martha cooked two days before we left, and which now wears a furry 14-day Satanic mantle. Everywhere are dirty plates. And newspapers – probably the only things Peter has brought in from the outside world.

Peter can't see dirt either. He can't see anything clearly. He has a grief filter over his eyes, and another of cynicism, another of self pity. Very little light penetrates. Candice is resolute about their split and he tells me divorce proceedings are imminent. They aren't talking at all now, and his only contact with her is when he collects and drops off the boys twice a week. It's like exchanging prisoners on a bridge in a John Le Carré spy movie, he says. It's as much as he can do to find his roll-ups, without worrying about whether there is milk in the fridge so his hosts can have a cup of tea when they get back from holiday.

But Martha's hurt. If it had been her left at home she would have filled the fridge up with essentials and cooked a welcome home meal. I know she will forgive Lowell for his youth, and also because he is busy organising his move in a couple of days to university in Exeter; and Europa because she is batty, and because she is going to Exeter too (we tried to dissuade her but she is insistent). But as far as Peter is concerned, Martha's affection for him has been damaged. She knows exactly what he is like. She has witnessed his behaviour for years. She expects him to turn up late, to forget birthdays and to let us down when he has said he will come to help us move a piano, but always in the past, there has been the payback of his wit. Now the wit is not enough. She's being used, overruled and ignored in her own home.

'How could he?' she keeps saying. She will never forgive him sitting in our house watching the pot plants die. 'How could he?' I stretch my own credulity devising excuses, but I know it is already decided. She won't do anything overt about it; she will continue to be polite to him, to laugh at his remarks, cook for him, help him when she can; but I know she has cast Peter adrift. Martha withdraws affection from people, and sometimes they don't even know. The thought of that makes me shiver.

Simpson is curled in the chair, manifestly unthrilled by our return, but I can't find Jack. He is in none of his places. When I do find him he is in a new place, the one place I don't want him to be. Someone has opened a drawer of the big chest in my study, and not closed it again. It's the drawer in which I keep all my press cuttings. This is where I find him. I can see he's been in there for days because the cuttings are filthy and ripped to shreds.

I can't be angry, whatever I feel about what has happened to this ephemeral evidence of my working life. Jack's not well at all. His tongue's hanging out. He looks winded. He's unresponsive and grubby-looking, he can barely walk, and when you pick him up he's thin and lumpy, like a bag of blackjacks. Peter says he's sleeping in the bidet at night, which is odd for a cat.

We have a lot to do in a short time: the children go back to school tomorrow and Martha goes to work. *I* have a lot to do. Apart from anything else, this being Sunday, I have my first TV review after the holiday to write in time for the 7.30 a.m. deadline. I haven't watched any programmes yet. But first I have to find a vet that's open. Jack's too ill to care where we're going. The vet says it looks as though his kidneys are gone, and keeps him in overnight in to run tests.

Lowell leaves to start a degree course in Media Studies at Exeter this week, so I have to organise a method of getting him and Europa down there with all his stuff and all her shopping bags. Lowell has managed to rent a house, so he's taking most of his possessions with him. It pains me not to be able to drive them down myself, help them move in, buy them a welcome meal, and make something special of it, but I have no time to spare. Fortunately Sam has given me the number of a man with a small van, recommended by the nanny of a friend. I ring the number and, thank goodness, the man is able to do it on Tuesday. He quotes me £120 for the trip.

Next I drive to Victoria Coach Station to meet our new au pair from Spain, Belen. Like Europa she's older than the norm. She's 25, a teacher. She's au pairing in order to improve her English, so she can quit her job and find work in the tourism industry. She seems friendly and is keen to chat, though as far as I can see she has no English to improve. Also, she's wearing dungarees. Mungo should be safe.

Sam has been campaigning, as Sam does, for us to get a Swede. She says our lives would improve 100 per cent if we would just take that simple step. Rut has been a revelation. She is *terrifyingly* efficient and has the children organised from dawn to dusk. Her Cordon Bleu-style cookery has raised the kids to a new level of culinary sophistication, and her English is so advanced she's even teaching Tamara words. Every morning she copies fresh instructions in a little notebook which matches her handbag. She insists on doing the children's washing and has organised a bulb planting scheme for the front lawn. Rut has taken over their household like a benevolent Waffen SS.

By the time I get a chance to open my post, everybody's in bed. I've watched a programme about squid fishermen, and a documentary set in a suburban tennis club about the English at play, something no other nation does with so little style and so many knees. I haven't begun writing yet. I have a big pile of letters, circulars mostly, and those items which you put in a pile. There is also a large cheque from the *Evening Standard*, much of which is already spent, or earmarked for home improvements, and a parcel postmarked Angoulême. Three weeks ago Bernard packed up his *Aghast!* magazines and left this dreary nation for good. He has sent us a sweet note in one-syllable English, a jar of pâté, and a jar of rilletes. It occurs to me that I never arranged for him to try a Kennedy's sausage.

There is also a letter to me from Tom Kershka, Anna's father. He says Anna has told him about my admission. Being a trusting girl, she says she was the only one who believed my story anyway. He says he knew from the start that I was guilty. No other explanation made sense. 'I didn't let on to you, of course. Why should I let you off the hook?'

So there it is. Now I am beginning to wonder how much of Anna's account I should believe. For a start it's not true that she and her father aren't talking.

Mr Kershka says he hoped I didn't mind him passing Toby on to me, the former college mate of Anna's who was looking for somewhere to stay in London recently.

Chapter 42   VOODOO

It's 9 a.m., time to say goodbye. Lowell and Europa have filled the hallway with their stuff and are making cups of tea. Despite the clutter, or perhaps because of it, the house feels emptier already.

I'm standing in the study alone, looking blankly into the garden, when a bird thuds into the window pane. A young but fully grown thrush is on the sloping roof of the ground story beneath, stunned, staring up at me, gripping the tiles, her breast pumping violently.

I assume she will recover, but when I go out into the garden a few minutes later, I find her on her back on the lawn beneath, dead. I pick her up. She is beautiful, and unblemished. She's still warm. It seems impossible she's dead.

'The van's here,' Lowell shouts from upstairs.

I go downstairs and open the door.

'We meet again!' he says.

It's Bert. He holds out his hand, but snatches it away. 'That's a dead bird!'

'You?'

'Yes, isn't that strange?' He looks at the dead bird.

'It is. Strange and ... cruel.'

He smiles at me. The old Bert smile.

'Might as well get cracking then, hey? ... Oh, look, there's a small problem ...'

'What could that be?'

'When we talked on the phone, right? Well I know a price was mentioned and all, right ...'

'We agreed a price, yes.'

'Well, you see, it was a reasonable price *at the time*, but now it's not enough.'

'You said £120. We both agreed.'

'Yes I know I *said* that, but it's Exeter, you see.'

'I know it's Exeter. I told you last night it was Exeter. £120.'

'But that was before I had a chance to look it up on the map.'

He wants £140. I give him £130.

I kiss Lowell and Europa goodbye, but now, apart from the sadness I feel because of their leaving, I am haunted by a presentiment of doom.

The vet says Jack should be put down. He's almost there anyway.

I hold Jack's head in my hand while the vet injects him. He doesn't feel the needle. His eyes look at me, and know me, and then they turn to glass.

'Do you want five minutes alone with him?' the vet says.

No, he's only a cat, I think, but I do want five minutes alone with him. I sit with him, with his head in my hand. For 13 years he's been my closest companion, in a spatial sense. I've never thought of it like that before. He followed me around the house, slept on my bed all night and sat on my desk all day. He was always there. He was easy. Such an easy friend to have; you didn't think about it. I used to curl him up in a ball and hold him on my head – 'the new Russian hat,' Peter used to call it. Once when we were drunk we laid him on his back on the polished table and played spin the cat with him. He didn't resist.

I find quiet moments to tell the children. Mungo goes quiet for a moment, then carries on. I'm worried about how Amelia will take it. They grew up together. I wait until she's sitting down in the living room.

'Jack died today,' I tell her. 'He was put down at the vet.'

She pauses for a second, then she leans forward and pats me on the knee. 'Oh well, plenty more cats in the sea,' she says.

It's so misjudged, I'm shocked, I'm appalled, briefly, but then I realise: everything in her life is misjudged at the moment, her clothes, her shoes, that strange make-up round her eyes. She's trying to find herself in there, I know that, trying to find the form that fits her mixed up old/young feelings.

About 3 p.m., I get a call from Lowell. He's in Newbury. Bert's van broke down on the motorway, two hours ago. They walked to a rescue point and Bert called the AA, but when they came they said they couldn't help because Bert wasn't a member. The AA man gave Lowell and Europa a lift to Newbury, where they are in the process of hiring a van. They need my credit card.

I sort it out with the hire company. It's expensive, but there's no choice. Then I talk to Lowell again. 'You'll be all right now?'

'Yes. Look, Dad, when I go back to get my stuff out of Bert's van, should I give him some money or something. He's stranded there. I feel sorry for him ...'

'Don't you dare!'

For a second when Lowell rang, I was horrified, but now it's sorted out, I couldn't be happier about this development. I'm delighted that Bert's out of the picture. Now Lowell can go to his new life without that albatross around his neck.

'Good luck, Lowell.'

'Bye, Dad.'

I go up to Lowell's room. Hell, it will smell better now, if I get rid of all the trainers. I see how empty it is, yet how full still of things he didn't rate worthy of taking. It's derelict.

Peter comes upstairs with the paper in his hand, to tell me that a vegetarian has died of CJD, after unwittingly licking lard off the breasts of a juju woman in a voodoo ceremony.

It's been a difficult day.

Chapter 43 SMALL

It's 2 a.m. and I'm woken up by Mungo's little figure at the bedside, crying. Something has frightened him. I hold him for a bit. 'Don't cry. No need to cry. Don't play the water trumpet.'

Half a giggle percolates through the crying. I take him to his room, put him back to bed and sit next to him, holding his hand.

'I can't go back to sleep now.'

'It doesn't matter.'

'I can't.'

'It doesn't matter whether you sleep or not. Just lie there and think. Sometimes when you try to sleep it's hard, so it's best not to try. Think of something nice instead. Have you got something nice to think?'

'I think so.'

We sit in silence for ten minutes. I don't know about him: I'm drifting off. Suddenly Mungo says: 'Some of the smallest things in the world are really very big.'

'What are you thinking about?'

'I'm thinking about the ants. Some things which are small to us are very big to them.'

Silence again. Then he says: 'We like bread, but every time we eat bread we leave a lot. To an ant one crumb is a lot.'

'It depends how you look at things; from what perspective.'

'What's that?'

'The point of view. What something looks like from where you're looking. We all look at things from different places and in different ways. Do you remember on holiday, when Rufus thought he heard a giant bee?'

'No.'

'It was early evening and he was out on the patio, alone. He heard a loud buzzing noise. Because he knows that bees buzz, he thought it must be a bee, and because it was *very* loud, he thought it must be a giant bee, and because it was coming from the direction of the pool, he thought it must be in the pool. He ran into the kitchen very excited, shouting: "Everyone come quick! There's a giant bee in the pool!"'

'I remember.'

'From his perspective there *was* a giant bee in the pool. But because he is very small, and because the house was set higher than the surrounding fields, he couldn't see over the far edge of the pool down into the field beyond. When I came out, because I'm taller, I could see that a teenage boy was riding a moped round and round the field. I told Rufus it wasn't a bee, it was a moped. This was even more exciting to him than the bee had been. He ran back into the kitchen shouting: "Everybody come quick! There's a moped in the pool!"'

Mungo laughs the condescending laugh of the maturer person, then concentrates on sucking the thumb which isn't curled in my hand.

How fabulous the world looked from Mallorca; how bright and fair and full of promise. Now my perspective has changed, and the vision is winded and spent, like the Streatham summer. We were gods in Mallorca, two-week immortals, holding our temporary destiny in the palm of our hand; carefree in Arcadia, sun-lounger heroes, bronzed by candlelight. In Mallorca there was nothing more taxing to do than frolic, and no one and nothing against which to measure our deficiencies. Slipping into the satin pool in the long evening, I was a dolphin, a glorious drunken dolphin – unerring leaper, silver-sided submarine, standing on water on my tail – and I can barely swim.

And Mungo, whenever the furniture called timeout, hunkered down with ants, empathised with ants, squinted along ant sightlines, pondered ant thoughts, planted ant feasts by ant trail-ways, peered into the epic ant world of unmarked tragedies and unreported genocides, of Herculean toil, and gargantuan booty the size of a crumb.

The ants always looked surprised when they stumbled across a crumb; it seemed to me that they did an ant double-take. 'Good God!' they seemed to say, 'a loaf of bread the size of Pavarotti! I'll risk my life carrying it home across the vast patio between the pounding human feet.' And that's what they did, without consideration of danger, with heroic endeavour, at huge risk to themselves, followed every arduous step of the way by a curious seven-year-old King Kong.

Ants don't consider themselves to be tiny, any more than President Mugabe does, though he is dwarfed by the African elephant. A butterfly on the North Circular Road thinks nothing of its own insignificance. Its joyful flight is all to it. Then – *pash* – it is a smudge of iridescent powder on a windscreen. When the butterfly ambulance gets to the spot they can find no trace of it.

'I'm sure it happened here ...'

Pash!

'Just think Mungo, you and I think nothing of leaving a pea on our plate at dinner time ...'

But Mungo is asleep, curled like an embryo around his thumb. I'm on a roll now: a pea roll. I am in the mind of the pea. At a conservative estimate there must be 60 million peas idly left on plates around Britain every week. In a year Britons leave enough peas on their plates to fill Birmingham Town Hall.

Yet if an ant finds a single pea he will spend a whole day rolling it home to his city of twigs. A detachment will come out to meet him – a pea detail – and together they will help him to haul it in, sacrificing their lives if necessary, to fend off vicious raids from other insects. They do it selflessly, for no reason other than the common good. There is no other reward available, not even celebrity. The chances of David Attenborough happening along with his film crew are really very slight.

Yet small things matter, to the ant, to Mungo, to me – *to history*. History pivots on a single bullet. Heaven and Hell reside in the detail. The Japanese understand this. Despite a misleading penchant for Sumo wrestlers, small is big in Japan. When their economic miracle began, the Japanese made oil tankers, but it didn't take them long to see the post and packaging advantages of downsizing. They found that small sells: personal stereos, wafer memories, palm computers, pocket-monsters ... In Japan, the smaller you get, the bigger you get.

As things get smaller, so the world shrinks, or appears to. It is part of the modern consumer ideal that everything we need in life should be at arm's reach, even information. Getting information used to involve library steps and effort and heaving around of boxes of files. Now it's all there, shimmering beneath the fingertips.

I read in the paper that a British inventor has produced a prototype digital memory system which can store 17 million books on a wafer the size of a credit card. Fantastic, but what if you lost it?

'Have you seen my books I've been storing?'

'How many books?'

'Seventeen million.'

'What do they look like?'

'A credit card.'

What if they were snatched by a pickpocket?

'What did you get?'

'Seventeen million books.'

'Anything good?'

'Nah.'

If they'd known about this system when they built the British Library they could have saved a lot of space, not to mention time and money. They could have got away with a biggish shoe box, and some tiny librarians.

'Can you show me the way to the British Library please.'

'It's right there, by your foot.'

Waging the modern war is not very different from any civilian job. Hours, conditions and safety expectations are similar. Most soldiers in Western armies do their fighting in comfort, from behind a desk. No foot-slogging like before, or getting on and off horses. Today the theatre of war is viewed from afar through a macro lens. We like to think we are the centre of the world, those of us with the information, the money and the lifestyle, the tiny phones and computer systems; that everything radiates from us; that we are gods. We are wrong. You only have to wake up in the night in panic, with your heart slapping your ribs, to know that. Your perspective is only one of many. In fact the world is as big and as terrifying as it always was, and relative to the world, each of us is as insignificant, and as important, as a smudge of iridescent powder on a windscreen.

We read about 11-year-old boy soldiers in the Sudan, the Congo and Sierra Leone, who have become the desensitised, fearless and carefree fighting machines of rebel warlords. The foreign journalist, adjusting our zoom lens, may provoke in us an iota of pity for them, yet even as we are considering their plight we are switching ourselves off from it; changing channels; surfing away. They're too different, too far away, too far gone, too small. They are with the ants in the driveway. It is as hard for us to love them, as it is for them to love us.

Yet Daniel was rescued. Daniel was a boy soldier in the Sudan, who was captured and taken into the care of the UN. Now he is 14 and trying to live a normal life. He says that however brutalised he was, however black his heart became, he carried a tiny light inside him that survived the horror and the blotting out. He carried the memory of the bright button on his mother's blouse. It returned to his mind again and again. He barely knew it for what it was, or what it represented, yet it was there, shining and sweet, and it is there still, for life is, if anything, even harder for him now. 'It is a small thing,' he says, 'but bigger than the world.'

Love for another. Love of another. These are our massive sustaining crumbs. Easy for me to say – I have Mungo's little hot hand in mine.

Chapter 44 BELEN

She came from outer space. Well, she might as well have done: I can't understand a word she says. And she came in friendship. Had she been hateful – had she come uttering threats – I'd have known to take avoiding action; scatter garlic, get the gun out.

I've had hateful au pairs before. I'm used to that. What I can't cope with is love, and Belen is *so* loving, *so* excessively, ecstatically, pathologically affectionate it's driving me mad. Belen loves ... the children, me, Martha, the cat. She loves us to death. She shows her love by slapping me on the shoulders, which hurts. She's a big girl. It's like having a euphoric great Dane in the house, wearing dungarees.

Nothing on her application form prepared me for this. Belen was Spanish, well educated and played an instrument. She described herself as 'helpful, cohesive and domestic'. Next to 'Can you cook?', she had put 'VERY!' Naively, I interpreted this as a good thing.

What the form didn't say is that she has a colossal milk intake, that she saws frozen mackerel into cylinders, eating the middle section and leaving the heads and tails in the fridge, that she plays 'Caimanera' on the trumpet of an evening, serves children saucers of cream crackers in warm milk and gobbles my expensive Parmesan ('good hard Spanish cheese,' she says) spread with marmalade. Belen breaks the Edam rule.

Most au pairs see children as a necessary evil and get on with them splendidly. Belen wants children to love her, so they hate her. She doesn't notice. *Things* don't like her either. Chairs shy away from her, glasses throw themselves off shelves at her approach. She has only to touch a curtain for it to fall on her head, making her bark with laugher.

Everything makes her laugh: children, pets, the washing machine ... *'Marteen!'* she hoots, making me dash anxiously from my study. I find her laughing at the washing machine. Then she explains the joke: 'Wash. In. Ah. *Circulation.* It I no. Yes?'

Not really. I haven't a clue. Most au pairs pick up elementary English. Not Belen. She is an intellectual – another problem. She has committed to memory 'glottal stop', 'sibilance', 'vocabulary' and 'circulation', but can't assemble them in any order that makes sense. She always gets the sex of people wrong. She has no linguistic capacity whatsoever. She writes shopping lists for items like 'hubbas back' and 'polish for the minnows'. Today she told me a long story about an animal called a hockney. She had me pinned for half an hour. She's a Manuel, but with balls.

For an easy life I have started nodding when she speaks and laughing when she laughs – a mistake, I now realise, because it makes her think I am a kindred spirit, and slap me on the shoulders even harder. Now she's got me laughing at the washing machine too. 'Let's coffee!' she whoops, dropping tea bags in cups of milk and putting them in the microwave. On my birthday she presents me with a large purple orchid. It's sweet of her, but alarming nonetheless. As far as I can see it's a vagina on a stick.

Sadly Belen's language problem doesn't stop her talking. She must proclaim her joy at all times – even when alone. From every point in the house I can hear her gabble of *non-sequitur* pidgin Spenglish. Every now and then she yells *'Marteen!'*, bringing me racing from my study. *'Putting!'* she says, *'Oh, putting!'* There she is putting something in the bin. 'Ah, putting! Ha-ha!'

Belen's happiness condition places a weight of infuriation on this house. With effort I can ignore my name being called (sometimes, I tremble to note, from inside the bathroom), but it still shocks me when she claps me round the shoulders, especially when she creeps up behind me in the study, making me shout profanities into the phone. I can't shout at her though: this is a girl who spends her spare time helping out at a centre for Guatemalan orphans.

So I am doomed to her oppressing presence. I start to think the talc on the bathroom floor might be a milk by-product – after all it has her footprints in it. I lay awake at night, haunted by an image of her asleep, full of milk and fish middles, blowing white bubbles on the pillow. I worry that maybe she is a man; or else a small, rhapsodic pony.

Other au pairs I have disliked with a free conscience. Not Belen. Even as I list these petty resentments, I picture her playing 'Caimanera' on her trumpet to a group of radiant Guatemalan urchins and I feel shamed. I cannot sack her; she is an innocent; so I am trapped. All I can do is increase my milk order.

Still, out of chaos comes opportunity. After telling the story of Belen to Martha's friend Mo, who works on *The Times*, she suggests it would make a good article for a column on the paper called Life Rage, and she gives me the name of the appropriate editor. I ring the editor and she agrees. I write the piece, and it is accepted.

Chapter 45 NUDE

The only reason why anybody would want to go to a nudist colony is to observe the genitalia of women. Well, maybe not *anybody*, but I do speak here for every small boy. And for the small boy in every man.

Every man that is, except the nudist, who tends to deny such honest motives. Ask him why he opts for the clothing-optional lifestyle and you will hear talk about being 'at one with nature', about the breeze on the bottom: that sort of guff. You will not hear the word lust.

Which is fair enough. Why should you? This is a lifestyle, after all, not a Saturday night rampage. On the other hand: how dull.

The reason I'm here at Costa Natura, and some might say it's foolish (in fact, Martha said it's foolish; in fact, everyone said it's foolish), is because I'm getting increasingly dissatisfied with my professional situation. It's not the Sisyphean task of TV reviewing in itself. Every day it shuttles me between abject despair, barking panic and brief reckless moments of relief; but the work is my work. I feel at home with this, and it's earning me respectable money at last. What's bothering me is the lack of perspective. I have no idea where it's leading. I've been doing it for ten weeks now. I've covered the gamut of British TV, from Andrew Marr's ears to Jilly Goulden's ailerons, incisively analysing their relative merits, yet I still have no idea whether I'm good, bad or indifferent at it; whether they think I'm a likely choice for permanent reviewer or whether they are scraping round frantically to find someone else. The longer this goes on, the less likely the first option sounds. It's making me nervous.

The *Evening Standard* is as inscrutable as a stone Buddha. Each day it gobbles my copy, but the bland expression on its face never changes. 'Ask them,' says Martha. 'Just ask them.'

Last week I rang my contact and asked as casually as I could, how I was doing. 'Fine,' was the reply. It didn't sound like they meant 'fine', as in, *exquisitely rendered craftsmanship*, however creatively I try to interpret the inflection, more like 'fine', as in *it'll do*. I get no encouragement from readers either. 'Sir,' the last letter said, 'Would you oblige me, by return, with the postal address of Cilla Black.'

So I am thinking I should now start to look beyond the *Standard* TV page, and pursue other opportunities. I've been taking it too seriously, working too intensely. Maybe I should loosen up. After all, this run could stop at any moment and I'd be left with nothing. *The Times* using my au pair piece has encouraged me that there is life outside the *Evening Standard* arrangement.

I needed to get out of the house too. I was desperate to escape the cumbersome and clattering juggernaut of family life, the kids, Belen, and in particular, Peter, who has begun to get on my nerves. He slopes around the house all day doing nothing, and is relentlessly downbeat. My conversations with him, which used to be such a welcome distraction, are oppressive now that they are following me round the house. They never lead anywhere; it's just comment, comment, comment. I'm so resentful of his presence that I've started taking his bike from the dining room, where it is doing no harm, as the room has been stripped ready for painting, and dumping it in the garden. I realise this is irrational, and probably a bit hurtful, but every time I see it there I have to get it out of the house, and it's better than throwing it on to the railway embankment, which is what I really want to do.

Peter's head is overfilled with information about this and that, but when I ask him what he's planning to do about his life, it goes blank, and he stares into the middle distance. I've made suggestions. I've suggested distractions. I've even suggested that he rings Eloise. It's just possible that she might like some witty company at lunchtime from time to time, and she's got an expense account. I've given him her number, though I know he won't do anything about it (and I'm not sure she'd thank me if he did).

The omnipresence of the extreme and polar personalities of Belen and Peter, one gratuitously optimistic, the other doggedly pessimistic, is leading me to work more at night, and sleep through the morning. Most days, this is my routine now, though it puts extra strain on Martha and the kids, and she resents it. It's the only way I can guarantee time to myself to think. At least I'm earning money.

The other thing that has depressed me lately is that Simpson died. She walked out into the road and was hit by a car. I miss the perverse old grimalkin. It seems incredible for this to happen so soon after Jack's death and it reminds you how quickly and easily things you take for granted can spin out of control. Martha was disorientated by it too. After we'd taken the body to the vet, we didn't go home, but drove to a carpet shop and ordered an £800 carpet for the stairways and landings. We'd been putting this decision off for some time, and it was good to do something positive together.

All this was going on in my head when an escape opportunity dropped into my lap – an escape, what's more, in the company of very many naked women. The *Observer* Magazine wanted an article about this naturist resort in Southern Spain. I was off to experience every boy's dream: the ultima Thule of carnal discovery. My ideal of combining naked women and work was finally to be realised.

I didn't have time to write a week's TV reviews in advance, though I was able to call in a week's worth of preview tapes and watch them all. I packed a week's worth of careful notes and shorthand comments, and also a portable computer. It's irredeemably autumn in England. I was encouraged by the hope that there might be a bit of sun left in Spain.

Underneath the ravishing banks of hibiscus, the glossy rubber trees, and the handsome palms, oozing elan, Swedish firemen sit with their big compliant wives, gazing sadly at their testicles. So many of them are Swedish firemen, or English provincial bank managers. It's not a pleasant sight.

I too am stark naked. I'm sitting on the patio, by the swimming pool, surrounded on every side, by the naked. It has taken all this for me to realise I don't like being nude in front of other people; not when I'm sober anyway. Far from being liberating, nudity is making me claustrophobic. I feel like I'm in a strait-jacket. I miss Martha and the kids. I miss Peter! I miss Belen! I've never felt so lonely in my life. I'm lonely for my family and my friends; I'm lonely for my clothes.

Lonely for lust. Remember lust? Hard to work any up here. So far as can be judged from outward appearances, lust is the last thing on the nudist's mind. He prides himself on his limpness in the presence of naked women.

His most noticeable erection at Costa Natura is the high wall with which he surrounds his ideal community, in order to frustrate prying eyes. He bans single men outright. If it wasn't for the fact that he walks round stark bollock naked, I would say that the nude was a prude.

As a single man, I am an exception. At the gate a video camera scrutinised my clothed self while an invisible security man inside tried to uncover my inner motive. I smiled as nudely as I could and waved my letter of dispensation.

Then I was in, struggling not to stare. There is no place in the world where is it ruder to stare, and no place where it is harder not to. I could argue that the place would be rude even if you didn't stare, but the nudist of course, would disagree.

In place of lust, the nudist substitutes an intense emphasis on family life, Phil Collins music and volley ball. The perfect nudist family unit, with its oddly well-behaved children, disports itself on manicured lawns, in Costa Natura's immaculate garden setting, in set-piece scenes reminiscent of God's eternal kingdom, as revealed to me by the Jehovah's Witnesses (except that here, of course, the people are naked, and there is a rule banning tigers). Volley ball is a genuine part of nudist life, not just nudist jokes. Take it as read: everything you have ever heard about nudism and volley ball is true. There's nothing new that can added.

What hasn't been said about nudism is this: women's genitalia are not generally visible, even in this most promisingly compromising of environments. Women are not the up-front naked people every small boy would wish them to be. They are intrinsically discreet, even when unclothed, however hard you stare. Women have to sit, or rather lie, in an unnaturally spreadeagled position to reveal the bits you want to see. You can wait forever for them to do this, watching illegally out of the corner of your eye through your sunglasses, with your head cranked at an uncontroversial angle, as though you are really examining an interesting piece of roof guttering. It has taken me (I realise with some embarrassment) 45 years to realise this would be the case.

While women retain a certain genital mystique, men are everywhere revealed. It isn't hard to spot the biggest penis in the resort supermarket, even when you don't want to. From my experience locked inside Costa Del Nude I can tell you that male genitalia vary enormously. One of the things naturists like to say, is that, naked we are all equal, but we are not equal at all. They say size doesn't matter, but some men – ha! ha! – are pathetically small, and vexed looking, while others are fat and blond.

The oddest things are the testicles, which appear to grow bigger and heavier with age. On old men, seen from behind, as they lean forward against a wall – to watch a game of mini-ten or volley ball for instance – they hang down like boulders in voluminous pale sacks, inconveniently knocking against the backs of the legs, as though they don't belong there, like things borrowed from an elephant, pinned on for a joke.

There is a poignant contradiction in the life of every nudist, for though he may genuinely desire a more innocent existence, unconstrained by artificial, value-laden, status-conferring, inhibition-forming clothes ('the rags of shame', as a US naturist poster refers to them), the practice of it leaves him clothed – so to speak – in a manner which brings to mind to the rest of us, the sex act. That incongruity is irresistibly funny.

Funny or not, half a day at Costa Natura is enough for me. As soon as the thrill of not being arrested wears off, I want out. I want something harder, more cynical. Something *obscene* would be nice. Most, I long for sexual allure. You may not think yourself a sexual animal but when the everyday, sly, allusive references to sex are taken away altogether, you realise just what a beast you really are.

This place is as asexual as disinfectant. The first four hours here, I worry that I'm going to have an erection. Everywhere I go, I take a broadsheet newspaper with me, in case I need cover. That oh-so-visible thermometer of male sexual arousal may be greeted with applause in the Masters and Johnson observation suite, but on a family sun terrace it would get short shrift. If during an unguarded moment – while sleeping off lunch perhaps – an uninvited carnal jelly fish were to swim lazily into the mind, and it raised its ugly head among the children and the ice creams, it would leave a shadow on the reputation longer than the one it casts across the sun deck.

After four hours I worry that I am *not* having an erection. It just *doesn't happen*. It is as though you pass through an invisible force field as you enter the compound. You are turned off at the gate: the penis remotely deactivated, the sexual mechanisms shut down. In normal life men get erections at parish council meetings, funerals and Slurpex Absorbent Household Cleaning Products demonstrations. Why don't they get erections when surrounded by naked women?

There are several reasons for this. One is that nothing destroys female mystique more surely than the sight of tomato ketchup spills on breasts. That sort of thing happens all the time at Costa Natura.

Another is that there are bits on most people's bodies that are, frankly, pig ugly. Oh they may have a certain coarse charm in the height of sexual frenzy (when they can serve as a much needed antidote to the Simply Red music) but you wouldn't want to look at them while buying cheese in the supermarket, which is what you have to do at Costa Natura. Naturists claim that the naked body is beautiful. In rare cases, and in the case of most children, this is true, but looking at all those sagging breasts, clumps of Ken Doddish pubic hair, operating scars, warts, pimples and cellulite rolls, makes you realise why God invented underwear. The truth is, naturists don't take off their clothes because it *looks* beautiful, but because it *feels* beautiful (to them), an important distinction. I am reminded of thinking, at the zoo, how much nicer it would be if the monkeys put some underpants on.

It's been 40-or-so years since I last appeared in public in my birthday suit, and I find that it has shrunk a little in some places and gone baggy in others (unlike a conventional suit, it doesn't go thin on the bottom – just the opposite, in fact). Even so, I am Adonis compared to some of these nudists, however beautiful they may feel. When naked people lie down, their pubic hair sticks up in pathetic tufts, like snagged tumbleweed, or something designed for Andrew Neil's head. Every kind of abomination is here: whipped-cream hips, leather dugs, hairy nipples ... Nothing's perfect, not even in the garden of Eden. The irony of Costa Natura's idyllic scenery is that it isn't natural at all. It's cosmetic. It's intensively husbanded by a tireless maintenance crew. But its human scenery is neglected. A bit of body grooming would improve the view, even cosmetic surgery; a tuck here, a nip there; in some cases a full bobbit wouldn't hurt none. Now here's something you don't necessarily want to know: naked people fiddle with their pubes. Fact. Because they're there, I suppose.

The other reason lust is absent is that even the most skimpily attired body is more interesting than a naked one. I realise that now too. In fact, the skimpier the layer, the more dramatic the effect on the imagination. That's why fashion houses can charge £3,000 for the merest figment of tulle – that's £3,000-worth of feminine mystique, and the way I'm thinking at the moment, worth every penny. The sexiest thing to happen so far at Costa Natura was when a pretty woman walked up to the bar fully clothed, and while she was waiting for her drink, casually undressed. It was incredibly titillating, right down to the last white flag. But the second she pulled off her knickers, she disappeared into the greater sea of anonymous nakedness. It was incredible. I couldn't see her any more. What wouldn't I have given for a wisp of tulle. I would have wrapped it around that lovely young woman, to flatter and to treasure her perfect figure, and then I would have asked her if I could buy her a drink. She would have been the envy of the whole sagging camp.

It's not nudity which is dangerous after all; it's clothing which is dangerous. In the film *The Piano*, the hole in Holly Hunter's stocking was sexy because the stocking was there. Well, let's hear it for danger. Put on your red dress baby. Live a little.

I slip the leash in the evening and gun the hire car, windows down, the short distance to Estopona. It is such a relief to get into the real world that I'm singing and shouting at the top of my voice, though in fact, this stretch of coast is far from real. It has been given up to tourism niche marketing. One after another I pass walled ghetto paradises dedicated to sybaritic minorities: East End criminals, yacht-people, 18–30s yobbos, naturists ...

I make straight for the gewgaw lights of the bars at Puerto Deportivo yacht basin. I eat tapas marisquera. Clams piled on the counter stick their lascivious orange tongues out of their shells, making the heaps shudder. Suddenly my world is full of flavours, salty, sharp and bright. I'm drawn to the corny tourist bars on the front, to sit at a bar stool on the pavement and watch the comings and goings. Here the holiday-makers dress up. At the Christopher Columbus karaoke bar they're belting out 'La Bamba' and 'Suspicious Minds'. There's a cheap and easy glamour, the beer tastes good and all the girls are on show.

I need to renew my faith in female allure. It doesn't take much. A hoicked hemline; a slit of midriff; the way one stockinged leg spirals around another; the ribbed welt of a tank top that emphasises the clutchable narrowness of a waist, a white blouse open one button at the neck, revealing a triangle of warm skin; the barely discernable curve of a bottom under a light skirt ...

Two girls from Port Talbot come and sit with me. They're giggling and warm, sparkling and sexy; generous spirited; abandoned to the holiday. When one of them leans across my back to tell the other something, I feel her breasts whisper against my shoulder. It doesn't take much.

At midnight I return reluctantly to Costa Natura. I still have my review to write up for the morning deadline. I feel like The Prisoner returning to The Village after an aborted escape attempt, to face the smug superiority of Number Two. Puerto Deportivo was still buzzing when I leave, but Costa Natura is silent, but for the susurration of sprinklers watering the immaculate tropical plants. There isn't a single human voice, not even Phil Collins. Everything is in darkness; the shutters of the poolside bar are lowered. With nobody around, the place looks exotic and tranquil, sexy even. Nudists go to bed early after their play, and get up early to catch the morning sun, unfearful of the UV menace, or the cynical eye.

I write my copy when I get to my apartment in Costa Natura's Calle de Maria Del Mare. I don't mind working at night. Here at least, I'm in control. I send it off at 5 a.m. I'll sleep in tomorrow morning, and write the next batch of copy during the day, so I can spend less time nudely interacting.

The phone wakes me at 7 a.m. It's the *Evening Standard* production editor. He's frantic. He says the copy isn't right. He says I've got the days muddled up. The TV programmes are all wrong. I've sent him tomorrow's copy, not today's. He says I've got half an hour to put it right.

I scream silently. I hold my head. I walk up, I walk down. Once again, inconceivably, I am paying the price for being early. I am the early worm awaiting the arrival of the bird.

Untangling a lucid thread from my dense mass of shorthand notes is almost impossible in the time I have. I know there's good stuff in there, but where is it exactly? I have 23 sheets of A4 paper here, covered with shorthand scribble, much of which appears to be about old ladies. Why do I keep writing about old ladies? How come the old ladies are eating carrion? Or are they wildcats, eating Koreans? I have no time. When I send my copy, half an hour later, it's still in half note form. I pray there is a very clever sub-editor on duty today.

A little later the copy is faxed back to me as it has appeared in the first edition, with a note telling me to rewrite it ASAP. It's appalling. I don't know why I thought the sub-editor might be able to cope with what had already evaded me. Here's an extract. In case you're wondering, it's about a natural history programme.

The first to cotton on to this need for dental diversification, curiously, was a little shrew-like creature with an expression rather like John Major, that scampered among the bones of the extinct dinosaurs and practised its survival techniques. From little Cimolestes all carnivores are descended, including the sabre-toothed tiger, which interestingly, has died out and evolved itself back several times, and the cat. For all we know they are evolving back to ferocity. The kittens being born behind your sofa right now, might be on their way back to hoplophoneus again. They might not be content to snag your stockings, no sir. They would be after snagging the washing machine, and instead of a decapitated sparrow on the hall carpet of a morning, you might find a pony. Curious to think that generations after John Major's loins could spring a race of sabre-toothed MPs, sharp of fang and claw, that will prowl down the future corridors of Westminster with deadly grace.

What does it mean? What does anything mean? What do Peter Greenaway's films mean? What do Professor Stephen Hawkings's books mean? – we only have his word for it that they make sense. What do Peter Dobbie's *Daily Mail* columns mean? When Peter Dobbie says,

Blair knows of the car's potency. How it is relished as a personal palace with prized fixtures and fittings and brochured glossily in the language of warfare: cruise control and remote locking. That if the Englishman's home is his castle, then the car is the moat. Quite simply, a capsule of selfishness.

what does it mean? I don't know what it means. I don't know what any of it means. But I do know, with deadly clarity, that I will never work for the *Evening Standard* again.

And I'm still here. For two more days I'm bored, listless and bolshy. I've been to Subbuteo conventions that were more interesting than this. I want to shout. I want to sit by the pool in an overcoat, or bondage gear. Instead I start drinking. I start naked drinking, though I loathe the bar staff, who stand apart in their catering uniforms and who treat their nude clientele with a condescension tinged with contempt, as though we are the inmates of an institution for the mentally subnormal. I have seen waiters patting people on the head, like pets or retards. Nobody complains; their pitiable nakedness renders them vegetable-like. I envy the waiters their clothes, their confident, superior, go-anywhere, godlike strides. I acknowledge the first law of fashion: in the land of the naked, the man with synthetic trousers is king.

In two hours I will be gone. I've drunk four beers and I'm sitting half dozing on the bar terrace in the hot morning sun, facing the wall.

There's a cough at my shoulder. I turn round to see a big matronly woman looming over me. Her crotch is a foot away from me at eye level, and for a second I have the mindless impulse to reach out and tweak her pubic hair. It's the Mayfair Art Gallery syndrome all over again, though here the nudes are real.

'I gather you are new to naturism,' she says.

'Yes.' How does she know? Do I look so green? Have I got (look down ...) an erection?

'I have to point out the first rule of naturism: always bring a towel to sit on. We always sit on a towel.'

'Oh I see – to stop you getting a striped bottom from the chair slats?'

'No,' she says.

'Well ...?'

'For hygiene reasons.'

My stomach turns. I'm forced to think about things I haven't even considered. The word 'seepage' enters my mind and hangs around. All those bottoms, even the lovely ones, are now condemned in my mind as the vile enemies of hygiene, rendered still more pathetic than they look by the indignities of naturist bureaucracy. I look around me. Everyone except me is sitting submissively on a towel. I rise to my feet with as much dignity as I can muster, hoping I'm not swinging too much.

'I'm not sitting on a towel for you or anyone,' I say.

This seems defiant when I say it, but as I watch it register on her astonished face, I realise how pathetic it sounds. I walk away. I will pack my case and leave right now. I crave the world of the textiles, the beguiling trickery of clothes, the freedom of zips and buttons and lapels and turn-ups to go where I want to in.

On the beach below the bar, a fat middle-aged man and woman, both naked and shaped like blancmange humming tops, are walking through the shallows in matching white baseball caps and white rubber shoes, hand in hand. How mindlessly happy they look.

Chapter 46 UNDER... AND OVER

I was nervous again, when I flew in to Spain, but coming home, with this overwhelming sense of disintegration, I can't be bothered enough to be scared. In fact, I'm asleep almost as soon as we leave the ground. I dream of Ursula. I don't see her face, but I know it's her; I recognise her cloppy shoes, her clothes and scent.

I am lying somewhere hot – Spain perhaps – exhausted, and naked, on a bed, or perhaps the floor. She comes in, says nothing. I can hear her taking her clothes off. I can hear her removing her underwear. She walks over and stands astride me, then squats down over my legs and does nothing for a while, as though absorbed in meditation. Then very slowly I feel her crutch touch my leg, ticklish, it is so faint; and it's gone again; then back it comes, pushing more firmly at me this time. Slowly, still squatting, she covers my body with little vaginal licks, gently and scrupulously, like a grooming cat, working her way from my legs up my stomach, from my chest to my face, where a new urgency, almost violence, enters her movements. She shudders, and presses herself hard against me, till I wonder how I am going to breathe, then abruptly raises her leg and gets off.

'I'd like a coffee,' she says.

I smell gorgeous.

'Seat belt, sir,' says the air hostess, shaking my shoulder.

The plane is lining up to land. I feel different. Enchanted. I'm carnally enchanted.

I hate arriving home from long trips during the day in the week, because nobody is there to greet me. Even Peter isn't here today. There's a message on the answering machine asking me to call the *Standard* urgently. I put it off for an hour. I walk round the house, open post. I make myself another cup of tea. Then I phone the *Standard*.

They want to let me know that they've engaged a permanent writer for the TV review page. I won't be needed any more. Thanks very much – so much – for all my work.

I have no work planned; nothing. I'm right back were I started. There's just one small bit of unfinished business. I phone *The Times*. National newspapers normally pay automatically, but I haven't received a payment yet for my au pair piece.

'I did an article for you a couple of weeks ago about an au pair. I need to know your rate, so I can invoice you.'

'It was the Life Rage column you did, wasn't it? I thought so. No, there's no fee for that column.'

'Is this a joke?'

'No, you see, in that column we normally run one of the longer letters sent in by a reader, so you see there's no budget for it.'

'But this wasn't a reader's letter. I'm a writer. I suggested the idea to you and you asked me to write it. I've never written for *The Times* before, and the only reason I didn't negotiate a fee beforehand was because I assumed your rates of pay would be reasonable.'

'I'm sorry, that's the way it is.'

'I can't accept this.'

'There's nothing I can do. Look, I can get you a token fee of £50, if we put it through as expenses.'

Professionally, everything is dreadful. Everything is more utterly dreadful than even I could have imagined it being. I know that, but I am strangely distant from it. I am under a spell.

Ursula arrives at four in the afternoon to collect Weeny, but Weeny isn't here yet. Belen's taken them all to McDonald's after school. I invite Ursula to come in and wait, and she hesitates for a second. She has only been in our house a couple of times in the whole time we've had Weeny. This is a level of involvement she has always resisted.

But she comes in today, and walks into the middle of our kitchen and stands there incongruously in all her dashing flight clothes, elegant, but awkward, like a beautiful statue that is waiting to be shipped to its rightful setting. I start making tea, which she doesn't want, but I have to do something. She sits at the table and we talk stiffly for five minutes about Weeny. We have almost nothing in common. Even my observations of Weeny are of a different nature to hers. An etching of a fish in profile, which hangs on the kitchen wall, catches her eye. It's a lovely primeval shape, a black, moodily muscular soul, swimming through a square of darkness.

'That's good,' she says, getting up. 'Who's it by?'

I stand behind her.

'The artist is Chris Salmon.'

'Any relation?' she says.

I laugh, though I need to concentrate hard to comprehend what she is saying. I am standing looking over her shoulder at the fish. She smells exotically of Boeings. I realise I am shivering.

'The fish is not a salmon.' My words sound robotic.

I put my hand on her shoulder and pull her towards me. It gives half an inch, then resists. Stupidly, wishfully, for two seconds I keep the pressure on. I am like a man trying to move a piece of furniture that has turned out to be heavier than he anticipated. The artificiality of the act is absolute. I have had no signal from her whatsoever, no sign of compliance or come-on, no lowering of the eyelids, no *double entendre*, not a whiff of pheromone. She has deposited no token nest material on my attractive blue feet.

I am acting solely on the basis of lunatic information brought to me in a dream, a random hallucination generated by my own exotic urges. As soon as I touch her, I know it is wrong. This sexual madness I am experiencing resides exclusively in me. This is as wrong as a car accident. It is awkward, clumsy, crunchy. It is not even elegantly or dashingly wrong. It is an act of gross misalignment, and it is not covered by insurance.

Ursula looks at me. Briefly the certitude is gone from her eyes. Here is something she wasn't expecting, and doesn't like. That is clear. A second later, her visor clangs down again. The smile returns, cold.

'I don't think so Martin,' she says firing off the words precisely, like notes picked out on a xylophone. Then she walks out. She walks with little determined steps to her car and drives off.

An hour later when Weeny is back, Ursula returns, and gathers up Weeny's school bag and hat in silence.

'Ursula ...' I say.

'I don't think we need continue this arrangement,' she says, and walks to the door looking straight ahead.

'I have to jiggle Weeny on the lights ...'

'You'll have to find someone else to jiggle from now on.'

I'm a fool. I don't really want Ursula. I can see that clearly now. The infatuation has gone. I don't care. But I do care about Weeny, and now she's gone too.

I tell Martha that Ursula doesn't want Weeny to come here any more. She's incredulous.

'Why?'

'I don't know.'

'Why so suddenly?'

'I think she must have a more convenient arrangement or something.'

'Didn't you ask?'

'No, I didn't think.'

Martha's baffled. And now she's seriously concerned. She knows there must be more to it than this. I tell her what happened in Spain and that distracts her. That dismays her. This is agonising. We're alone sitting in the kitchen. Martha's in her dressing gown. She's pale and tired looking.

She asks a lot of questions, but I can't talk honestly to her. I don't want her to be upset, though now it seems inevitable one way or another.

'Look she says. Something's not right. I don't know what's going on and I'm not sure I want to know, but for the moment, I'm going to bed.' She gets up and walks to the door, then turns. 'One thing I'll insist on though: Peter's got to go. I don't care how you do it, but I can't cope with him on top of all this.'

Chapter 47 SNAP

The holiday snaps came back this week and, God, what a dull time we appear to have had. Looking at these, I'm beginning to wonder why we bothered to go at all. I'm resolving (as I have before) never to take another snap in my life. Live for the moment. Let the future take care of itself.

I'm already having difficulties interpreting them to friends. 'Just look at the sea,' I say, 'it was the colour of that vase there on the mantelpiece.'

'Here's me!' I say. And it is me. I can't deny it. I can't deny the stooped shoulders, the cannelloni tummy and the resilient Inner London pallor that shines forth from the photograph like a beacon of dullness in Paradise. At the time I thought I was as brown as Harry Belafonte, the very picture (if anyone had bothered to take it properly) of rude health.

It hasn't been easy persuading people to look at the snaps. As soon as I bring them out they look at their watch and shuffle their feet. These are my happiness trophies and nobody cares. Had I been *unhappy*, now that would have been different. Had someone managed to take a snap of me being assaulted by a bandit with a machete, I would have gathered a queue of eager viewers all the way to London Bridge, all of them saying, 'And the sea is such a lovely colour' or, 'You really were very brown' to disguise their morbid curiosity.

Unfortunately Boots only sent me pictures of Martha embracing a blurred statue, Mungo on a funny toilet, me with my feet sticking out of a sand mound and a group shot of some new-found friends-for-life, none of whom I'll ever see again, peering with red eyes from the gloom of a forgotten bar.

Judging by the snaps of my neighbour Mr Loveday though, which he insisted on showing me in the street, I had quite a nice time. The arrogance of the man gets to me. He thinks he's part of a Bacardi advert, though his snaps clearly demonstrate otherwise: another beige sunset, another grey paella, another small mountain.

What makes mountains small in snaps? I don't know. All I know is that the mountain in the snap is never the same as the one that made you stop the car in awe to take a picture that day. That's why, in the throes of back-to-reality depression, we stuff our holiday photos into shoe boxes and throw them in the corner of the study, behind the broken speaking scales. And there they sit. Rubbish though they are, they exert a curious hold on us. They become part of our emotional and physical baggage which it is our fate to cart around for the rest of our lives.

I have one picture of my grandparents, 10 of my parents, 40 of me as a boy and thousands of Amelia and Mungo. Already I can't look at Mungo on the funny toilet, or Martha embracing the blurred statue, even the red eyes of the new-found friends, without feeling my heart will break. I cannot throw these snaps away, and the more I have to look at, the greater is my sense of loss.

The garage is the place to be alone. The garage is as remote as it gets in a city household, especially when it's at the end of the garden. No one in their right mind goes to the garage. It's dark and it's freezing cold. There are no happiness relics. There isn't Martha's reproachful face, or Peter's hollow talk.

It's a good place to lick your wounds. I've been here an hour now, standing among the mess. My head's full of mess too. I'm cold, but the cold is the bit I like best: the cauterising cold. I like its clean and resolute design. You can lean on it.

I don't remember things being this bad. Things are worse than they were this time last year. Last year things seemed hopeless; now they're all broken. The *Evening Standard* gave me the best break I've ever had and I blew it. I don't know if I can ever recover professionally.

I also had the best chance to make Martha happy – to be the man she wants me to be – and I blew that too. She's disappointed, and I resent her disappointment because it hurts me so much. I've hurt her too. I've hurt her more than even she knows.

A bond of resentment is growing between us. We are coming to depend on it because there are no finer emotions to sustain us. I can't talk to her. What is it? Is it pride? What have I got to be proud about?

It would be easier if I didn't care, but I do. I fell in love with her a long time ago and it's too late to unfall now. Love is not in question. What is in question is the future and whether we have one together. She would like me to get a job of some sort on a small magazine, cut my losses. I'd hate to do that. I'm beginning to think she'd be better off without me.

I am aware of someone walking down the garden towards me. It's Amelia, with something in her hand.

'Are you all right down here?'

'… I'm looking for something.'

'I saw your torch. I thought you might like a cup of tea.'

I put down the fish slice I'm holding (I don't know why – I saw it in the lawn mower hopper in the torchlight and picked it up absent-mindedly) and take the hot tea. 'Thanks.'

Amelia is silhouetted against the house lights. I can't see her face but I can see her warm breath all around her.

'Don't stay out too long, Dad,' she says. 'It's *freezing* out here … Right. I'm going in.'

She goes back. As she turns I see her profile briefly against the hard clear back-light. She looks fresh and young and beautiful.

Chapter 48 WALLOW

Effort is counter-productive in the art of drunkenness. Children and teetotallers can accomplish it with ease, but drunkards find it difficult, though they practise every day. The bottles keep coming, but the giggle rush that I love so much keeps evading me.

Our nights are like this now. Martha goes to bed around 11 p.m. and Peter and I stay up drinking wine, and talking, or watching TV into the early hours; not because I want to necessarily but because I can't bear to go to bed: because I've done so little during the day, because that's where Martha is, or to spite myself – I don't know why. I'm in limbo.

I've hardly seen Martha in the two weeks since Costa Natura. The closest we've been for a long time was when we briefly clutched each other in horror today, after the carpet layers had gone. That carpet we ordered to cheer us up after Simpson's death: it's dark maroon. It's morbid, funereal, cat-grief maroon.

Well, at least we have a carpet. The house may look like a mausoleum, but we no longer have to explain to guests that we are floorboard modernists, or slightly Dada.

The carpet goes well with late-night horror films. Peter and I have seen a lot of these lately. They're all bad, but they have built-in compensations for the wine-dulled. Horror is a more forgiving genre than humour, for while horror that isn't frightening often makes you laugh, humour that isn't funny never gets a laugh, and it isn't frightening either.

Tonight, because I have been toying with a new novel, Peter and I are in the study. We have a bottle of whisky. I'm at the keyboard on the desk and he's in the armchair, reading extracts from the local paper. The new novel is even shorter than Codpot.

'Do you want to hear the book I'm writing?'

'Are you going to read it to me?'

'Yes,'

'OK.'

'The working title is Wispy.'

'Snappy.'

'"His hair wasn't ..."'

'What?'

'No, this is it ... I'm reading the novel.'

'Ah.'

'"His hair wasn't the slightest bit flopsy-mopsy – more wispy, if at all."'

'... Is that it?'

'Yes. What do you think?'

'I hope you don't mind me being frank.'

'Not at all.'

'It's overlong. If you want, I'll edit it for you.'

'No way. You're a philistine. You'd tear the heart out of it.'

'Heart-tearing is what it needs. It's begging for the editor's knife – or blow-torch.'

'Do you not think it has the ring of veracity?'

'I think it has the ring of rubbish. Listen to this ...' He leafs back through the paper.

'"Slum Caused Dad to Snap" – that's what people want nowadays: the complete picture in five words. This was good too: "Bird Wot Woz A Dad ..."'

'What's that about then?'

'It's about a bloke who had a sex change. The point is, it's all there in five words: sex, human interest, family tension, paradoxical contrast ... Yours is twenty words and you're still in somebody's hair.'

'Thirteen words.'

'You can't have a thirteen-word book.'

'Why not?'

'It's unlucky.'

'Well, flopsy-mopsy is hyphenated.'

'Flopsy-mopsy is evil. It has to die.'

'You're heartless. You have no compassion for your friends – for my flopsy mopsy – but when it comes to Candice, who hates you, you're as soft as a lime barrel.'

'Ah, Candice.'

'There you are – you never criticise her.'

'That's not true.'

'You never stood up to her. Your epitaph should read: *I Did It Her Way*.'

'I did stand up to her. Once.'

'When did you stand up to her?'

'When she was pregnant and asked me to wear one of those things: those belly things.'

'Those what?'

'An empathy belly. They strap them on fathers-to-be. They weigh the same as an unborn baby, and they wriggle and make you hot and unnecessary, just like a real pregnancy.'

'You wore that?'

'No, I *didn't* wear that – that's the point.'

'What did Candice say when you refused?'

'She called me a coward. She said a real man would want to experience the pain of womanhood.'

'Did she offer to experience the pain of manhood in return?'

'No. ... What pain?'

'I don't know ... I know – when you sit down sometimes and your trousers are wrong or something, and you get, you know – that thing with your testicle.'

'Oh God yes! Ball twist.'

'That's it! Everything goes black ...'

'You can't move.'

'You can't speak.'

'It feels like your testicle's gone up into your lung. Ooooh!'

'Ooooh!'

'And you can't explain it to the people you're with – especially women. You can't say you've just sat on your testicle.'

'Empathy Testicles. They should start making them now.'

'With a *Ball Twist* button.'

'Women wouldn't wear them.'

'They're too smart.'

'More whisky? Peter what are your plans now? Now that you've rebelled against Candice and been kicked out?'

'I dunno.'

'Don't you think it's odd that you should be living in Streatham, which you despise so much?'

'Yes, it is odd, but beggars can't be choosers. Besides, Brixton's not the same any more. The Moldi's Reliance Café has closed down.'

'What about that shop which nobody could work out what it sold?'

'The Kuru Globe Centre? Gone. And Mr Cheap Potatoe has had its spelling mistake corrected.'

'No?!'

'That graffiti – *Is Emotion Beguiling You?* – that's gone too. *The Miners Will Win* is still there though.'

'What are you going to do now. Have you thought of getting a job?'

'You sound like Candice. She said it was time I stopped pretending I could act.'

'Well, maybe it is. Why don't you get a job?'

'Oh I dunno. I'm going to be 50 next year. What could I do?'

'You could do anything. Even working in a bar might be enjoyable, make you feel you were contributing. It would be better than sitting around doing nothing.'

'You can talk.' He picks up a *Guardian* appointments section. 'Let's see what's going. Corporate Strategic Planning Manager – that doesn't sound too hard does it. This is me: Creative Buyer ...'

'No, they'd want someone like Europa.'

'I couldn't work in an office again anyway. I'm a dinosaur. I'd knock over the flo-chart with my tail ... Sedimentologist – that sounds fun.'

'You could be a mini cab driver.'

'I haven't got the cataracts, or the old Volvo with the bob-sleigh motion and smoking dashboard ...'

'They could be acquired.'

'I'd have to buy some cheap aftershave, and an A–H London street guide ...'

'Martha wants me to get a job too. I can't think what I might do, apart from being a boatman for a minor bishop, on some balmy, reed-bound broad. I'd row him to church every week, in dappled sunlight, with long, leisurely strokes of the oar.'

'There's no such job.'

'None of the best jobs exist. Except divot replacers. They exist.'

'At some fair-weather racetrack.'

'I'd go out between races and put the divots back. I'd be on TV.'

'In your charismatic old geezer hat.'

'Or bean spooner.'

'What's that?'

'There were two at the Heinz baked bean factory in Wigan. I was on a guided tour. I was writing about beans. They stood one either side of the conveyer belt of baked beans holding ordinary desert spoons. There was no mystique to the job. They had to pick out the bad beans.'

'What sort of beans are bad?'

'You see, you'd be good at it – very relevant question. The odd kidney bean gets through, I suppose, an occasional black-eye—'

'Any with teeth.'

'Yes see! You'd spot beans that had been getting past the other spooners.'

'Beans with evil intent.'

'Rowdy beans.'

'Bean cop-killers.'

'When I saw the bean spooners, I envied them their job: standing there seven hours a day, watching the beans go past, thinking their noble thoughts.'

'It's a discipline worthy of a fakir.'

'After twenty years of it, you'd become wise.'

'People would come seeking audiences.'

'And you'd say: "Never start a new milk until the old one's used up."'

'"Never sit next to people eating popcorn if you are wearing brushed nylon."'

'You'd never have to make a decision again.'

'Long way to travel. Do you think I could do it?'

'I think they'd give you a try-out.'

'It would be on the CV: Would-be actor. Bean Spooner ...'

'Good urinator ... This is depressing.'

'Yes it is.'

'What time is it?'

'3.16 a.m.'

'We're sitting here night after night reinforcing each other's hopelessness.'

'Yes.'

'Look Peter. You've got to leave.'

'I was wondering when you'd say that.'

'Tomorrow?'

'OK.'

Part V

WINTER

Chapter 49 HUMPS

It's just me and the computer most days. Peter's been gone a month. I'm missing him now. Belen's day is filled up with outside activities. I sit in the middle of a city joined to the world by phone and email, and I feel utterly alone. Until my kids come home from school, but I have little energy for them nowadays.

I've tried to place story ideas but none has been taken up. I left messages on four answering machines this morning, at four different offices. With each advance in communications technology, people become less accessible. One answering machine asked me to send a fax.

Friends call me out of duty nowadays. I have no appetite for small talk. I'm bad company because I think I'm bad company. I'm not really interested in anything either. I can sense them panicking as they run out of questions. Then they ring off.

The phone lays dead mostly.

The conviction of professional and personal failure intensifies. It wouldn't be so hard if it wasn't my fault. I once thought (glibly, it turns out) that I could cope with failure – that it was mediocrity which was to be feared – but now I'm feeling the full force of its oxygen-sapping, confidence-eroding presence. A little mediocrity would pep me up.

If it wasn't for the prostitutes on my route up to the High Road shops, with their routine, 'Want business?', nobody would speak to me at all some days.

I have to get out. Some days I wander over to the tea hut on Tooting Bec Common, where all the dog people go. There are sometimes twenty dog people there at once, including jolly dog ladies from the Heaver Estate, who say 'Hello that Dorothy' to each other, and have ancient dogs with rigid legs. One of the dogs – a bull terrier – can only move diagonally, very slowly, like a walking table. I am the only person with no dog, apart from the man with the Tennents lager can and the 'Party Person' T-shirt, whose dog Benny died at Christmas. I am an impostor here. I am a late cat man.

This morning I walk up to the High Road, braving the cold, to buy wine, some Kennedy's sausages and maybe an apple to eat on the way back. I am a man of simple needs, I tell myself. As I go by the sleeping policemen on the side road, I think of Weeny. Peter claims that nobody but me calls them sleeping policemen any more. They are *traffic calming measures*, he says, *road humps*, in the vernacular. Sleeping policemen are members of the police force who have had a bit of a fright – seen a criminal or something – and are on permanent sick leave on full pay. He may be right, but I like the name, and names are important. I like to think that at some time in the rosy past real policemen lay dutifully across the road, on low pay, but with willing hearts. Lambeth Council put these in here to deter kerb crawlers, though I can't see the logic. After all, a hump is what they're after.

They make me think of Weeny because Weeny always used to talk about them when we walked up here. The first time I told her they were called sleeping policemen, she said, 'Are they policeman's eggs?'

'Yes. They're laid by Panda cars. They're waiting to hatch.'

'Like the eggs we saw on TV?'

'More or less. And when the baby policemen hatch they struggle to their feet and run down the road calling "Nee-naw, nee-naw!"'

'Why?'

'To find their mummy.'

'At the police station?'

Computer innovation erodes conversation even in shops. It's a serve-yourself wonderland at the hi-tech greengrocer. No fat ladies with brown paper bags and innuendos, just a meek girl with a computer cash terminal. I want an apple, but there are so many on display that I lose my appetite. A notice on the pile says 'PLEASE DON'T SQUEEZE ME TILL I'M YOURS'. I baulk and buy a banana. The girl presses

'BANANA' on the till touch-panel and grunts. I grunt. We are hi-tech apes.

Now I'm in the wine shop. It has fences on the inside, in front of the counters, so that the assistants and the wine are locked together inside a giant cage. The assumption is that the customer is a bloodthirsty sadist. This may be true of Amanda Loveday, but it's not true of me. Not yet anyway, though I can feel my resentment building as I press my face painfully against the bars, trying to read the wine labels. I can't. Neither can I decipher the handwritten hosannas stuck to the bottles for the benefit of people who don't speak wine (but have good eyesight). I like to feel the bottles, weigh them in the hand, invoke their essence, imagine myself to be Jilly Goulden in a supersonic dress.

As it is I can only stand in barren isolation while the assistant smiles at me from inside his cage, as though that is a perfectly normal thing for a wine merchant to do. I resist the urge to jump against the fence shouting and growling – that would only confirm his prejudices. Instead I take out the banana and eat it slowly in front of him.

And now my sausages. I can't have my favourite sausages. I can never have my favourite sausages again. The supersonic supermarkets have triumphed again; as if they don't have enough. Kennedy's has closed down. The beloved little half shop with its marble tops and pink scrubbed girls in white aprons and old ladies with shopping bags has gone. After hundreds of years of exquisite joy, it has died.

The shop is locked up, a goodbye letter Sellotaped to the window.

There's something awaiting me from the outside world when I get in. My answering machine carries a message from someone called Zena, inviting me to appear on the TV discussion programme *The Time ... The Place*, to discuss big breasts. Apparently I wrote something once about liking small breasts and the word has gone round. I ring back and find myself talking to a robot which can only speak algebra. 'Who do you want to speak to?' it says. 'For Q press 7. For Z press 9.'

What is it saying? I don't know. It doesn't know. It doesn't care. I yell 'Long live humans!' into the mouthpiece and slam the phone down. I haven't time to answer riddles from a machine; I'm a busy man; I have to talk to a woman about big breasts.

I ring Kennedy's sausage headquarters at Peckham and a real person answers the phone in the old-fashioned way, using her voice. It throws me for a second. I'm floating in unreality. I ask her what has happened to the Streatham shop.

'Well, the shop landlord didn't want to let out his shop in half units any more – there's not much demand for them apparently. He wanted us to take on the whole shop, but we don't really generate enough income to justify it. We still have six shops in South London.'

'But not in Streatham.'

Zena rings me again, so here I am, a day later, on *The Time... The Place*. I know what I want to say: something about small breasts being full of promise under pullovers and how any woman, however imperfect her body, can be full of promise, and a neat point about the off-putting effect of excessive quantity, like when you stand in a sea of naked breasts on a Spanish beach, wondering if you should have opted for Mini Golf. Eve tempted Adam with an apple, not an applethon. I try to remember that line.

We are in a studio full of opinionated people, mostly women, ranging from bitter women in resentfully tailored dresses, to hen party horrors with enormous breasts scooped into orange and cerise stretch tops. They are all arguing about implants and size 58s and breasts being the shock troops of the disco front line and what the fellas really want, and who cares what the fellas want anyway? Why am I here? Eventually John Stapleton, checking his notes, moves towards me. Everyone swings their breasts in my direction: '... because over here we have Martin Plimmer, who happens to be in favour of small breasts.'

'Any sort of breasts are fine by me,' I say.

He doesn't want to hear this.

'The trouble is,' I say, 'there are far too many of them on some beaches. It's like a pile of apples. You can't eat them all ... All you want is one ... or two, maybe ... in this case.' I started with elan, but now weird things are coming out.

'Hmmm?' says Stapleton. I can see him losing interest. My mouth goes dry.

'After all – and who can deny this – under a jumper they are like sleeping policemen, full of mystery ...'

Stapleton gives the sort of frown which, in films, precedes the phrase, 'Call security', and hastens away. Why am I here?

By the time I get off the tube train at Brixton it's three o'clock. It's Tuesday and I have nothing to do. I find myself walking up the hill to Weeny's school, like I have so many Tuesdays. Feeling out of place, I stand with the women at the school gate, keeping behind them so that Mr Monaghan doesn't spot me. I can see Weeny in her little hat, in the line. A woman I've never seen before picks her out and they walk past me.

'Hello Weeny,' I say as they go past, and Weeny turns round, smiles and waves her little hand at me, as though it wasn't the end of the world.

I go for a drink on the way home, in one of the cheap, empty pubs on the high road. It's a prosaic business, drinking by yourself. No glamour to it at all. There are others like me, dotted through the bar. Strange too, to indulge your thoughts so lavishly like this for one and a half hours, when you have so little to think.

Martha is sitting in the kitchen talking to Ursula when I get back. I know what they're talking about. I go upstairs and wait.

Chapter 50 EDGE

This is it. This is our argument. Martha and I don't argue much and even now we are talking. Or Martha is talking. She is very upset. God, she is upset. And she is completely in the right. We are in the car; stupidly in the car, because tonight we were invited for a meal with a colleague of Martha's. We can't pull out at this point, Martha said, but already we are grounded; we've pulled over to the side of the road and it's clear we're not going to go any further.

Martha is crying now, sobbing deeply and pitifully. She's crying and I feel curiously remote, callous almost. This is my fault. I have done it and there's nothing I can do to put it right, because I'm the wrong person. I'm not the organised, responsible sort of person who builds homes and careers.

There are questions from Martha; lots of questions I can't answer satisfactorily. What is going through my mind? What am I thinking? What was I thinking?

'Look at me!' she says. 'I'm breaking down and you won't help me. You can't even put your arm round me.'

She's right. I can't. I'm empty. I can't comfort her because I'm the cause. It would be like Hitler hugging the Jews. I have never felt so miserable. And I'm sure she will hate me more now. I would hate me.

'I don't see how this will end happily,' she says. 'I don't want to see you again.'

I drive her home. We put the children in the car and she drives over to Clive and Sam's without me.

I don't like my trousers. I can buy a shirt and wear it indifferently, or even become attached to it. Not so trousers. I always dislike them. There's something difficult about trousers. Something tricky. The crutch is too high; the waist too low. They are too tight or too baggy. Or they are a bad colour, or not even that: almost a good colour. In my life I have only owned two pairs of trousers which I haven't resented. I wore those until they dropped.

A good pair of trousers is hard to find, and I don't have one this morning; I haven't had one for some time. I don't like my trousers. When I am in the depths of despair, I look at my trousers and I think, 'Whose are those trousers?' and it makes me sad.

Is it just them or is it me? I choose the least offensive pair, close up the empty house and go out. I catch the coach outside the Odeon.

I have a suicide philosophy, formulated years ago. It goes like this: if ever you feel like suicide, stop what you're thinking for a second and think instead of all the things you haven't yet done. There are many of them; so many in fact, that they will dazzle you. Your life will look like a mean and narrow track in a broad and glittering landscape. This, of course, might be the reason you are committing suicide.

But some of those dazzling things you haven't done – maybe one or two of the lesser, or more obscure dazzlers – will be within your reach. They may not have been possible before, because of some perceived risk, or social stigma, but now you have nothing to lose. The experience may just be extraordinary enough to put you back in the bigger picture. It will at least make life – what's left of it anyway – more interesting.

It's called the Ketchup Man Contingency. I name it after an incident 25 years ago, in a café in Aylesbury High Street. It was a wet day and the café was packed with shoppers and office workers eating lunch. It was the perfect setting for the unexpected to happen, and it did. There was a man in there you would not have looked at normally. In fact, being overlooked was probably the predominant theme of his life, until that point. He had arbitrary hair and ramshackle clothing. He looked as though he had been dressed by blind people. Anyway, this man leapt into the spotlight from nowhere that day, suddenly and dramatically in that café full of people; he pushed his chair back from the table suddenly and stood up. In each hand he held one of those giant plastic, tomato-shaped tomato ketchup dispensers. He inhaled greedily and with a wild and exultant look on his face, wheeled around in a circle, blasting the room full-on with both containers. The world went red.

What a glorious moment that was! I may not remember who John Pilger is, but I will never forget the Ketchup Man. He is dead now, or running an international corporation, or sitting up a tree on a Grecian Isle. Whatever, I know he is content. I believe the Ketchup Man can save us all.

So when I get off the coach at Brighton, I go into a café. It's a cold wet day, and the café is cosy, full of shirking homeworkers. I order a tea and find a table. There are no big plastic tomatoes. In fact, now I come to think of it, I haven't seen a plastic tomato in a café for years. Each table has a collection of soy sauce bottles, chili oil, salad dressing and a tub of mustard. I could sprinkle soy sauce around, or smear mustard on people with the little wooden paddle, but it would be a painfully drawn-out process and would appear sadistic, if not perverted.

Oddly enough, I don't care. For the first time in my life the Ketchup Man Contingency doesn't seem an attractive option at all. Nothing seems attractive. My brain's numb. Rationally, I know there are things which are good; I'm aware of them vaguely, as if through a mist. But I can't precisely shape them in my mind. It's like trying to fix an idea in your head when you're falling asleep. It slips away.

Anyway, let me make this clear: the reason I'm going to Beachy Head is not because I'm suicidal. I'm going to Beachy Head because I need to get away. And also because I've never been there before. I know about it of course, like everybody knows about it. I know it's one of Britain's most beautiful landmarks and that it's just a couple of hours' drive from Streatham. But I've never been. It's as though I've been saving it for a special occasion, like this.

After making enquiries, I take a 712 Eastbourne bus out of Brighton and alight near Beachy Head. It's a long walk to the cliff along the footpath from the road, and it's raining solidly. I don't care. Nobody's about. Sheep graze by the path. A ditty comes into my head: *Maresydoats and doesydoats and liddlelambsydivy...*

Well I'm here now. At the edge. On the edge. It's bitterly cold up here, and wet, and awesome. I'm in the habit of thinking of England as a small and petty place, but balancing on top of this great solemn white slice of it, I see what a pretentious little upstart I am. In fact I'm slapped in the face by it. I'm utterly terrified! I drop on to my stomach in the grass, and crawl slowly to the edge and look over. Down it goes in a swirl of water drops and white. What is it – 500-plus feet? I know that one person a month on average goes the distance. It's one of those facts that stick in your head where times and appointments sometimes don't. I feel tiny here, and presumptuous, a speck in the landscape, yet daring to be intimate with the vast, mushroom-white flesh of my country. On top of the terror pinning me to the earth, I feel the lift of exhilaration! I didn't expect such feelings. I didn't expect *any* feeling, other than the dull pain of self-loathing that has entrenched itself in me these past few weeks.

I didn't think fear came into it. I thought people who stood here were beyond all that. What frightens me is that very sense of expectation and excitement, and the questions which came into my mind for the first time in the instant that I looked down into the abyss and instead of bleakness there, saw rapture. What is it that makes them take that last awful step? Is it the numbness that was, or the exultation that is? Is it what brought them here, or what they find when they get here? Is it the prospect of killing themselves, or of fully living for six seconds?

I have barely begun to get to grips with these feelings when there is a fundamental noise: a rumbling, elemental noise that registers not only in the ears, but through the body. I feel it coming up through the ground into my belly. The earth is vibrating. The whole of the rump of England is shaking, and as I turn my head, a hundred thousand tons of chalk leaves the cliff face a quarter mile up the coast, and drops, thrashing and roaring, into the sea. It didn't care that it was supposed to be soaring and steadfast. It didn't care how many people might have been trying to jump off it at the time. It saw its chance and down it came.

I rise shakily to my feet, but my fear has subsided. I feel strangely calm now. The moment of drama is gone. How still it is now, and how wet. The rain piles solidly down, heavier than ever. It is the same rain at the foot of the cliffs as it is at the top. The elevation is immaterial now. The whole world is connected by water. The sky and the sea are a blur, as though the sea might be moving upwards. I am in the middle somewhere, cocooned by water; still grounded, but only by my feet; wet and tranquil and deliciously cold.

I no longer wonder why I'm here. I can walk slowly backwards from the sweet lip, from the final step into the landscape. I look seawards, at the world waiting to be vaulted, and then down along the delirious coastline, and back at the walkable land. Visibility is worse now and I realise that as well as the greyness of the downpour, it must be starting to get dark. I set my back to the sea. Suddenly I've had enough of Beachy Head. I want to go home. I start the walk back.

It takes a long while to get back to Brighton, but all the way I'm thinking of my children. I'm thinking with fresh clarity of all those good things which were so indistinct to me just a short while ago.

I'm thinking of Amelia at eight, one summer's evening, whirl-dancing to 'Sweet Home Alabama', in the white lace dress I brought her back from Mexico, across the Streatham lawn; of Mungo, my dream child, saying, 'When will I be a girl?'; of Lowell, aged five, bawling among the pious plane spotters at Heathrow Airport Observation Platform, because the planes scared him; of Mungo, four years old, telling me that God was a small purple ball ...

I'm thinking of the night I took Amelia and Tamara into town on the bus to see *Cats*, and all the way there, Tamara was teaching Amelia the dip rhyme, *Eeny meeny macaraca, rare eye pacaraca, chicaraca, picaraca, om pom PUSH!* It took Amelia half an hour to learn it, bit by painful bit, over and over, with many a slip-up along the way. Finally she recited it correctly from start to finish, without a mistake. '*YES!*' they both said, and then they both sighed, and there was a long silence while they digested the satisfaction.

Then Amelia said, 'D'you know which bit I like best, out of all of it?'

'Which bit?' said Tamara.

'Rare I,' said Amelia.

Tamara nodded. 'Me too,' she said.

I'm barely aware of what I'm doing, I have so many thoughts going through my head, but in Brighton I get on the coach to London and sit in a fug of steam. I'm barely aware of the little dormitory towns we pass through, with their neat Christmas lights and civic trees. I hadn't realised Christmas was so near. I'm keen to get home, but when I get off the coach at Streatham Odeon I remember that the house will be empty, and the thought of being there – just me and Hubert Pinkney's post – is daunting. So I go to the Marrakech Coffee House instead and linger over strong coffees.

As I sit there, surrounded by tables of convivial Moroccans, another memory returns to me with poignant vividness; not an old memory, or one I've ever considered before, but a memory of an incident which I haven't given a second thought since it happened a few weeks ago, so overwhelmed have I been by my own stupid underachievement. It is the image of Amelia bringing a cup of tea down to me in the garden that cold night when I stood feeling sorry for myself in the garage. Amelia had barely talked to me in the few months before that, let alone done anything so thoughtful. And then I remember the glimpse I had of her face as she turned in the light, and how fresh she looked, and I realise, now, that Amelia is changing. She's shedding a skin. She's coming through that teenage frumpy stage. She's less awkward, she's taking part in conversations more, her dress sense has moved beyond the youth uniform. She's finding her real self and I'm missing it. The thought brings a lump to my throat. And Mungo? I'm shocked to realise that I don't really know how he is, except that, even in the summer, I was aware he was showing signs that he was moving out of his Mummy's boy phase. He is a sensitive little soul, not hardy like Amelia, and he needs me right now. And Martha …

I leave the café abruptly. I don't know what I can do about all this, how I can get back, make amends; but I know I have to get back to the house, back to base. I'm tired and cold now. I walk the ten minutes home. I feel as though I've been gone days. I'm dreading this.

The house is as dark as I expected, but as I get closer, I think I can see the car outside. It is. I go in. Mungo is asleep in his room, and Amelia in hers. Martha is in our room, asleep on the bed. I lean over and kiss her hair.

'Martha,' I say. 'I'm here. Martha, I'm here.'

It's all I can say, 'I'm here, I'm here, I'm here …'

She turns over and pulls me to her. I am sobbing. I am crying like the bear. 'I'm here.'

'I know,' she says.

Chapter 51 REGRET

'I wanted you, Martha. More than anything I wanted you to be here.'

'I thought you might somehow. We came home to wait for you.'

'There's been so much rubbish going on. I'm so sorry ...'

'Where were you today? I tried to ring you.'

'I went to Beachy Head.' Martha looks startled. 'I'd never been there. I saw a cliff commit suicide. I'm not kidding – there was an enormous rock fall. It was lucky I wasn't standing further along.'

She sits up in bed and puts on the light. 'What are we going to do now?'

'I don't know, but it's got to change, hasn't it. *I've* got to change.'

'Yes. It's too important to let it go on as it was. But what are you going to do?'

'I don't quite know. The trouble is ... I feel incapable of pleasing you now.'

'I'm not so hard to please.'

'You are. You have so many *requirements* – the house and everything, carpets, kitchen refits, annual foreign holidays ...'

'Well, you like all that stuff too.'

'Yes, but you get so aggravated ... so angry if it doesn't happen. You only seem happy when I'm earning money.'

'That's not the only thing that makes me happy. I want good things for the house and for the children. Who wouldn't? But they're not the most important things. And I've waited this long, if you think about it. Mostly I get angry because you're unhappy. I'm frustrated I don't know how to help.'

'Am I unhappy?'

'Yes. Oh *yes*. You've been very unhappy.'

'I have been thinking about it. If we can bear to put everything on hold for a while longer ... I'd like to write my book and to hell with it. I don't care if anybody reads it or not, or if anybody likes it. I just want to get it out of my system. Then we can look to the future.'

'I wish you'd done it a long time ago.'

'I've been putting it off. That's what my life has been about. A delaying tactic. I was scared.'

'What were you scared of?'

'That I had nothing to say.'

'Ninety-five per cent of books have nothing to say.'

'But the other five per cent are frighteningly articulate. Even self-destruction seemed a reasonable option compared with writing a book with nothing to say.'

'Has that changed?'

'Not really. Well, one thing's changed: I don't think being scared is a good enough reason not to do it any more. I'm going to do it anyway; see what happens. Besides, I think everybody has something to say. Journalism has taught me that. If you can be honest enough, it will come out. You've just got to do it. I've been thinking about something you said to me once: "The people who succeed are the people who don't accept failure." I've always been too quick to accept failure.'

'I sometimes think you're bewitched by it.'

'I thought it was preferable to mediocrity. And perhaps, routine. But I've seen the light.' Or rather, I've glimpsed the darkness.

Mungo doesn't budge when I kiss him, but Amelia's arms shoot up in her sleep to hug me, like they always used to. I bring tea up to the bedroom. Martha and I talk for a long time. We talk about regrets.

'I hate that song "My Way",' I say. 'How can all those celebrity singers be so cocksure and smug about themselves. It's not like the song at all. If I had my time again I'd do everything differently.'

'Everything?'

'Well, not everything.'

'What do you regret?'

'I regret not having a white wedding,' I said.

'You? You wanted a white wedding! Why?'

'Because they're beautiful. And everybody remembers them for ever. And everybody has a chance to formally fall in love with the bride.'

'Why didn't you say at the time?'

'Because you'd already told me you would find a big wedding embarrassing.'

'That's incredible. I had no idea.'

'What about you?'

'I wish I'd become a teacher.'

'Are you serious?'

'Yes. I keep seeing the teachers at Mungo's school and more and more, I think: that's a great thing to do.'

'But you're not a teacher sort of person at all.'

'That's what I thought.'

'I don't mind if you become a teacher. But there's something else I'd like you to do first. Simpler perhaps.'

'What's that?'

'Let your hair down occasionally; get mad with me; have a drink ... you know – loosen up. You've been too grown up all your life. Don't be quite so responsible.'

'It's hard to be irresponsible when I've got you to compete with. On the other hand ...' She goes to the cupboard and comes back with a shoebox. She takes a pair of trainers out and throws them on the bed.

'I'm going to do some exercise. Maybe go running with Amelia.'

'They're horrible.'

'Yes they are, but you want me to loosen up.'

'I wasn't thinking that kind of loosen up.' I've never seen Martha run in my life.

'Any more regrets while we're at it?'

'Well, this is no surprise but a very big regret nevertheless. I regret losing Weeny.'

'I know you do. It was your fault you lost her.'

'I know.'

'And she's probably gone for good.'

'I know.'

'But ... maybe, we can work on Ursula.'

'I don't think Ursula will talk to me.'

'I said, maybe *we* could work on Ursula.'

I love my wife.

Later, she says: 'What's the single thing you'd most like to happen, this week, say?'

'I'd like to be darlinged by Audrey Hepburn. Anything by Audrey Hepburn really.'

'That's something you've got to stop.'

'What?'

'Glib answers. Your always avoiding, avoiding. You even avoid the nice things, if they involve making a decision.'

'I just made a joke.'

'Yes but you always make a joke, and not everything's a joke, is it? There's always some funny comment getting in the way. You need to engage your passion instead of your wit. You skate across the surface. You need to dive in sometimes. Just when I'm expecting something real, a funny thing comes out instead. Not always funny either.'

'No.'

'Let's try again. What's the single thing you'd most like to happen? Something achievable?'

Now I think about it, the question's not that hard. 'I'd like to be in a roomful of dancing friends.'

'Me too. Let's throw a party.'

Chapter 52 DANCE

My house is a friend magnet. It's a throbbing music pot. It's one week before Christmas and everybody's coming, children too. Lowell is here, back from college. He ran up the path and hugged us all. Amelia and Mungo jumped up and down, squeaking loudly, and were instantly shy when he asked them a question. Then he ran through the house appreciating all the things I take for granted. Lowell loves this house, and he's missed it. To him it's a rock. To me it's a moment in entropy, a figment of willpower and plaster dust, but no less precious for that. It's home.

In 500 years' time when there is nothing here at all – no shelves, cupboards, wall dividers ... no walls – people will look at it and say nothing. Or maybe they won't even look. I don't care. I'm living for now, and now is great.

There have been changes. Nothing you'd notice, no makeovers or rebirths. Nevertheless I've shed things – ways of thinking, attitudes – they've all been ditched, along with the still unfinished *The Underground Empire: Where Crime and Governments Embrace*. I've had a haircut too. Martha prefers it razed; otherwise, she says, I start looking like a social worker. She likes her men brutal. Martha's happy. Right now she's being irresponsible on the dance-floor with Rufus. Every morning she runs around the common. You've never seen anything so funny in your life.

Tony's here. He slipped in without me noticing. That's because he doesn't look like Tony. If I've changed, then Tony's transformed. He must be three stone lighter than when I saw him a few months ago, and he's dressed as Marc Bolan, in flared velvet hipsters and a swirly, ruffled shirt.

'It's not a fancy dress party, you know.' You would never imagine, to look at him, that this man has built a jigsaw puzzle dumb waiter in his living room.

'I've lost weight.'

'I can see that.'

'Fortunately, I never throw old clothes away, and these still fit me.'

'Where's Janet?'

'I've left her. I've finally done it!'

'What?'

Next thing – and this is the big surprise: he squeezes my bottom. 'Nice arse,' he says.

Howard and Beth are here. I ask Howard how he's enjoyed his first year of retirement.

'With the right attitude, it's good,' says Howard. 'You have to say to yourself you're not going to miss your old lifestyle. You have to accept your Karma, slow down to the new reality and enjoy.'

'No regrets?'

'None whatsoever.'

That's the terrifying thing about Howard: no self-doubt – not an iota of it. 'You could have been a captain of industry if you'd lived your life differently Howard. You could have run Disney, or British Airways.'

'Maybe, but I wouldn't have had so much fun.'

Clive and Sam are here. They're incredulous. They've been incredulous all week, since Sam discovered that Rut, their au pair, had been systematically stealing her clothes, and much of her underwear, and taking them back to Stockholm on her trips home.

'Be careful if you talk to Tony,' I tell Clive, 'he's just pinched my bottom.'

'You too?' says Clive. 'Thank goodness.'

'And me,' says Sam. 'I wasn't going to tell anybody, but as we're all in it together.'

I want to dance but people keep arriving.

It's Peter and ... I don't believe it: Eloise is with him. Peter looks sheepish, but smugly so.

'You never told me you had such witty and charming friends,' says Eloise.

Peter shrugs his shoulders. I know he's my friend and all, but I hate to think of him turning her taps on with his feet.

Nadia is here, Mo, Laura, and Wendy from next door, Katherine is here, and Eithne. Harvey Solomons, my accountant, is here. Even Amanda Loveday pops in briefly, and the man who complains about the music. Mungo is dancing with Beth. Tony is dancing with Belen, waving his hands in the air like Melanie. Belen has dyslexia of the legs. Peter is dancing, very seriously, with Eloise. A notice has been stuck on his back: 'SLOW DANCER – PLEASE PASS'.

And now I am dancing too. I am dancing with my daughter. Look at her – how beautiful she is. She's so stylish. She's wearing a flared skirt she bought at a charity shop and jazzed up herself with bits of material. She's got taste. She laughs at my jokes!

She dances like a dream. Always has. Never stops. Can't stop. Dances in her sleep, up and out the bed and across the room. I'm forever picking her up and putting her back. Sometimes I wonder if one day she'll want to stop, but won't be able to. And I worry that she'll blame me.

It is my fault. If the way you put a baby to sleep affects their personality, then it's my fault. Babies who are soothed to sleep, grow into calm adults, babies who are shouted at, become customs officials. For the first thousand nights of her life I danced Amelia to sleep. Now she can't keep still.

I danced with my daughter because I had wanted a daughter so much. When Amelia came, wriggling and angry, into the world, I was ecstatic. All I could do was dance. I scooped her up and beamed at her furious face ... and rocked her. That started it. That moment launched her into perpetual motion, into a rhythm from which there is no escape.

I couldn't help myself. Dancing with my daughter was the best thing life could offer. When Martha went to put Amelia to bed, I snatched her away. Every night I danced her to sleep in my arms. Sometimes I put on jazzy lullabies, but more often than not I cranked the rock 'n' roll up. A few choruses of the Beastie Boys' 'No Sleep Till Brooklyn' and she was gone.

Or gone as Amelia ever got. She was never still, even in sleep. She never stopped rolling. She danced even there, twitching and spinning, uttering Cossack yelps, stamping wild flamenco feet on the invisible floor, flinging arms above her head. I would go into her room and find her lying in a different place to where I had left her, as though a giant bird had idly picked her up and tossed her across the room.

At ten months Amelia found her feet and never looked back. At every social gathering Amelia danced. She turned her friends into Busby Berkeley chorus lines. She started ballet classes, then contemporary classes, then choreography. It was *The Red Shoes* all over again. She can't stand still. While waiting to dance, she transfers elasticated bands from her hair to her elbows and back again in an endless cycle, like all dancers do. Her body fidgets for action.

I weep when I see her dance on stage. Nothing else plugs so directly into my emotions. I'm like a shopgirl at a wedding. She'll dance all of her life, whatever else she does, and I'll try and keep up with her, panting for breath, like tonight, at parties with Martha and Mungo and all my dancing friends, dancing together to David Lindley & El Rayo-X, singing 'El Rayo-X', spinning through the room, wheeling the world around.

Chapter 53 LUCKY

I have a letter from Amelia Thorpe, Managing Director of Ebury Press. She says she enjoyed my Life Rage piece in *The Times*, about my au pair, and wants to know if I would consider writing a book.

I would.

But first I have another party to attend. Once again it's my only work-related party of the season. I wouldn't miss it, even if it wasn't Mark Borkowski's. This year it's a more intimate affair, at the Nazrul Indian restaurant, in Brick Lane. The place is packed. Gerry Cottle, the circus owner is here again. I ask him about Lucky, the turkey.

'Lucky's dead.'

'Not so lucky then. What did he die of?'

'Complications. The thing is turkeys are bred to eaten. They're bred to be big, not to walk around, so he reached a point where he was too heavy for his legs. He was just unfeasible as an animal ... or bird ... Or anything really, apart from a Christmas dinner.'

'You could have had him in the show in a wheelchair.'

'No, that would be exploiting a vegetable.'

'What was he like – as a pet?'

'Not very interesting.'

Someone prods me in the back: 'You were right about the Mona Lisa.'

'Lisa!' It's the girl I met here last Christmas. She's carrying a tiny baby, a couple of months old. 'And ... baby.'

'I just popped in to show her round. You gave me the idea, you know.'

'I didn't?'

'Who knows. Something must have planted it in my mind.'

'I wanted you.'

'I know.'

'You were fantastic.'

'You were crazy.'

A man joins her, still in his coat, wet with rain. I remember him.

'You were here last year, weren't you?'

'Last year I was the illusionist.'

'Oh yes.'

He takes the baby from Lisa, holds it formally and proudly, like a darts trophy. 'But I got lucky.'

'So you did. The baby's fabulous. Can I hold her?'

There's a prostitute on the path through the woods. I can see her silhouette on the bench, in the light of the one street lamp on this part of the common. She must be a prostitute. No other single girl would stand in such an isolated place, alone, in the dark.

'Hello!'

She walks beside me as I reach her, and keeps pace. She's younger than most of them. She doesn't look desperate, or hard.

'Do you want to be sexed?'

'No thanks,' I say. Then stupidly: 'I'm on my way home.'

Normally they turn away now, with a sniff.

She says: 'OK. Take care.' She stops.

I stop. I turn to look at her. She's very young, perhaps no more than 17. Maybe four years older than Amelia.

'You take care,' I say. She smiles. 'You know you shouldn't be out here. It's very dark here. It's dangerous.'

'I'll be all right. I know what I'm doing.'

But she doesn't know what she's doing. I don't know what else to say.

'Goodbye then.'

'Happy Christmas.'

The prostitute in the woods is the first *moment* of Christmas, but a sad one. She touched my heart when she told me to take care, and she made me feel useless. I will never forget her. I will always wonder whether I shouldn't have done something for her; whether I shouldn't have gone back, entered her life, tried to help her. Impossible, I tell myself. It would be potentially disastrous, fraught with extraordinary problems. She's probably too far gone. She wouldn't be as she seems. She's probably a drug addict. She would resent you, drag you down, drag down your family, spit on you. And why should she want your help anyway?

But these are the sort of parameters which begin the best stories.

And she said take care.

I ask myself: where does the story of my book start. Will it, like the story of the prostitute, never start at all? This is what this last year has been about: the search for a beginning. Where does my story start? Stories can finish at any number of points. It's the starting that's so hard.

Chapter 54 STRONG

It must be one in the morning. I've just got in and I'm sitting on the stairs, on the maroon carpet, tired, in that sublime hiatus between actions; in that blink between days, in that stillness of nothing. I'm still in my coat, looking serenely at my shoes, revelling in nothing at all. There's no past, no future, no ambition, no regret; just coat and shoes, shoes and coat.

The phone rings: Manjit Singh from Leicester, a Punjabi muscleman with a needlework habit. I don't know that yet.

'We're in!' he says. 'We're in *The Guinness Book of Records*!'

'Congratulations,' I say.

'Oh, I am so sorry ... I think I am dialling the wrong number. I hope you are not disturbed.' The chink of conviviality; the energy of close friends in a small room, pulses down the line.

'No trouble,' I say. 'I'm not in bed.'

'Ah, bed. I should be in bed. But my friends are here. I have told them I have to sleep. I woke up five a.m. this morning! And I start training tomorrow! They said no Manjit, we must celebrate!'

'What?' I say.

'We made the world's longest wedding dress – 86 feet!'

'Are you a tailor?'

'No, not actually.'

'That's some wedding dress,' I say, '86 feet! The bride will still be in the car when she reaches the altar.'

'It was eleven days of hard work. My smallest girl Daljinder is really small; she is only two years old. If we put some beads on it, she just takes the beads out. We're putting on, she's taking out!'

'Who is the dress for?'

'Nobody.' He laughs. He says his eldest daughter Gulminder, is only eleven, so she can't wear the dress (though she stitched 500 yards of gold lace), and it is the wrong colour for an English girl's wedding. It's scarlet, richly flowered and sequinned. And 80-odd feet long.

'Asian girls wear red things for weddings. They put red things on their hands as well. On their foreheads they put red things. Red is ... I don't know, I must ask somebody. Anyway, City Garments of Leicester has offered me £1,100 for the dress, but that won't cover my costs.'

'Why did you make it?' I ask him.

'Why not? It's for my daughter Gulminder Kaur and my wife Molinder Kaur, because I wanted their names in *The Guinness Book of Records*.'

'I thought you said your name was Singh?'

'All men from India, Punjab, got name Singh, all the girls got name at end Kaur. We get mixed up always. We have lot of problems. They say, why is wife's name not Singh at end? All the ladies are Kaur, all the men Singh.

'Anyway, it started ... my little daughter found a wedding train dress in *The Guinness Book of Records* 75 feet long, and I had an idea out of that ... well, I thought I can make better than that. Then I made a plan ... I drawed it on a big piece of paper. Then I said, "This is too much!" I said, "We can't do this!" ... And then we did it anyway!' He laughs.

'Why did you want your wife and daughter to be in *The Guinness Book of Records*?'

'Well, I am already in *The Guinness Book* – three times! This dress is my fourth time. I am world champion of parallel bar dips for one hour: 2,735 dips in one hour. And also for one minute – 155 dips in one minute. And I sat against the wall, which is called a static wall sit, like sitting on a chair, but it is not under your knees, you know – underneath. I sat 90 minutes against the wall like that! And the world record was 76 minutes at that time. That wedding dress was the fourth record. The whole family is credited now for that.'

'Are you a Keep Fit fanatic, Manjit?'

'No, not really. But I am going to attempt the Free Squat record – sit down and stand up, sit and stand, sit and stand, 1,810 squats in one hour – just sit, stand, sit, stand, sit, stand, like that. I'm hoping to do more. I'm hoping to do 2,100 ... or at least 2,000 squats in one hour – we're going to set the date tomorrow.'

I picture Manjit with his big muscleman physique, sitting on an invisible chair in the centre of his world of extraordinary laborious achievement, surrounded by diaphanous red billows, sewing the last flower with a tiny needle, on a magnificent dress no-one will ever wear.

'Are you happy?'

'Quite contented, yes. Except my friends are here now. I said I needed some rest, but they said no Manjit, and here they all are with bottle of champagne – you can hear the noise of this ice!'

I can hear the friends' distant laughter. 'Hell, Manjit, if I had half your energy, I'd be rich!'

'Man does not live by bread alone,' he says. 'And now I have to go. I start training tomorrow. Dial 1471 for my number. Give me a ring sometime. Anything you need, I'm always here.'

And he is gone.

My family is in bed, asleep. I love the way this house absorbs us all. I don't mind any more that it sways in the breeze. Movement is what it's all about. Without movement there is no life. Movement is my theme now. I'm 46, and it's about time I did some.

I'll put the doorknobs on. I will. I'll get round to it. It will be the last DIY job I ever do.

I want to get into bed with Martha but there's something else I have to do tonight, something nagging and new and utterly irresistible. I go upstairs and switch on the computer: the damnable machine. For once it looks exciting, important. I feel comfortable. I open a blank document and I write.

This is a story of a year in the life of a man on the edge. I say 'edge', but the word already sounds out of place, because his condition is so amorphously middling as to make the idea of edges seem very remote ...

The End